Second Language Learning in a Foreign Language Environment:
A Pragma-Discoursal Account

Asha Tickoo is Associate Professor of English Linguistics at the University of Gothenburg. Her areas of specialty are Pragmatics, Discourse Analysis, and Second Language Acquisition. She uses discourse-pragmatic principles to analyse the structure of written language, and examines the prose of both skilled and unskilled writers,. often in comparative ways. While she is interested in the formal study of written language, one of her major goals is also to show that rigorous discourse-pragmatic analysis of language data is a rich resource of information for language pedagogy.

Second Language Learning in a Foreign Language Environment:

A Pragma-Discoursal Account

ASHA TICKOO

University of Gothenburg, Sweden

TERRA FIRMA

Second Language Learning in a Foreign Language Environment:
A Pragma-Discoursal Account

TERRA FIRMA, INDIA

Registered Office
Terra Firma, 201 Manasa, 43 13th Cross Road, Malleshwaram, Bangalore 560003, India

Distributed by
Orient Blackswan Private Limited

Other Offices
Bengaluru, Bhopal, Chennai, Ernakulam, Guwahati, Hyderabad, Jaipur, Kolkata, Lucknow, Mumbai, New Delhi, Noida, Patna, Vijayawada

This edition first published 2016

ISBN 978 81 920475 9 1

Typeset by
Anand George at Trinity Designers & Typesetters, Chennai 600041
in Adobe Caslon Pro 11 pt.

Printed at
Rasi Graphics, Chennai

Published by
Terra Firma
201 Manasa, 43 13th Cross Road, Malleshwaram,
Bangalore 560003, India

Acknowledgements

The author wishes to thank the following for the papers in this book, first published by them:

John Wiley for Indefinite Reference Framing, published in the *International Journal of Applied Linguistics; Prospect: a Journal of Australian TESOL* for The Acquisition and Use of the Past Tense: Understanding Selective Marking; Elsevier for The Felicitous Use of 'Then'/'After that' published in *System*; John Benjamins for On the Structure of Enumeration published in the *Australian Review of Applied Linguistics*; John Wiley for The Encapsulating Sentence and Text-Building, published in *World Englishes*; De Gruyter for Variable Temporal Passage in Storytelling, published in *Text*; the English and Foreign Languages University, India, for Narrative in Support of an Opening End-state Statement published in *The EFL Journal*; the Institute of Advanced Studies in English, Pune, India, for Information Design and Language Learning, published in *Pragmatics (2006)*, edited by Ashok Thorat; the English and Foreign Languages University, India, for Message Undercoding and Language Learning, published in *The EFL Journal*.

Contents

For my parents

Introduction

In the act of message framing rather distinct dimensions of the total meaning are made 1) by lexical means, 2) propositionally and 3) by selection amongst dissimilar information-packaging options. Selection between packaging alternatives puts in place established kinds of contrast, and therefore distinctiveness in structure or design, which serve to generate pragma-discoursal levels of effect on meaning. Packaging options, implementing dissimilarities in information design and the resulting pragma-discoursal impact, exist for the entire hierarchy of levels that constitute discourse structure.

The aspects of prose composition that are addressed in this collection of nine papers are treated as unique modes of packaging that produce well-distinguished informational configurations, each with its distinguishing pragma-discoursal effect. Each of the first seven papers individually addresses a core composing skill which poses difficulty for high-intermediate EFL learners, and examines how learners tackle the very particular information-packaging directives or constraints it conforms to. These seven papers cover a range of composing skills posing challenge to the learner, from the micro-level to the more macro-level. The eighth paper attempts a more general assessment of the information-design challenge that these aspects of composing collectively constitute, and the last paper identifies, and also accounts for, a common information design strategy that learners adopt to tackle this challenge.

1. INDEFINITE REFERENCE FRAMING

The first paper examines NP reference framing, a skill crucial to the act of communication. The paper first argues that to facilitate effective reference, information must be packaged to make the intended referent unique amongst like entities. It is suggested that learners successfully adopt this information packaging directive in framing definite reference, where both the communicator and interlocutor can see, or already know, the referent, and therefore also know what makes it unique amongst like entities. But learners do not apply this packaging directive effectively in framing indefinite reference, for which neither the referent nor, therefore, what makes it unique is known to the interlocutor. Indefinite referring expressions are examined in a sample of learner narratives by L1 users of Cantonese. Evidence is presented of three different kinds of departure from the standard packaging constraints, suggesting the adoption of three separate hypotheses on the means to making the referent unique. These are shown to constitute three levels of mitigation of the established informational constraints on indefinite reference framing, correlating with three levels of proficiency. Pedagogical implications drawn from these findings are then discussed.

2. THE ACQUISITION AND USE OF THE PAST TENSE: UNDERSTANDING SELECTIVE MARKING

The second paper deals with another basic composing skill, that of signalling location in time, by examining Cantonese learners' use of the past tense in a sample of their narrative prose. It is shown that the past tense poses a challenge for these learners, and argued that this is because English marks it categorically, on all qualifying happenings, whereas a comparable aspectual marker in the learners' L1 is routinely used selectively to signal an informational contrast in narrative discourse. In this case, therefore, learners apply informational constraints to past tense marking that do not in fact monitor its use in English. Pedagogical implications are examined.

3. THE FELICITOUS USE OF 'THEN'/'AFTER THAT'

This paper examines the most widely adopted means to the marking of temporal passage, namely, the use of temporal 'then'/'after that'. It first delineates the informational constraints on the standard use of 'then'/'after that' to show that it marks a very particular kind of passage through time. It then shows how the use of 'then'/'after that' differs in narratives by L1 speakers of Cantonese and Vietnamese. Learners' usage is shown to mitigate the stringent informational constraints on the standard use of 'then' and 'after that', influenced by the use of a comparable temporal marker in L1.

4. ON THE STRUCTURE OF ENUMERATION

This paper first explores the informational constraints on enumeration, generally regarded as the most basic means to text incrementation and responsible, therefore, for the construction of the simplest of text-types. It then examines Cantonese-speaking learners' attempts at enumeration, to identify three kinds of nonconformity. Each of these departures from standard practice mitigates the informational constraints on this means of incrementing the text, to a degree suggestive of a differentiated level of English proficiency. Pedagogical implications follow.

5. THE ENCAPSULATING SENTENCE AND TEXT BUILDING

This paper first describes the informational constraints on the use of 'encapsulation', a way of incrementing the text that is diametrically opposed to text-building by means of enumeration. The paper then examines text building in expository prose by learners who use Cantonese as L1 to demonstrate that, because they learn enumeration first, incrementation by encapsulation becomes a challenge. Packaging constraints are violated where they most blatantly contradict earlier learned means to building text, using incrementation by enumeration. Pedagogical implications are discussed.

6. VARIABLE TEMPORAL PASSAGE IN STORYTELLING

This paper revisits the marking of temporal passage, examining its character and impact not just inter-clausally, as was done in paper 3, but at the more macro-discoursal level. It suggests that while temporal passage is a defining feature of all narrative prose, in the sub-genre of story, it is informationally regulated to appear in a variable, undulating or wave-like manifestation. It then examines stories by L1 users of Cantonese to suggest little evidence of such variable temporal passage and a concomitant diminished story-like quality. Learners are shown to mitigate the stringent informational constraints applied to the sub-genre story, upholding only those which apply to the broad genre of narrative.

7. NARRATIVE IN SUPPORT OF AN OPENING END-STATE STATEMENT

This paper first examines defining informational constraints that monitor the complete textual design (that is, both the macro- and micro-developmental features) of a sub-genre of narrative which is frequently used in academic writing tasks, referred to as 'narrative in support of an end-state-statement'. In this kind of narrative, an opening end-state statement (e.g. 'Edwardsville is now a ghost town') prospects a following sequence of events that brought it about. The paper then examines attempts at this genre by L1 users from three language backgrounds —Spanish, Mandarin and Swedish—and finds a common pattern of departure from established usage-norms. Whereas the macro-design is effectively implemented, micro-developmental features pose a common area of challenge. It is suggested that this argues against the current widespread neglect of narrative in English language instruction, in college and university curriculums.

8. INFORMATION DESIGN AND LANGUAGE LEARNING

This paper makes a general assessment of the challenge that composing poses to the high-intermediate EFL learner. It argues that a common information-design principle—the 'make meaning informationally distinctive' directive— regulates, in somewhat different realisation, the earlier examined composing skills: 1) reference framing, 2) the marking of past tense, 3) the marking of temporal passage by means of 'then' and 'after that', 4) the distinct intersentential means of incrementing text by means of enumeration and encapsulation, and 5) the variable realisation of temporal passage in the narrative sub-genre of story. It suggests that an assessment of its overall implementation in these areas shows that it poses a challenge in the following circumstances: a) when it must be applied to new, rather than known to the interlocutor, information (as in indefinite reference framing); b) when its application goes counter to an established, and so competing, seemingly relevant L1 alternative (as in past tense marking and 'then' and 'after that' use); c) when it is applied at the more particular or more specialised level of structure rather than the more general (as in the marking of temporal passage in the narrative sub-genre of story) and d) when its application contradicts the directives of an earlier learned realisation of it (as in the use of encapsulation, after enumeration has been mastered).

9. MESSAGE UNDERCODING AND LANGUAGE LEARNING

The final paper interprets learners' common relaxation of information constraints in the above-assessed composing skills. It proposes 'undercoding' as a general strategy adopted by learners in the EFL context in their implementation of information packaging conventions, and demonstrates its use in 1) indefinite reference framing, 2) the marking of past tense, 3) the marking of temporal passage by means of 'then'/ 'after that', 4) the use of enumeration and encapsulation as means to building text, and 5) the utilisation of variable realisation of temporal passage to signal the narrative sub-genre of story. It then argues that the learning conditions in the EFL context, in particular the almost exclusive reliance on the teacher as interlocutor, encourage this kind of meaning making, because, as interlocutors, EFL teachers are both adept at making the discourse context relevant to the interpretation of the learner's meaning, and also accommodating of greater than normative message-processing load. The result is successful message transfer, in spite of message undercoding. Undercoding, therefore, appears to learners less demanding, in time and effort-investment, and so more efficient than full coding.

1

Indefinite Reference Framing

First published in the *International Journal of Applied Linguistics* 12 (2) (2002), John Wiley

INTRODUCTION

An aspect of noun phrase reference which is of considerable interest to researchers of language acquisition and/or pedagogy is how referring is achieved when there is no readily available term with which to identify the intended entity. Scholars have made mention of a number of referent identification strategies that are put to use in these circumstances, including description of the identifying characteristics of the referent ('the thing with three legs'), its identification in terms of similarity to a comparable namable entity ('the object that looks like a star'), and its identification in terms of its function ('the thing that is used to open a can') (cf Krauss and Weinheimer 1964; Krauss and Glucksberg 1977; Carroll 1980; Yule 1981, 1982; Brown and Yule 1983; Faerch and Kasper 1983; Krauss 1987; Mangold and Pobel 1988; Derwing 1989; Pechman 1989; Bialystok 1990; Poulisse 1990; Kasper and Kllenuan 1997). General principles of communication that underlie effective referent identification by these means have also been described. It has been claimed that to successfully identify the referent, the referring expression must be framed in terms of information that is shared knowledge between speaker and interlocutor (the Shared Knowledge Principle). Krauss and Fussell (1990:112) state that 'any communicative act rests on a base of mutual knowledge'. Earlier studies have also made much the same claim, referring to the need for 'common ground' in the act of communication (cf Clark and Marshall 1981; Clark and Carlson 1982). It has also been claimed that for effective identification, the referring expression must be framed in terms of the right *amount* of information, neither too little nor too much (the Economy Principle). This principle is discussed by Poulisse (1997) in its application to L2 use. The relevance of the notion to Ll use has been discussed by a number of scholars, including Grice (1975), Leech (1983), Levinson (1987) and Sperber and Wilson (1986).

This paper will suggest that advanced ESL learners show differential mastery of the act of reference, depending on how the Shared Knowledge and Economy Principles must be put to use in reference framing. These principles do not appear to apply in exactly the same way to every act of referring. They apply differently to the following two types of referents:

- referents that are *physically present* at the time of reference, as in the boldface NP in 1a, or already *known* to the interlocutor at the time of reference, as in 1b. (Sometimes they are made known in the preceding discourse, as in the underscored NP in 1c, or because they belong to a generic class, as in 1d.

1.

a. **The man in the corner** was asking about you.

b. **The man who came to see you yesterday**...

c. A couple I've never seen before came in to see you yesterday. **The man**...

d. At this point **a can opener** will come in handy.

- referents that are *neither physically present nor already known* to the interlocutor:

2.

When I arrived I found I didn't know anyone. But the following day I met **a man who befriended me**.

Advanced ESL learners appear to refer effectively to physically present or known referents, but have considerable difficulty framing reference to new referents. I will argue that this is because reference to a physically present or known referent (cf la–d) requires use of the general formulations of the Shared Knowledge and Economy Principles of communication, given above, in which manifestation these principles pose no difficulty for the advanced learner. However, when the language user is required to evoke a new referent (as in 2), the task of referring is not fully addressed by the general versions of these principles. Rather, it requires use of a specialised version of the Shared Knowledge and Economy Principles.

In what follows, I will first examine referring expressions in 60 samples of writing by a group of advanced learners of ESL, to show that while they have no difficulty referring to known referents, they are systematically challenged by reference to new referents. I will then compare the acts of referring to given and new referents to point to the ways in which the Shared Knowledge and Economy Principles are dissimilarly observed. Finally, I will examine representative examples of learners' references to new referents to identify the key nonconformities in their application of the Shared Knowledge and Economy Principles.

THE INFORMANTS AND THE DATA

The study looks at the referring expressions in the narrative prose of a group of 60 Cantonese speaking freshmen enrolled in the humanities programme of a Hong Kong university. The referring expressions examined in this study appear in their written recalls of W. Somerset Maugham's short story *The Dream*. These learners studied English as a foreign language a few hours a week from age three or four to age twelve, and then started using it for most of their classes.

By their freshman year in college, they had about fifteen years of exposure to the English language.

The students were given fifty minutes in class to read Maugham's short story and were then asked to rewrite it from memory in the following fifty minutes. The written recalls were first drafts of the students' work.

Referring expressions to known and new referents were identified and examined for felicity of use in their discourse context. In all, 516 references to given referents and 60 to new referents were identified. In examining reference to new referents, the study looked exclusively at learner attempts at first-time reference to the principal protagonist of Maugham's story.

In assessing the references to new referents, it is relevant to note that Maugham himself narrates the story in the first person and uses the following referring expression to introduce the protagonist of his story: 'a man whose appearance entertained me'. This first reference to the protagonist is immediately followed by a detailed description of him:

> He was a Russian, a tall fellow, but amazingly stout, and he had so vast a paunch that he was obliged to sit well away from the table. His hands, small for his size, were buried in rolls of fat. His hair, long, dark, and thin, was brushed carefully across his crown in order to conceal his baldness, and his huge sallow face, with its enormous double chin, clean-shaven, gave you an impression of indecent nakedness. His nose was small, a funny little button upon that mass of flesh, and his black shining eyes were small too. But he had a large, red, and sensual mouth. He was dressed neatly enough in a black suit. It was not worn but shabby; it looked as if it had been neither pressed nor brushed since he had had it. (Maugham 1975: 227)

This description is important because while learners very rarely attempt to reproduce Maugham's own choice of referring expression, they draw from the body of descriptive detail about the protagonist which follows this first reference.

FINDINGS OF INITIAL DATA ASSESSMENT

Assessment of the total body of referring expressions showed that learners have no difficulty with reference to known referents. References to known referents did not fail to identify their referent, nor were they in some other way infelicitous though they successfully identified the referent. This was in marked contrast to the references to *new* referents: 87% were regarded unacceptable by skilled users of standard academic English. (Acceptability judgments were elicited from 15 graduate students and 35 faculty members of the English department of an American university.)

DEFINITE, INDEFINITE NONSPECIFIC AND INDEFINITE SPECIFIC REFERENCE

It is possible to explain this difference in the learners' proficiency in framing given and new referents by looking at the different ways in which the Shared Knowledge and Economy Principles govern the well-formedness of these two types of referents. The above-stated standard versions of these principles account for the felicitous framing of given referents. But a specialised version of these principles appears to monitor the felicitous framing of reference to new referents. It is this that poses a challenge for learners.

A comparative assessment of the following three sets of referring expressions—A (definite referring expressions), B (indefinite nonspecific referring expressions), and C (indefinite specific referring expressions)—suggests that modified versions of the Shared Knowledge and Economy Principles are called for when the referent is newly evoked rather than present or known. The full nature of these modifications will be discussed further below.

A. **Definite Referring Expressions**

1. **The man** isn't eating anything. He looks like he is about to leave. [The others are not men.]
2. **The fat man** is the quietest of the lot. He looks like he is about to leave. [The others are not fat.]

3. **The man of extraordinary size** has a voice to match his size. He looks like he is about to leave. [The others are less fat.]

B. **Indefinite Nonspecific Referring Expressions**

1. **A man** must meet his obligations. *He looks like he is about to leave.
2. **A fat man** has the advantage of reserves of fuel and energy for hard times. *He looks like he is about to leave.
3. **A man of extraordinary size** is exceptional at least in this respect. *He looks like he is about to leave.

C. **Indefinite Specific Referring Expressions**

1. ??This morning I saw **a man**. He came into the store.
2. ?This morning I saw **a fat man**. He came into the store.
3. This morning I saw **a man of extraordinary size**. He came into the store.

There is comparable information content in the like numbered referring expressions of each set, e.g. A1 is informationally comparable to Bl and Cl, and A2 is informationally comparable to B2 and C2. But the referring expressions in A have referents that are physically present (and thus known) at the time of reference, and those in B have referents that are known to the interlocutor at the time of reference, since each one of these refers to a known generic class. The referring expressions in C, on the other hand, are new, at the time of reference. Also, while all three referring expressions in A are equally felicitous, as are also all three in B, this is not the case with the three referring expressions in C, even though there is comparable information content in like-numbered referring expressions in all three sets: C3 is more felicitous than C2, which itself is somewhat more felicitous than C1.

Further, in all three, felicitous referent identification is facilitated by a process of selection from a set. In Al, A2 and A3, each referring expression makes a selection from a present (and therefore known) set of entities. The three examples in B also each select a generic class from other known generic classes. In C, we again find conformity to the same principle, since the felicity of the more acceptable referring expressions is based on their interpretability as a selection from a set. C3 is the most felicitous, because it best qualifies as such a selection. Cl is the least felicitous, because it cannot be interpreted as such a selection, while C2 lies somewhere in between, because its ability to qualify as a selection from a set lies somewhere in between.

In addition, the selection in each set is facilitated by the use of shared knowledge about the selected item, in conformity with the Shared Knowledge Principle. This shared knowledge about the selected item distinguishes it from the other members of the set to which it belongs. But the nature of the shared knowledge used in A and B is significantly different from that used in C. In A, a shared knowledge distinguishing feature separates the selected known entity from a set mutually known to speaker and interlocutor. For example, by using shared knowledge about the referent of A1 that he is distinguished from the others physically present (and therefore mutually known) by being a man, the language user is able to effectively identify this individual. Likewise, by using the shared knowledge about the referent of A2, that he is distinguished from the others present (and therefore mutually known) by being fat, the language user is able to effectively refer to this individual. (A shared knowledge distinguishing feature also separates the selected known entity from a set mutually known to speaker and interlocutor when the referent is of the type that Prince (1987) refers to as an 'inferable' (as in A4):

A

4. I went to the supermarket this morning. **The cashier/The person working at the cash register** refused to take my credit card.

Here the referent is not present but is known because it is inferable from the preceding discourse. Here, too, a shared knowledge distinguishing feature—working at the cash register—separates the selected known entity from a known set: the people who work at 'supermarkets'.)

In B, a shared knowledge distinguishing feature singles out a known generic class from other known generic classes. For example, by using the shared knowledge about the referent of B1—that it belongs to a class of human beings distinguished by maleness—the language user is able to separate it out from other known generic classes. (This process of achieving referent identification holds even when the speaker is trying to refer to a generic class that the hearer may be less familiar with. In making the assumption in B4 below that the hearer is not familiar with linguists, the speaker still must use the most likely shared knowledge distinguishing feature of a linguist, that is, B4′ rather than B4″ or B4‴, to separate this generic class from other known generic classes:

B4′: A person who studies the system of language is not necessarily a polyglot.

B4″: A person who attends the LSA convention is not necessarily a polyglot.

B4‴: A person who emulates Chomsky is not necessarily a polyglot.

This type of reference could arguably pose a greater challenge for the L2 learner than reference to generic classes better known to the hearer, but the process of referent identification is not fundamentally different.)

In C, because the referent is new information to the hearer, it is not possible to use shared knowledge about the referent to distinguish it from the set to which it belongs. Yet its use still plays a crucial role in the referring process. The descriptor used for the referent is not something that is mutually known about the referent. But it must be shared knowledge about the descriptor used for the referent that it is *capable* of evoking the referent as a *well-distinguished* element from a set to which it belongs. The descriptor 'a man of extraordinary size' in C3 can distinguish the referent from the set of other men. The descriptor 'a man' in Cl cannot separate the referent from the set of other men. This means that we have shared assumptions about what common features exist between elements of an acceptable set and what distinguishing features can single out any one element from the set to which it belongs. It also means that every language user is constrained by these shared assumptions when framing a referring expression. In judging C3 as more felicitous than C2, we are also referring to shared assumptions about what type of descriptor can more effectively evoke a referent as a well-distinguished element of its set.

When we examine the applicability of the Economy Principle to the process of referring in sets A, B and C, we find that this also appears to monitor the well-formedness of referring expressions in sets A and B somewhat differently from the way it governs the well-formedness of those in set C. For sets A and B, it is appropriate to say only as much as is necessary *to identify* the known referent and misleading to say more than this. This is evident in the definite referring expressions in set A. If I am referring to the only man in the group, it is sufficient to say 'the man' even if he is not only male but also fat, because reference to his maleness is sufficient to identify him. If I do refer to him as 'the fat man', the information which is *not* needed in the task of referring will be interpreted by the interlocutor as carrying some other communicative purpose than identification. In set B, more than the essential amount of information will fail to identify the right generic class; this is evident from the fact that 'a man' in B1 identifies one generic class, while 'a fat man' in B2 identifies another.

When we examine the referring expressions in set C, we find that the Economy Principle again holds but, as with the Shared Knowledge Principle, in a somewhat different form. Again the difference stems from the need to evoke a new referent rather than identify a known one. The right amount of information is needed to *evoke* a new referent as a well-distinguished selection from a set to which it belongs. The infelicity of '*a* man' in C1 suggests that information used to frame the referring expression is insufficient in this regard. But in

C2 and C3, increasingly more information is used—'fat' in C2 and 'of extraordinary size' in C3—to delimit set membership among the set of all men and better evoke a new well-distinguished referent.

In summary, category A (definite) referring expressions and category B (indefinite, nonspecific) referring expressions select a known referent from a known set by utilising shared knowledge distinguishing information about it which is sufficient in amount to achieve *identification.* Category C (indefinite specific) referring expressions *evoke* a new selection from a set by utilising information which is mutually recognised as *capable of* properly distinguishing the element from the set to which it belongs. The information is also used in the amount deemed *capable of* properly distinguishing the element. The choices in A and B, that is, are monitored by what is known about a particular present or known element and the set to which it belongs. The choices in C, on the other hand, are monitored by a shared body of abstract conventions which define what is a well-distinguished selection from a well-formed set.

The implication of these differences is that referring expressions that evoke a new referent are likely to constitute a greater challenge for ESL learners, because the language user *cannot* rely on shared knowledge about a new referent, but must be knowledgeable about abstract conventions specifying what constitutes a well-distinguished selection from a well-formed set.

DIFFERENTIATED SENTENTIAL STATUS

There is an additional dimension of complexity to the referential task when referring expressions must evoke new referents, stemming from the fact that new referents are not a homogenous group. Discourse internally reference to new referents can realise one of two kinds of information status in the sentence. This is apparent in a comparison of Cl (repeated below) with C4:

C1. ?This morning I saw **a man**. He was...

C4. This morning I killed **a man**. He was...

The boldface referring expressions in both Cl and C4 are indefinite and specific (in that they evoke a particular individual rather than point to a generic class). They are also informationally identical. Yet, the referring expression in C4 is felicitous in its context of occurrence, while that in Cl is not fully felicitous. If we examine the information status of each of these NPs in its respective sentence, we find that the referring expression in C4 occurs in the context of a high-content, focal verb (that is, a verb that is the new information of key significance in its sentence; cf Gundel 1993). As a result, it is not itself the focal constituent of its sentence. On the other hand, the referring expression in Cl occurs with a low-content, nonfocal verb, and it is therefore itself the focal constituent of its sentence. Its infelicity then appears to derive from the fact that it does not properly qualify for focal status in its sentence.

If we return now to our initial set C specific indefinite referring expressions (repeated below), we find we have a set of *focal* specific indefinite referring expressions:

C

1. ??This morning I saw **a man**.
2. ?This morning I saw **a fat man**.
3. This morning I saw **a man of extraordinary size**.

All three specific indefinite referring expressions accompany the same low-content, nonfocal verb 'saw' and are therefore required to function as the focal constituent of their sentences. The differences in felicity of these referring expressions are determined, then, by how well they qualify as the focal constituent of their respective sentences. The referring expression in C3 is best suited for this status, while that in Cl is the least suited.

Our earlier claims about the Shared Knowledge and Economy constraints on specific indefinite referring expressions only apply, therefore, when the referring expression carries the information status of focal sentence constituent. That is, when the specific indefinite referring expression is the focal constituent of its sentence, the information used in framing it must be mutually recognised as capable of evoking the referent *as a well-distinguished selection from its set,* and in an amount deemed capable of doing this. When the referring expression is not the focal constituent (C4), these constraints do not appear to monitor its well-formedness. (In such cases, the speaker selects a shared knowledge feature that identifies it as an *undistinguished* member of the known set, and by doing so separates it from members of other known sets. That is, the speaker is using shared knowledge about a known set, rather than relying on abstract notions about conceivable sets, about what qualifies as set membership and what distinguishes any one element from the other elements of the set.)

Specific indefinite referring expressions, then, can carry one of two sentential statuses—focal or nonfocal—and are differentially constrained for information content in accordance with their status. This again adds to the complexity of the referring task when the learner is required to evoke a new referent rather than identify one that is already known. The learner has to gauge the information status of the referent in its sentence before s/he can decide how to frame an appropriate referring expression for it. In the writing samples analysed here, there were 30 instances of nonfocal specific indefinite referring expressions. Learners did not show evidence of any difficulty in framing these. The difficulties were exclusively in the proper framing of focal specific indefinite referring expressions.

In what follows, I will examine learner attempts at *focal* specific indefinite referring expressions to identify the key referring strategies they adopt and to assess how this differs from standard usage.

THE CONSTRAINTS ON FOCAL INDEFINITE REFERRING EXPRESSIONS

In first reference to the protagonist of Maugham's story the referent is new information to the reader and also the focal sentence constituent. Therefore, it must conform to the specialised manifestation of the Shared Knowledge and Economy Principles given above. That is, the information used to frame the expression must be mutually recognised (by speaker and hearer) as capable of evoking the referent as a well-distinguished selection from its set, and in the right amount to do this.

The data suggest that learners are aware of this and that they use well-formulated hypotheses about the nature of sets, what constitutes set membership, and how to effectively represent a well-distinguished selection in a set.

The data also suggest that learners' selections of information for reference framing are guided by one of three distinct hypotheses. These are described below.

The lowest common denominator

The underscored NPs in examples 3 and 4, taken from two separate learner samples, are representative of one way in which our learners refer to the protagonist of Maugham's story. In both instances, the NP is a specific indefinite referring expression accompanying a low-content nonfocal verb and is therefore the intended focal constituent of its respective sentence. By the Shared Knowledge and Economy Principles, the information selected for the referring expression must be mutually recognised as capable of evoking a well-distinguished selection from its set, and deemed appropriate in amount to do so.

3. There were a lot of people. I needed to share a table with **a man**.
4. The restaurant was crowded and small, so he shared the table with **a man**.

In 3 and 4, however, both the quality and quantity of the information are inappropriate, since, as suggested earlier, the chosen information—'a man'—does not evoke a well-distinguished selection amongst other men.

The governing learner hypothesis at work here appears to be that the lowest common denominator amongst set-defining features will evoke a well-distinguished selection from its set. That is, if we list some qualities/characteristics of a possible subset of men—man, weighing 200 lb, 6ft tall, basketball player, good basketball player, Hall of Fame basketball player—selection of the earlier listed items means that more men are included. But as we move down the list, fewer and fewer men are included. By choosing the lowest common denominator, namely the feature of maleness alone, however, one is not in fact in a position to distinguish the referent from other same-set entities at all.

TABLE **1.1**

	STRATEGIES		
Means	**Lowest common denominator**	**Increasing delimitation on set membership**	**Discriminating selection**
Length of recall	410	395	407
Clause length	8.0	7.5	7.0
Full NP length	2.5	2.0	2.5

Thirty-one percent of the learners' referring expressions showed adoption of the lowest common denominator strategy. The data was assessed to rule out the possibility that what appeared to be adoption of the lowest common denominator strategy was in fact mere lack of fluency in the language. To this end, the mean length of the written recall, the mean clause length and the mean length of full noun phrases were assessed for users of this strategy. These values were then compared to values of comparable categories for users of the other two strategies (see Table 1.1). There was no correlation between the length of the written recall, clauses and full noun phrases and the use of the lowest common denominator strategy. That is, the group using this strategy did not on average produce shorter rewrites, shorter clauses or shorter full noun phrases than users of the other two strategies.

Clearly, selection of the lowest common denominator of set-defining features, or, in other words, saying so little that the referent remains indistinguishable from same-set entities does not work. But does it follow from this that increasingly delimiting set membership by including more features not shared by the larger group of members improves the acceptability of the referring expression?

The increasing delimitation on set membership

This is the second hypothesis that learners adopt in framing referring expressions. The increasing delimitation of set membership is illustrated in 5b–e:

5.

a. This morning I saw a man.
b. This morning I saw a man weighing 200 lb.
c. This morning I saw a man who was 6 ft tall, weighing 200 lb.
d. This morning I saw a man who was a 6-ft-tall, 200-lb basketball player.
e. This morning I saw a man who was a 6-ft-tall, 200-lb weight, Hall of Fame basketball player.
f. This morning I saw a Hall of Fame basketball player.

It is also illustrated in the learner referring expression in 6a:

6.

a. He shared a table with **a tall Russian, with a small nose, [small] hands, long thin hair, black eyes, double chin and large red sensual mouth, in a shabby clothes**.

Sixteen per cent of the learner referring expressions used the increasing delimitation on set membership strategy. Again, there was no correlation between the mean lengths in Table 1 and the use of this strategy: that is, users of this strategy did not on average generate longer rewrites, longer clauses and longer full noun phrases.

Hence it is not suggested that learners who appeared to use this strategy were in fact just more wordy than learners who used the other two strategies.

While one would logically expect this increasing delimitation on set membership to work, it does not in fact result in fully acceptable referring expressions (cf 5b-d and 6a). 5b–d would only be acceptable if both speaker and hearer regarded the description in each of these referring expressions as in some way out of the ordinary. In the USA, a man weighing 200 lb is not uncommon, nor is one who weighs 200 lb and is also 6 ft tall, or one who is a 200-lb, 6-ft-tall basketball player. The delimitation on set membership only works in 5e because one of the included features makes the referent salient in the set to which it belongs, that he is a Hall of Fame basketball player. Example 5f shows that leaving out all but this feature works equally well, suggesting that the other set-delimiting features are not in fact needed to achieve acceptability. The ineffectiveness of the increasing delimitation on set membership is also evident in 6a, which contrasts with 6b and 6c, where there is use of only a select feature (or features) which makes the referent salient:

6.

b. He shared a table with a man whose shabby clothes forced one to take note of him.

c. He shared a table with a man with the most extraordinary black eyes and a pair of very full, very red, very sensual lips.

What achieves effective reference, therefore, is neither selection of the lowest common denominator nor a maximal delimitation of set membership, but rather the selection of those features which make the referent informationally salient in its set.

We can also interpret the inadequacy of these hypotheses as resulting from their violation of the right quantity of information condition. Both too little information (by the use of only the lowest common denominator) and too much information (by inclusion of more and more set delimiting information) is ineffective; the right amount makes the referent informationally salient.

The discriminating selection

The third hypothesis, evident in the learners' framing of focal indefinite specific referring expressions, is the selection of a saliency-achieving feature. Fifty-three per cent of the learner referring expressions use this strategy. Again, this strategy did not show any correlation with the length of the written recall, clauses and full noun phrases (see Table 1).

In using the discriminating-selection strategy, learners adopt a principle that is normatively applied in standard usage. Yet their reference framing still is not consistently acceptable. Only 6 per cent of such referring expressions are fully acceptable. In the rest, learner choices of referent-distinguishing features do not readily make the referent salient, because they do not adhere to shared notions of saliency or newsworthiness (cf 7 and 8 below):

7. He shared a table with **a fat man.**
8. He shared a table with **another man dressed neatly.**

The underscored referring expressions of 7 and 8 appear childish precisely because only children are likely to perceive the chosen descriptor as making the referent salient. In normal circumstances, a man is not singled out by being either fat or neatly dressed. If we compare 7 with 7′ and 8 with 8′, we see that the shared assumption is that a man's weight can single him out only if it is exceptional; likewise his mode of dress can distinguish him only if it is significantly out of the ordinary:

7′. He shared a table with a man of extraordinary size.

8′. He shared a table with a man who was so immaculately dressed that people were compelled to look up and take notice.

So effective reference is achieved if the referring expression uses a distinguishing feature that delimits set membership by making the referent salient in its set, using a conventionally shared notion of saliency or newsworthiness.

Two additional constraints on framing focal indefinite specific referring expressions are also rarely upheld in this body of data.

The observer's bias

A referent must be presented in terms of the world view/perspective of a particular observer. When this observer is someone other than the speaker/writer, the observer (A) must himself/herself appear salient in the text in order for the referring expression used to evoke the observed referent (B) to be perceived as fully acceptable. This is not the case in 9, below:

> 9. One day **a man** (A) went from New York to Petrograd...he met **another man who was dressed neatly** (B).

We can alter this text to make the descriptor used for the observed individual (B) properly salient in its set, as in 10.

> 10. Yesterday **a man** (A) met **a man he will never forget** (B).

An unforgettable man is by convention singled out amongst other men. But the absence of a salient observer (A) still makes the sentence unacceptable. When the observer (A) is also made salient, however, the sentence does become felicitous (as in 10′ and 10″):

> 10′. Yesterday **Bill Clinton** (A) met **a man he will neyer forget** (B).
>
> 10″. Yesterday **a man of some considerable standing in our community** (A) met **a man he will never forget** (B).

Our data suggests that learners do not uphold this constraint.

Temporal and logical considerations

The referring expression is also constrained to be information about the referent that is known to the observer at the depicted point in time, and regarded informationally significant by him at that time.

11. **I settled** down in my chair with (at) a small **table**. Then **a Russian** came in and shared the table with me.
12. I shared a table with a tall and **funny** Russian.
13. I shared a table with a strange, ugly but **well-educated** Russian man.

The choice of 'a Russian' suggests this is the salient distinguishing feature about the individual so referred to. It suggests that the observer first noticed the individual with whom he shared his table because he was Russian. But, whereas the individual in question was Russian, it is not true that this was what first caught the observer's attention.

Likewise when he first meets the individual in question, the narrator/observer in Maugham's story does not know that the individual he is observing is either funny or well-educated (cf 12 and 13). Our data suggests that learners do not observe such logical and temporal constraints on reference framing.

PEDAGOGICAL IMPLICATIONS

This study shows that advanced learners of ESL have difficulty framing focal indefinite specific referring expressions in expected ways. Such referring expressions must evoke a referent that is new, using information of the right kind and amount to make the referent salient in its set, in accordance with conventionalised notions of saliency/newsworthiness. Further, to be perceived as salient, the focal indefinite specific referring expression must be in the purview of a salient observer, and therefore constrained by the knowledge and perspective of that observer, at the time of referent observation.

To help the learner achieve full competency in the use of focal indefinite specific referring expressions, classroom instruction should, therefore, consider drawing attention to the following areas of noun phrase reference:

1. the difference between focal and nonfocal indefinite specific referring expressions;
2. the difference between a referent that is evoked as a well-distinguished element of its set and one that is not well distinguished (The learner should be made conscious of the crucial role played by saliency in this. Learners should become aware of shared notions of salience and how to judge the right type and amount of information);
3. the need for a salient observer in the successful representation of a salient referent;
4. the need to frame the referring expression with an awareness of the observer's knowledge and perspective at the time of reference to the observed entity.

References

Bialystok E. 1990. *Communication Strategies.* Oxford, England: Blackwell.

Brown G and Yule G. 1983. *Teaching the Spoken Language.* Cambridge University Press.

Carroll J. 1980. Naming and describing in social communication. *Language and Speech*, 23: 309–22.

Clark H H and Carlson T B. 1982. Speech acts and hearers' beliefs. In N V Smith (ed), *Mutual Knowledge.* New York: Academic Press.

— and Marshall C E. 1981. Definite reference and mutual knowledge. In A K Joshi, B Webber and I Sag (ed), *Elements of Discourse Understanding.* New York: Cambridge University Press.

Denving B. 1989. Information type and its relation to nonnative speaker comprehension. *Language Learning*, 39: 157–72.

Faerch C and Kasper G (ed). 1983. *Strategies in Interlanguage Communication.* London: Longman.

Grice H Paul. 1975. Logic and conversation. In P Cole and J L Morgan (ed), *Syntax and Semantics: Speech Acts, Vol 3.* New York: Academic Press.

Gundel J, Hedberg N and Zacharski R. 1993. Cognitive status and the form of referring expressions in discourse. *Language*, 69: 274–307.

Kasper G and Kellerman E (ed). 1997. *Communication Strategy Research: Psycholinguistic and Sociolinguistic Aspect.* London: Longman.

Krauss R. 1987. The role of the listener: addressee influences on message formulation. *Journal of Language and Social Psychology*, 6: 81–98.

— and Fussell S. 1990. Mutual knowledge and communicative effectiveness. In J Galegher, R Kraut, and C Egido (ed), *Intellectual Teamwork.* Hillsdale, NJ: Lawrence Erlbaum Associates.

— and Glucksberg S. 1977. Social and nonsocial speech. *Scientific American*, 236: 100–105.

— and Weinheimer S. 1964. Changes in reference phrases as a function of frequency of usage in social interaction. *Pyschonomic Science*, l: 11–34.

Leech G. 1983. *Principles of Pragmatics.* London: Longman.

Levinson S. 1987. Minimization and conversational inference. In M Papi and J Verschueren (ed), *The Pragmatic Perspective.* Amsterdam: John Benjamins.

Mangold R and Pobel R. 1988. Informativeness and instrumentality in referential communication. *Journal of Language and Social Psychology*, 7: 181–191.

Maugham W Somerset. 1975. *Collected Short Stories.* Reading, PA: William Heinemann.

Pechman T. 1989. Incremental speech production and referential overspecification. *Linguistics*, 27: 89–110.

Poulisse N. 1990. *The Use of Compensatory Strategies by Dutch Learners of English.* Dordrecht, Netherlands: Foris Publications.

— 1997. Compensatory strategies and the principles of clarity and economy. In G Kasper and E Kellennan (ed), *Communication Strategy Research: Psycholinguistics and Sociolinguistic Aspects.* London: Longman.

Sperber D and Wilson D. 1986. *Relevance: Communication and Cognition.* Cambridge, MA: Harvard University Press.

Yule G. 1981. New current and displaced entity reference. *Lingua*, 55: 41–52.

— (1982) The objective assessment of aspects of spoken English. *World Language English*, 1: 19–39.

2

The Acquisition and Use of the Past Tense: Understanding Selective Marking

First published in *Prospect: A Journal of Australian TESOL*, 2001

I. INTRODUCTION

Current opinion holds it that there is a common explanation for the way in which the past tense is acquired in L2, for all learners irrespective of their L1. The here-examined body of data suggests that English past tense acquisition by L1 users of Cantonese is not properly accounted for by the so-called universal explanation. Our data shows that the learner's L1 plays a significant role in the acquisition of past tense in L2, raising the possibility that the universalist explanation is in general a less tenable proposition.

Highlighted by this finding is the need, by both researchers and language educators, to properly acknowledge the potential impact of L1 in the acquisition of L2. Two secondary implications are also found to emerge for both research and pedagogy from the particular language-analysis techniques used to facilitate this more accurate assessment of past tense data. In this study, proper data analysis is effected by use of qualitative assessment of the language use of the individual learner, in place of the more frequently used, often exclusively, collective and quantitative evaluation of the performance of groups of learners. A proper data assessment is also found to depend on the examination of the learner's use of past tense in the discourse context in which it occurs, rather than in isolation from its context of use. Of relevance hence to both research and classroom instruction is the suggestion that learner syntax is only fully understood when there is appreciation of the role it plays in the bigger enterprise of text generation and the facilitation of the speaker's communicative intent.

The universalist hypothesis about past tense acquisition in L2 claims that the past tense is acquired in developmental stages, in which verbs that are lexico-semantically more event-like (e.g. 'write a poem' and 'shut the door') are marked for tense first, followed in well-demarcated stages by the marking of increasingly less event-like verbs (e.g. 'run', 'talk', 'feel' & 'know') (cf Andersen 1989, 1991; Bardovi-Harlig 1992; Bardovi-Harlig and Reynolds 1995; Bardovi-Harlig and Bergstrom 1996; Kaplan 1987; Klein 1986; Kumf 1984; Meisel 1987; Robinson 1990; Shirai 1991; Shumann 1987; Trevise 1987; Veronique 1987; von Stutterheim and Klein 1987; amongst others). I will show that this developmental pattern does not describe the past tense acquisition of ESL learners whose L1 is Cantonese.

I will examine past-tense marking in a large corpus of narratives by ESL learners at three different proficiency levels in Hong Kong. I will show that these learners do not move gradually from the selective marking of past tense on verbs that are more event-like to the inclusion by stages of less event-like verbs. Rather, across all three proficiency levels, some learners are found to use selective marking to signal grounding distinctions (i.e. differences in informational salience) in the text, while others use the uniform marking of past tense on all verbs, in conformity to the target language grammar. I will give evidence to suggest that what changes as these ESL learners advance in their academic career is the number of students using uniform marking over selective marking. This number, as might be expected, increases gradually. The idiosyncrasy of this pattern of acquisition will be interpreted as resulting from the transfer from these learners' tense-free L1 of a feature of its temporal system.

2. THE OUTPUT OF A REVISED METHODOLOGY

In this study past-tense marking was examined in a total of 120 narratives, 40 from each of the three learning levels: Form 3 (age 12), Form 6 (age 15) and the second year of university (age 20). Students from all three classes started learning English at about age four as a school subject, and from about age twelve were required to use it for many, though by no means all, of their courses. Like almost all other groups of language learners, these students were encouraged to write narrative prose in their early exposure to English. Therefore Form 3 students were still writing narrative prose. But by high school the emphasis was on expository and argumentative prose, and more generally on different forms of academic writing.

The narratives used in this study were all produced as in-class written assignments on topics set by the class teacher. Students were given about 50 minutes to write the narrative, and the written samples were therefore first drafts.

The initial examination of this data was carried out as part of a project funded by a Baptist University faculty research grant. In this initial examination, the data was assessed for its conformity to selective marking of past tense according to the lexical aspectual category of the verb, on the pattern of the many previous assessments (cf Andersen 1989, 1991; Bardovi-Harlig 1992; Bardovi-Harlig and Reynolds 1995; Bardovi-Harlig and Bergstrom 1996; Kaplan 1987; Klein 1986; Kumf 1984; Meisel 1987; Robinson 1990; Shirai 1991; Shumann 1987; Trevise 1987; Veronique 1987; von Stutterheim and Klein 1987; amongst others).

Researchers who adopt this lexical-aspectual assessment differentiate between verbs of different lexical aspectual classes: states, activities, accomplishments and achievements (see Table 2.1). These four lexical–aspectual categories are characterised, and differentiated from each other, by the use of three semantic features: punctility, telicity and dynamism. Punctility, occurrence at a single point (as in 'begin to sing'), is in contrast with durativity (as in 'sing'). Telicity, the property of having an end point (as in 'sing a song'), is distinguished from the condition of having no end point (as in 'sing'), and dynamism (as in 'play', 'read', and 'talk') is set apart from stativity, the condition of being nondynamic (as in, 'seem', 'know' and 'be').

Using the three semantic features of telicity, punctility, and dynamism it is possible to characterise, and distinguish between, the four above-referred-to categories of verbs: states, activities, accomplishments and achievements (cf Table 2.1). Table 2.1 shows that states (e.g. 'know' and 'be') are nonpunctual, atelic and nondynamic, activities (e.g. 'run', 'talk' and 'walk') are nonpunctual and atelic, but dynamic, accomplishments (e.g. 'build a house' and 'compose a symphony') are nonpunctual, but both telic and dynamic, and achievements (e.g. 'shut the door' and 'flip the switch') are punctual, telic and dynamic. Achievements and accomplishments, which are both telic and dynamic, are regarded as the most event-like verbs and often together referred to as events, to the exclusion of other verb-types.

Researchers have shown that the marking of past tense in L2 begins with verbs that are achievements ('I shut the door'). It later extends its scope to encompass accomplishments ('I built a house'), activities ('I slept') and states ('I knew it'), in that order.

TABLE **2.1**

SEMANTIC FEATURES OF ASPECTUAL CATEGORIES

LEXICAL ASPECTUAL CATEGORIES				
Features	**States**	**Activities**	**Accomplishments**	**Achievements**
punctual	–	–	–	+
telic	–	–	+	+
dynamic	–	+	+	+

(Source: Bardovi-Harlig and Reynolds 1995:109)

The project funded by the Baptist University faculty research grant aimed to test the validity of this claim for Chinese learners of ESL. The marking of past tense on verbs of different lexical–aspectual categories was assessed, noting both target-like use as well as non-target-like use. But, as is customary in lexical–aspectual studies of past-tense acquisition, this initial examination of the data then ignored all instances of target-like use and focused only on the pattern of nontarget-like use. Computing group averages for the marking of past tense on each lexical-aspectual category of verb, for each of the three levels of learning, it was found that the nontarget-like use of verbs did appear to reflect selective marking according to lexical aspectual categories: Nontarget-like use was more apparent in states and activities than in achievements and accomplishments (cf Table 2.2 below).

TABLE 2.2

PERCENTAGE OF NONTARGET-LIKE FORMS

	From 3	Form 6	Year 2 of university
Accomplishments	27	27	25
Achievements	20	22	18
States	41	44	39
Activities	38	39	35

However, there did not appear to be clear corroboration for the developmental sequence. That is, there was not clear support for the hypothesis that learners mark events in early stages and then gradually include less event-like verbs, since the percentages of nontarget-like marking remained relatively constant from Form 3 to Year 2 of university. This raised doubts about the appropriateness of the lexical-aspectual assessment of past-tense marking for this group of learners. It was difficult to believe that the acquisition of past tense could remain relatively unchanged over some eight to nine years of continuous study in spite of the improvement clearly evident (both in writing skills and general knowledge of target grammar) in year 2 of university compared to Form 6, and of Form 6 compared to Form 3. These quantitative findings were actually at odds with my personal knowledge of these learners as a teacher in Hong Kong. A significant number of my university students had no difficulty at all with the use of the simple past tense. Also, in contradiction to the above-described quantitative assessment, a simple reading of the narratives did in fact suggest improvement in past tense use with academic advancement. It seemed likely, therefore, that it was the mode of analysis that was at fault. Assessment for sensitivity to lexical–aspectual differences was in some way inappropriate, or at least inadequate, for a proper evaluation of this data.

There are other inherent problems with the manner in which the lexical aspectual studies have been conducted: 1) the focus on nontarget-like use, and neglect of the many instances of target-like use, has a significant impact on the interpretation of the data; 2) the failure to acknowledge individual learner performance also precludes an accurate assessment of learner behaviour, and 3) the failure to recognise the potential impact of discourse context on learners' use of tense marking also distorts our understanding of the data. In addressing the above-referred-to apparent lack of clear progress from Form 3 to Year 2 of university, three changes in methodology were made:

a. All realisations of verbs, both nontarget-like and target-like, were acknowledged.

   When this was done, it was found that the data does not show consistent patterning for any category of verb.

   If more event-like verbs are in fact marked for past tense before less event-like verbs, then verbs of any single lexical–aspectual class will be gauged either sufficiently or insufficiently event-like at any given point in the developmental process. In consequence, verbs of a particular lexical-aspectual class will be either uniformly marked for past tense or uniformly unmarked. For these three groups of learners this is in fact not the case.

When assessing tense marking by computing group averages, although more event-like verbs are found to be tense-marked more frequently (e.g. 'Yesterday he baked a cake' and 'Yesterday he wrote a poem') than less event-like verbs (e.g. 'Yesterday he feel bad' and 'Yesterday he is happy'), verbs of every category are sometimes tense-marked and sometimes unmarked (e.g. 'Yesterday he baked a cake and write a poem about it. He felt good; in fact he is very happy.'). This is indicated in Table 2.2, above. For all levels of proficiency, although accomplishments and achievements are marked for past tense in larger numbers, some accomplishments and achievements are not past-tense marked. Likewise, although fewer activities and states are past-tense marked at all levels of proficiency, some activities and states are past-tense marked. It is true that some learners at every level demonstrate strict conformity to target grammar for past-tense marking, and this accounts for some of the inconsistent marking for verbs of a given category, when group averages are computed. But this in itself does not account for all the inconsistent marking.

b. Individual learner narratives were examined.

When both target-like use and nontarget-like use is examined, and further all cases of tense marking are examined in the context of individual learner narratives, it is found again that *learners who use selective marking* do mark a larger number of more event-like verbs, but they do not categorically limit use of the past tense to any particular lexical–aspectual class. In fact, all verbs which should be in the past tense are sometimes marked for past tense and sometimes unmarked, irrespective of their lexical aspect.

c. Tense marking was examined in its discourse context.

The Chinese learners' use of selective marking of past tense was, therefore, found to both cut across all the lexical–aspectual categories, and to be consistently used for none of them. But this variability was not asystemic. It could not be explained by simple reference to lexical aspect, but it was found to be consonant with the grounding of the denoted situation. The learner who used selective marking differentiated between verbs which qualify for marking from those which do not by gauging the grounding of the situation they denoted.

Hopper's notion of grounding

Although there are earlier assessments of the L2 learner's past tense marking in terms of grounding (cf Kumf 1984, Veronique 1987, von Stutterheim and Klein 1987), these studies perceive it in somewhat different terms than here envisaged. It is recognised only as a discourse construct that acknowledges an informational dichotomy between salient and nonsalient components of the narrative. In the here-adopted Hopper (1977, 1979) treatment of it, grounding has added dimensions of systematicity.

In Hopper's terms it correlates with a discourse-based conception of aspect, which he defines in terms of a conglomerate of features of the denoted situation (features relevant to this analysis are listed and exemplified in Table 3). Plus-marked values of these features (listed under the category 'prefective') contribute to informational centrality to or foregrounding status in the narrative, and the negative values (listed under the category 'imperfective') contribute to situation backgrounding.

The key defining features of the semantic-feature assessment of eventhood, telicity and dynamism (see Table 2.1) are retained in the form of constraints 1 and 3 of Table 2.3, but other features are also added, including the assessment of givenness, in constraint 2, the assessment of overall informational salience, in constraint 4, and the assessment of the realis or irrealis realisation of the situation in constraint 5. The notion of discourse aspect which determines the grounding of the denoted situation, therefore, is not entirely disparate from a lexical conception of aspect; rather it subsumes the key features of this classificatory system.

TABLE **2.3**

Perfective	Imperfective
Constraint 1 (the telicity feature)	
View of the event as a whole, whose completion is a necessary prerequisite to a subsequent event (cf 1)	View of a situation or happening whose completion is not a necessary prerequisite to a subsequent happening (cf 2)
1. We completed the drive in 8 hours. Then in the early evening we stopped at a small motel.	2. We drove for hours. We passed a series of small towns.
Constraint 2 (the givenness feature)	
Unmarked distribution of focus in clause, with presupposition of subject and assertion in verb and its immediate complements (or other unmarked focus)(cf 3)	Marked distribution of focus, e.g. subject focus, instrument focus, focus on sentence adverbials (cf 4)
3. Most of us felt exhilerated.	4. But Sam did not enjoy himself.
Constraint 3 (the dynamism feature)	
Dynamic, kinesic events (cf 5)	Static, descriptive situations (cf 6)
5. We drove for 8 hours	6. It was a long journey.
Constraint 4 (the saliency feature)	
Foregrounding. Event indispensable to narrative (cf 7)	Backgrounding. State or situation necessary for understanding motives, attitudes, etc. (cf 8)
7. We drove for 8 hours.	8. We passed a series of small towns.
Constraint 5 (the realis/irrealis feature)	
Realis (cf 9)	Irrealis (cf 10)
9. He was sick.	10. It may have been something he ate.

(Adapted from Hopper 1979: 216)

Table 2.3 shows that clauses central to the narrative tend to denote events rather than states; they are likely to be happenings that are telic rather than atelic, those that are informationally new rather than given, and those that are realis rather than irrealis. The ultimate grounding status of any one situation, however, is a function of the *discourse context* in which it occurs. Thus, a denoted state may be foregrounded in a context in which accompanying denoted states have fewer perfective features than it. In example 11 below, in which the verb of every clause denotes a state, only the first clause carries new information; other clauses merely expand the information of the first clause. The denoted state of clause 1, therefore, has one perfective feature that the states of the other clauses do not possess, and is in consequence foregrounded in the context of these accompanying states.

11.

> She was by far the best candidate for his job. Her credentials were outstanding, and she had the requisite experience. In fact, she seemed to have no shortcomings at all.

Our data shows that it is this 'relative grounding' that governs past tense marking in the writing of those students who use selective marking. That is, students, in gauging the grounding of any one denoted situation, assess whether it has more or fewer perfective features than co-occurring denoted situations. If it has more perfective features than its co-occurring denoted situations, it qualifies as foregrounded in its discourse context, and is marked for past tense.

3. A CLOSE ANALYSIS OF SELECTIVE MARKING IN LEARNER NARRATIVES

In what follows selective marking is shown to be effectively interpreted in terms of relative grounding in three samples of narrative, randomly selected from Form 3, Form 6 and University Year 2, data samples. Clauses with tense-marked verbs have been underlined.

Form 3 narrative

[1]On the 24th of December at 10 o'clock. The suspects went to the National Bank. [2]Their robberyed many money and other things **[3]The suspects was two man and the robber dog.** [4]The one man is tall and thin and the one man is fat and short. [5] The dog is very big.

[6]On the 20th of december, the two robber read newspaper. [7]Suddenly, they saw the one advertisement. [8]The advertisement was wanted a watch-dog. [9]So they called the Banker Philips. [10]They went to the National Bank to visited the Banker. [11]The Banker gave the money to them. [12]So the dog in the bank for work, **but the dog was accomplice, it helped the robbers for robbery the Bank.**

[13]On 24th of December, the Bank was 4 o'clock closed. [14]But only the Banker and watch-dog here in the Bank. **[15]At the nine O'clock, the Banker went to home. [16]So the robber went to Bank robberyed money and many old vases. [17]They put the all things in the van.**

[18]On next day, the banker called the police.

In this narrative by a Form 3 student the separation of clauses with marked and unmarked verbs differentiates between the key events of the storyline (left-hand column, below) and subsidiary, noncentral detail (right-hand column).

On the 24th of December at 10 o'clock.
The suspects went to the National Bank.
Their robberyed many money and other things
The suspects was two man and the robber dog.

> The one man is tall and
> thin and the one man is
> fat and short.
> The dog is very big.

On the 20th of december, the two robber read newspaper.
Suddenly, they saw the one advertisement.

The advertisement was wanted a watch-dog.
So they called the Banker Philips.
They went to the National Bank to visited the Banker.
The Banker gave the money to them.
So the dog in the
bank for work,
but the dog was accomplice, it helped the robbers
for robbery the Bank.
On 24th of December, the Bank was 4 o'clock closed.
But only the Banker
and watch-dog here
in the Bank.
At the nine O'clock, the Banker went to home.
So the robber went to Bank robberyed money and many old vases.
They put the all things in the van.
On next day, the banker called the police.

When we assess the past tense marking in this passage, we find that whenever there is an unmarked verb it is the verb 'to be', a state. But it is not true that the verb 'to be' is consistently unmarked. Rather it appears to go unmarked only in informationally backgrounded clauses. By assessing the information status of the denoted situation in terms of the above-defined notion of relative grounding, it becomes evident that in sentence 3 the verb 'to be' is marked for past tense even though it is a state, because it constitutes new information in its context of appearance. By perfective feature 2, it qualifies for foregrounded status. In sentences 4 and 5 the same denoted state is now given information. Hence sentences 4 and 5 qualify as backgrounded information, and the verb 'to be' in each of these goes unmarked for past tense.

In this Form 3 passage there is not a lot of information that can qualify as supplementary detail, serving merely to amplify the account of the principal event sequence. For this reason there are few contexts where unmarked verbs can be appropriately used in conformity to the learner's selective-marking hypothesis. A point worthy of notice in this body of data is that as the learners' narrative skills improve, they provide more supplementary information in the form of comments on the central events of the storyline. Ironically, this concurrently creates more opportunities for the use of unmarked verbs.

> Form 6 narrative
>
> [1]When I look back at that time in my life, I am surprised that something so small should have been so important to me. [2]Although it was happened in three years ago, I remembered this clearly.
>
> [3]**When I was 14, once time I cleaned my bedroom.** [4]**During this time, I found out so many useless things.** [5]**Then I put them in a rubbish bin.** [6]Useless thing - in my mind, there are some of my primary school's friends letters and Christmas cards because of its dust. [7]So, I have taken a very stupid action and **threw them all away**.
>
> [8]I have met one of my primary school friends afterward. [9]**It was totally five times.** [10]**But we were missed all the chances** that we can gather together. [11]It is possible that both of we are afraid of the other side have already forgotten ourselves. [12]In fact, I am sure that **he remembered me and I also remembered him.** [13]**I was regretted** (the missed opportunity)...

In this extract from a Form 6 narrative, the separation of clauses with marked and unmarked verbs again differentiates between the key events of the storyline (left-hand column, below) and subsidiary, noncentral detail (right-hand column).

> (When I look back at that time in my life, I am surprised that something so small should have been so important to me. Although it was happened in three years ago, I remembered this clearly.)
>
> When I was 14, once time I cleaned my bedroom.
>
> During this time, I found out so many useless things.
>
> Then I put them in a rubbish bin.

Useless thing - in my mind, there are some of my primary school's friends letters and Christmas cards because of its dust.

So, I have taken a very stupid action

and threw them all away.

I have met one of my primary school friends afterward.

It was totally five times (that I met my primary school friend).

But we were missed all the chances

that we can gather together. It is possible that both of we are afraid of the other side have already forgotten ourselves.

In fact, I am sure that

he remembered me and I also remembered him.

I was regretted (the missed opportunity). ...

Here the stative verb 'to be' is again sometimes tense-marked and sometimes unmarked. As in the preceding sample, when the state denoted by the verb 'to be' is informationally new and therefore foregrounded, it is tense-marked (e.g. sentence 3). When on the other hand it is given information (e.g. sentence 6), it is backgrounded and therefore unmarked for past tense.

There is another context in which verbs go unmarked for tense in this sample. Verbs representing irrealis situations are backgrounded by perfective feature 5, and these are therefore unmarked for past tense. In sentence 10 the narrator states that s/he and his/her primary school classmates missed all the occasions when they *could* have gathered together. This irrealis realisation of the event of gathering together is represented by the unmarked verb 'can'.

It is important to notice that this Form 6 narrative has *more* instances of unmarked verbs compared to the Form 3 narrative. Of the total number of verbs used 22% are unmarked in this Form 6 narrative, whereas only 13% of the total number of verbs used were unmarked in the Form 3 narrative. This is because this writer's greater facility at developing his/her story (by providing supporting detail to flesh out the representation of the principal event-sequence) creates increased opportunity for the use of unmarked verbs.

University year 2 narrative

[1]**When I was about ten years old, I started to play the piano.** [2]I love playing the piano and so do my mother. [3]She put many pressure on me and have great expectation on me.

[4]One **event that I won't forget was happened in Form seven in Secondary school.** [5]I have to face with the Advanced Level Examination as well as the Advanced Piano Examination. [6]I don't know how to use my time, for studying or playing the piano. [7]**Finally I put much effort on studying instead of playing the piano.**

[8]In August, I have to participate in the piano Examination. [9]**It was really unfortunately that I was severely sick on that day.** [10]It may be due to too much nervous and stress and thus made me sick. [11]I cannot play the piano well, even the easiest part, **I made mistakes.** [12]**All the theories, musical histories were gone.** [13]I feel totally beaten by disappointment. [14]After the examination, I cannot stop crying.

[15]**Two months later, I received the result.** [16]**Both performance and theories were fail.** [17]Although I have enough preparation for the result I still very upset about this. [18]**My mother didn't scold me.** [19]**She suggested me to participate in the examination next year again only.** [20]Until now, I still haven't participate in the exam, may

> be I'm afraid of the failure. [21]This was an unforgettable event that make me a shadow effort. [22]It may erase by the passing of 5time.

In this narrative by a second year university student, the separation of clauses with marked and unmarked verbs once more clearly differentiates between the key events of the storyline (left-hand column below) and the writers comments on these, or on her/his state of mind at the time of their occurrence (right-hand column below).

When I was about ten years old I started to play the piano. One event that I won't forget was happened last two years when I was studying in Form seven in Secondary School.	(I love playing the piano and so do my mother.) I have to face with the Advanced Level Examination as well as the Advanced Level Piano Examination. I don't know how to use my time, for studying or playing the piano.
(Finally I put much effort on studying instead of playing the piano.)	In August, I have to participate in the piano Examination.
It was really unfortunate that I was severely sick on that day.	It may be due to too much nervous and stress and
thus made me sick.	I cannot play the piano well, even the easiest part,
I made mistakes. All the theories, musical histories were gone.	I feel totally beaten by disappointed. After the examination I cannot stop crying.
Two months later I received the result. Both performance and theories were fail.	Although I have enough preparation for the result I still very upset about this.

My mother didn't scold me or condemn me, she suggested me to participate in the examination next again only.	(Until now I haven't participate in the exam, may be I'm afraid of the failure.)
This was an unforgettable event	that make me a shadow effect.

The thematically noncentral comments (in the right-hand column) tend to be descriptions of feelings and therefore states, as in 'I feel totally beaten', and 'I don't know how to use my time'. But as in the preceding two narratives, it is clear here too that the marking of past tense makes no simple differentiation of verbs on the basis of their aspectual category. Verbs that are states are marked for tense in some contexts of their occurrence, e.g. 'It was unfortunate that I was severely sick on that day', and unmarked in others, as in 'I feel totally beaten'. Once again this marking correlates entirely with their grounding status in the narrative. Being 'severely sick' is highly salient in this narrative since it precipitates the bad performance; 'feeling totally beaten' on the other hand is merely an amplifying statement describing the narrator's disappointment on the occasion of the key event, the bad piano recital.

Unmarked verbs in this passage are also irrealis realisations of situations, which by perfective feature 5 are a part of the background. For example, the writer says in sentence 5 that s/he *had to* face the Advanced Level Examination, not that she faced it; in sentence 10 that the sickness *might* have been due to too much nervousness, not that it was due to it; in sentence 8 that s/he *had to* participate in the piano examination, not that s/he participated in it; in sentence 11 that she *was not able* to play even the simplest piece, not that she did not play even the simplest piece; in sentence 14 that s/he *was not able* to stop crying, not that s/he did not stop crying; and in sentence 17 that s/he *was given ample opportunity* to be prepared for the results, not that she was/was not prepared. In all these irrealis realisations of the situation, the verb goes unmarked for past tense.

It is again noteworthy that the total number of instances of unmarked verbs in this University year 2 narrative increases to 31% (of the total number of verbs used) compared to the 22% (of the total number of verbs used) in the Form 6 narrative and 13% (of the total number of verbs used) in the Form 3 narrative (cf Table 2.4). This increase is again because the writer is better able to provide supplementary information to develop the core event sequence which provides greatly increased opportunity for the use of unmarked verbs. Indeed, if this study were not an assessment which acknowledged the key role played by discourse context in the selective marking hypothesis, it would appear that these learners were regressing (as far as past tense marking is concerned) with academic advancement.

TABLE 2.4

	Total number of verbs used	Number of unmarked verbs	% of unmarked verbs
Form 3	23	3	13
From 6	22	5	22
Year 2	32	10	31

4. OVERALL ASSESSMENT OF DATA

The overall assessment of this corpus of narratives reveals that, for students at all three levels of learning, whenever there is selective marking of past tense, it, without exception, marks grounding distinctions, in the manner exemplified in the above-analysed samples. What, then, changes across the three academic levels is that there is progressive increase in the number of learners using uniform marking (in conformity to target-language syntax) rather than selective marking. As stated earlier, in the 120 narratives examined here (each by a different student) 40 narratives were taken from each of the three proficiency levels: Form 3, Form 6 and Year 2 of university. Out of these 40 narratives, in Form 3, only 15% use uniform marking. This number increases to 55% in Form 6, and to 75% in Year 2 of university (cf Table 2.5 below).

TABLE 2.5

	Total no. of narratives	No. using uniform marking	% using uniform marking
Form 3	40	6	15
Form 6	40	22	55
Year 2	40	30	75

Those learners who retain the selective marking hypothesis, however, evidence an increase in the number of unmarked verbs as they improve as writers, because, as stated above, improvement in writing skills means the learner is better able to provide more auxiliary, non-thematically central detail in the narrative, which creates increased opportunity for use of unmarked verbs signalling backgrounded information. So while there are in fact *fewer learners using selective marking* in Form 6 relative to Form 3 and in University Year 2 relative to Form 6, since the opportunity for use of unmarked verbs increases significantly for users of selective marking, it appears that the overall percentage of unmarked cases generated remains relatively constant across these three levels of learning.

4. ADDRESSING CASES THAT CANNOT BE EXPLAINED BY LEXICO-SEMANTICS

It is interesting to note that this grounding-based interpretation is able to explain two patterns of past tense marking that cannot be addressed at all in the lexical–aspectual approach: 1) the nontarget-like use of past-tense marking on modals, and 2) learners' failure to mark both the verbs of a compound structure denoting what can be interpreted to be a single real-world event, as in 'I got up and left' or 'She opened her mouth wide and shouted loudly'.

There are significant numbers of unmarked modal verbs in this data. There are also many compound constructions in which only one of the successive main verbs is marked for past tense (e.g. 'He unlocked the box and open the lid' and 'He opened his eyes wide and stare hard'). In the lexical–aspectual approach these unmarked verbs are not accounted for. As we have seen above, the current approach explains the failure to mark modals as the result of their interpretation as irrealis events and hence backgrounded information. It is able to explain the marking of only one of two main verbs of a compound structure, denoting only one real-world event, as the output of a learner attending to events rather than individual verbs and their aspectuality. In recognition of a single event, the learner who uses selective marking marks just one of the two verbs used in its denotation, if the event they together denote is salient.

6. THE ROLE OF TRANSFER

It is relevant to consider why this data fails to conform to the so-called universal developmental sequence: the marking of more event-like verbs before less event-like verbs; and why they show selective marking that is responsive to grounding, a discourse perception of aspect, rather than the lexico-semantic perception of it. This deviation from the universal pattern of acquisition appears to result from the transfer of a grounding-marking principle from this learner's L1. Language judgements elicited from my Chinese colleagues suggest that in Chinese the perfective particle '-le' is used to signal foregrounded situations in narrative. It is this that appears to bring about the grounding-sensitive selective-marking of English past tense.

Hopper says of grounding that it is a universal text-organisational phenomenon, and that across languages, therefore, information-saliency distinctions are overtly marked in narrative prose. But they are formally marked cross-linguistically by disparate means (cf Hopper 1977).

In Chinese the marking of grounding appears to be the job of the perfective particle '-le'. It has been claimed of '-le' that it carries the meaning of completed action (cf Chao 1968), and also that it refers to a situation in its entirety, with no assessment of its internal structure (cf Li and Thompson 1981), as in the event of 12, below:

> 12.
> qiche zhuang-dou -le daqiao
> car hit-down -le bridge
> 'The car knocked down the bridge'
> (Li Ping 1989, p 21)

In an attempt to assess whether '-le' plays a grounding-marking role in Chinese narrative, I used the following English transliteration of a passage first used by Hopper (1977) to show the role of the particle '-lah' to mark grounding distinctions in Bahasa Malaysia narrative. I gave this passage to five native speakers of Chinese and asked them to translate it into Chinese, underscoring any '-le'-marked verbs. They consistently used '-le' to mark the underlined verbs in the passage below. Interestingly, there was complete correlation with the use of '-lah' in the original Bahasa Malaysia passage. (It is relevant that both languages are tense-free.)

> One day Mr. raffles was talking with this secretary about wishing to send a reply to Prince Rambas, and suddenly <u>arrived</u> a Malay man bringing six pieces of durian, thinking Mr. Raffles wanted to buy durians, and brought them into the house. He stood at the door and Mr. Raffles <u>got</u> the smell of the durians, and immediately held his nose, <u>ran</u> he upstairs. And <u>amaze</u>d all people to see this thing of running; they didn't know he could not take the smell of durian. And after a moment he called to the sepoy who guarded the door, saying who brought the durian here? And he pointed to the Malay

> man and he ordered him outside quickly, and he gave order to the sepoy, no one allow to bring durian through this door. And from that day no one bold enough to bring durian again. And only them did I realise that Mr. raffles at that time under no circumstances could eat durian. And a moment later came down he downstairs, saying: Mr. head aches from the odor of the durians; a most evil food is that. And smiled all of us to hear his words because different his habits from other people. A thing which was liked by people was hated by him. And because of that, whenever there were people bringing durian, they were sent away by the sepoy.

As Hopper notes, if we separate out the clauses with particle-marked verbs, we get all and only the crucial information of the narrative:

> Suddenly there arrived a Malay man bringing durians.
>
> And Mr. Raffles caught the smell of the durian.
>
> And he ran upstairs.
>
> And everyone was amazed to see this thing of him running.
>
> And a little later he came downstairs again.
>
> And we all smiled to hear his words.

The parallel between the use of '-le' to mark foregrounding, and our students past-tense marking is unmistakable.

It is also relevant to note that in Chinese only one of the verbs used in compound syntactic constructions denoting a single real-world event (as for example 'I opened my mouth wide and shouted loudly') is marked with '-le', when that single denoted event is salient. The suggestion is that the complete grounding–signalling system of L1 is brought to bear to the task of past tense marking in English, and transferred in its entirety.

7. CONCLUSION

This data suggests that grounding, rather than lexical aspect, explains the Chinese learners' selective marking of past tense. It is suggested further that the hypothesis which monitors this selective marking derives from the transfer of a grounding–marking principle from the learners' tense-free L1. Learners use selective marking to signal grounding distinctions in conformity to the transferred L1 system until they, at some point in the acquisition process, reassess this tense-marking hypothesis. At this point, appreciating its difference from the target-language system, they switch to uniform marking. There is nothing in this data which would suggest a developmental sequence.

If this is in fact the case, Bardovi-Harlig and Reynolds' (1995) method of enhancing the learning of English past tense is not fully helpful to the Chinese learner. They suggest that learners must be given positive evidence of the appearance of past-tense marking with verbs which are lexico-aspectually low on the event-like scale (activities and states). For Chinese learners, however, positive evidence must demonstrate that verbs in backgrounded clauses are as well qualified as those in foregrounded clauses for past-tense marking, so that the learner's hypothesis that English past tense is used to show grounding distinctions can be dislodged.

The broader implication of relevance to the larger community of learners— L1 users of a variety of different languages— is that L1 should not be ignored in our efforts to understand and serve the needs of the L2 learner. Also, the method that served to facilitate an effective assessment of past tense marking here— a discourse-based, qualitative assessment of the individual's performance— needs to be incorporated into existing quantitative and collective assessments of learner syntax. The system underlying learner's use of L2 syntax can only be properly gauged when its textual role is appreciated, in the fulfilment of the learner's communicative goal.

References

Andersen R W. 1989. La adquisicion de la morfologia verbal (The acquisition of verb morphology). *Linguistica*, 1: 90–142.

Andersen R W. 1991. Developmental sequences: the emergence of aspect marking in second language acquisition. In T Huebner and C A Ferguson (ed), *Second Language Acquisition and Linguistic Theories*. Amsterdam, Netherlands: John Benjamins.

Bardovi-Harlig K. 1992. The relationship of form and meaning: a cross-sectional study of tense and aspect in interlanguage of learners of English as a second language. *Applied Psycholinguistics*, 13: 253–278.

Bardovi-Harlig K and Bergstrom A. 1996. The acquisition of tense and aspect in SLA and FLL: a study of learner narratives in English (SL) and French (FL). *Canadian Modern Language Review*, 52: 308–330.

Bardovi-Harlig K and Reynolds D W. 1995. The role of lexical aspect in the acquisition of tense and aspect. *TESOL Quarterly*, 29 (1): 107–129.

Chao Yuen-ren. 1968. *A Grammar of Spoken Chinese*. Berkeley: University of California Press.

Hopper P J. 1977. Observations on the typology of focus and aspect in narrative language. *Studies in Language*, 3: 37–64.

Hopper P J. 1979. Aspect and foregrounding in discourse. In T Givon (ed), *Syntax and Semantics Vol 12: Discourse and Syntax*. New York: Academic Press.

Kaplan M A. 1987. Developmental patterns of past tense acquisition among foreign language learners of French. In B VanPatten, T R Dvorak, and J F Lee (ed), *Foreign Language Learning: a Research Perspective*. Cambridge, MA: Newbury House.

Klein W. 1986. *Second Language Acquisition* (rev ed, Bohuslaw Jankowski, Trans.). Cambridge University Press (Original work published 1984).

Kumpf L. 1984. Temporal systems and universality in interlanguage: a case study. In F Eckmann, L Bell, and D Nelson (ed), *Universals of Second Language Acquisition*. Rowley, MA: Newbury House.

Li C and Thompson S. 1981. *Mandarin Chinese: A Functional Reference Grammar*. Berkeley: University of California Press.

Li Ping. 1989. Aspect and Aktionsart in Child Mandarin. Unpublished manuscript.

Meisel J M. 1987. Reference to past events and actions in the development of natural language acquisition. In C W Pfaff (ed), *First and Second Language Acquisition Processes*. Cambridge, MA: Newbury House.

Robison R. 1990. The primacy of aspect: aspectual marking in English in interlanguage. *Studies in Second Language Acquisition*, 12: 315–330.

Shirai Y. 1991. Primacy of Aspect in Language Acquisition: Simplified Input and Prototype. Unpublished doctoral dissertation. University of California, Los Angeles.

Schumann J. 1987. The expression of temporal Basilan speech. *Studies in Second language Acquisition*, 9: 21–41.

Trevise A. 1987. Toward an analysis of (inter)language activity of referring to time in narratives. In C W Pfaff (ed), *First and Second Language Acquisition Processes*. Cambridge, MA: Newbury House.

Veronique D. 1987. Reference to past events and actions in narratives in L2: insights from North African learners' French. In C W Pfaff (ed), *First and Second Language Acquisition Processes*. Cambridge, MA: Newbury House.

von Sutterheim C and Klein W. 1987. A concept-oriented approach to second language acquisition studies. In C W Pfaff (ed), *First and Second Language Acquisition Processes*. Cambridge, MA: Newbury House.

3

The Felicitous Use of 'Then'/'After that'

First published in *System*, 30 (1) (2002), Elsevier

1. INTRODUCTION

Because both the conceptualisation of time and its lexical and/or syntactic marking differ across languages, temporal reference is a daunting task for L2 learners, even at advanced stages of learning. But whereas the challenges inherent to the acquisition of morphological tense and aspect have been addressed in some measure in the SLA and L2 literature (cf Andersen 1989, 1991; Bardovi-Harlig 1992, 1992a, 1992b, 1992c, 1994, 1994a; Bardovi-Harlig and Reynolds 1995; Kaplan 1987; Klein 1986; Klein et al 1993; Kumpf 1982; Meisel 1987; Noyau 1990; Robinson 1990; Schumann 1987; Trevise 1987; Veronique 1987; von Stutterheim and Klein 1987), the same is not true for the acquisition of lexico-syntactic—that is, temporal adverbial—means of temporal reference.

The discourse-based, functional research on the acquisition of temporal reference suggests that temporal adverbials are used early in the acquisition process. In referring to the temporal order of past events (TOP), learners progress from its purely discourse-pragmatic representation—the placing of denoted events in strict chronological order—(cf Bardovi-Harlig 1992a; Klein 1984, 1986; Meisel 1987; Schuman 1987; von Stutterheim and Klein 1987) to the inclusion, by stages, of increasingly more formal means of marking it. Temporal adverbials are said to be used in the first formal representation of TOP (Meisel 1987; Schumann 1987). (Tense marking occurs at a later developmental stage [Bardovi-Harlig 1992a; Meisel 1987; Schumann 1987] .)

Because temporal adverbials are acquired early, researchers do not associate the complexities of the formal marking of temporal reference with its lexico-syntactic representation. For the morphological marking of tense and aspect it is claimed that interlanguage associations of form and meaning are distinct from the target language counterparts, 'it takes some time for form–meaning associations made by the target language to appear in interlanguage' (Bardovi-Harlig 1992, p 274), and formal accuracy often precedes functional felicity. This bifurcation of, and asymmetrical focus in, the learning process (cf Table 3.1 below) has not been shown to be true for the adverbial marking of TOP. This study will suggest that early acquisition of the temporal adverbials 'then' and 'after that' by Chinese and Vietnamese ESL learners does not imply accurate mastery of their function.

TABLE **3.1**

STAGES OF L2 ACQUISITION

	early	**more advanced**
target language	form	form and function
interlanguage	function	

While learners' use of 'then'/'after that' is entirely system governed, the constraints which define it are significantly different from those that govern standard usage.

In standard usage, 'then' and 'after that' are seen to share roughly the same function in the marking of chronological order and are therefore not treated separately in this study. There are some differences, but they do not relate to their core function in marking chronological order. One of the differences, for example, is illustrated in 1 below.

1.

a. All the children were quiet and fully absorbed in the story.
b. Then the lights went out, and all hell broke loose.
c. # After that the lights went out and all hell broke loose.
d. But then the lights went out and all hell broke loose.

In the context of 1a, 1b, which has a sentence initial 'then', is felicitous, while 1c, which has initial 'after that', is not. But the 'then' of 1b does not just signal temporal follow up to 1a; there is an inherent contrastive quality to the relationship of 1b to 1a, so that what is really clause initial is 'but then' as in 1d. When 'then' signals only temporal follow up, it, like 'after that', is constrained to accompany a denoted event which follows a preceding completed event (as in 2b).

2.

a. I kicked him.
b. Then/After that I kicked him again.

For this reason 3b below is not felicitous.

3.

a. It was calm and quiet in there.
b. # Then/after that it was calm and quiet again.

However, 'then' used with its contrastive implication would be felicitous after the state of 4a, as in 4b.

4.

a. It was calm and quiet in there.

b. (But) then it turned into a mad house.

The in-discourse use of temporal 'then'/'after that', in standard usage, marks chronological order for only informationally salient events. The key determinant of informational salience is event centrality to the narrative, but this is not its only determinant. In their use of 'then'/'after that' our learners also mark chronologically ordered situations of central importance to the narrative, but they do so with total disregard for two other deciding factors of informational salience in English narrative. (The term 'situation' conveys no commitment to a particular aspectual category—event or nonevent—that is, it is aspectually neutral.) For our learners 'then' is as felicitous in the 6b and 7b type of sentence as it is in 5b.

5.

a. I got home at five.

b. Then I took the children to the movies.

6.

a. I thought he was wrong.

b. # Then I told him so./And I told him so.

7.

a. The Johnsons had a baby.

b. # Then they called him Tom./ They called him Tom.

In this paper, I will give evidence of, and offer a possible explanation for, this difference. In section 2, I will first describe informational salience in terms of Hopper's (1977, 1979) notion of grounding, and identify the two grounding conditions that are violated by our learners in their marking of chronological order by means of 'then'/'after that'. In section 3, I will discuss representative samples of these violations from my data. And in a final section I will suggest that the difference in the learners' notion of salience emerges out of the transfer of a notion of salience and its formal marking from their tense-free L1s. I will conclude with a brief consideration of the pedagogical implications of these findings.

2. GROUNDING AND THE LEXICO-SYNTACTIC MARKING OF CHRONOLOGICAL ORDER

2.1. Defining the narrative clause

It is first relevant to mention that the constraints on the felicitous marking of chronological order by means of 'then'/'after that' match the conditions on narrative clauses for some definitions of narrative clause. But they constitute a subset of these conditions for other definitions of narrative clause.

A number of competing definitions of narrative clause exist in the extant literature. Common to all these definitions is the principal feature that the events of such clauses are represented in discourse in chronological order (Dry 1981; Dahl 1980; Labov 1981; Labov and Waletzky 1967; Hopper and Thompson 1980, 1979; Hopper 1977, 1979; Reinhart 1984, amongst others). Labov (1981) builds on this basic condition by postulating the temporal juncture condition (a relationship between a pair of clauses such that a change in their order also changes the order of the real-world events they denote), and the 'Then what happened?' condition, his 'critical test' of narrativehood. The potency of the 'Then what happened?' test is illustrated, for example, in 8b. While temporal juncture holds between 8b and 8a, 8b fails the 'Then what happened?' test.

8.

a. I left for school at 9 o'clock

b. (# Then) I arrived in the nick of time.

From a somewhat different perspective, Dry (1981) comments on the aspectual difference between sentential situations which push narrative time forward and those that do not, claiming that in general event sentences push the timeline forward, while nonevent sentences do not. For Dry, therefore, 8b would push the narrative time forward because it qualifies as an event, though it fails Labov's crucial 'Then what happened?' test.

Dahl's (1980) 'maximally short narrative discourse', 'Julius Ceasar's famous statement' (9 below), is also altered in an interesting way, specifically in the pragmatic force it carries, when individual clauses are modified to meet the 'Then what happened?' test (10 below):

9.
Veni, vidi, vici.
'I came, I saw, I conquered.'

10.
I came.
Then I saw.
And then I conquered.

The original text carries the suggestion of inevitable follow up at the completion of the first utterance, 'I came', and second utterance, 'I saw'. With clause-initial 'then' preceding the second and third utterances, the suggestion of inevitable follow up is lost. So, while Labov's 'Then what happened?' test is met, the outcome is by no means quite the same narrative text.

In Hopper's (1977, 1979) notion of the narrative clause again iconic representation of event order is not the only defining feature. Added is the crucial feature of informational salience in the discourse, which Hopper refers to as the grounding of the denoted situation in its discourse context (cf Reinhart 1984, for a somewhat different interpretation of grounding). Because Hopper takes the salience of the denoted situation into account, a clause denoting an event may not qualify as a narrative clause. The clauses of 11b, for example, are not narrative clauses, though they do denote events, because they are not salient to the narrative theme.

11.

a. The girl went inside and shut the door behind her.
b. The sky darkened and took on the shades of the night. An owl hooted eerily from its tree-top perch.
c. She hesitated for just a brief moment and then, with a resoluteness that was new to her, picked up the phone and dialled that dreaded number.

Clearly there is not complete agreement on the specific conditions that are required for narrativehood beyond the fundamental constraint of denoting events in chronological order. The same is not true for clauses that felicitously take temporal 'then'/'after that'. Whether 12b—repeated below from 8—qualifies as a narrative clause or not, its inability to accommodate temporal 'then' seems uncontestable.

12.

a. I left for school at 9 o'clock.
b. (#Then) I arrived in the nick of time.

2.2. Defining information salience

We have said that the in-discourse use of 'then'/'after that' marks chronological order for informationally salient events. Hopper (1977, 1979) refers to informationally salient events, those which are central to the narrative storyline, as Foregrounded events. He contrasts them with Backgrounded situations, which merely amplify or support the key events of the narrative. He defines grounding in terms of a conglomerate of binary features, and uses the cover term 'perfective' for the collection of plus-marked values of these features, referring to the compilation of their negative correlates as the imperfective (cf Table 3.2). Foregrounded situations have more rather than less of the plus marked values, i.e., are more perfective, and those that are backgrounded have more of the negative counterparts, that is, are more imperfective.

TABLE 3.2

Perfective	Imperfective	Constraints on the felicitous marking of chronological order by 'then'/'after that'
1. Strict chronological sequencing	1. Simultaneity or chronological overlap of situation C with event A and/or B.	1. Foregrounded situation
2. View of event as a whole, whose completion is a necessary prerequisite to a subsequent event	2. View of a situation or happening whose completion is not a necessary prerequisite to a subsequent happening.	2. Aspectual constraint: completed situation
3. Identity of subject within each discrete episode.	3. Frequent changes of subject.	3. Given/new constraint: new situation
4. Unmarked distribution of focus in clause, with presupposition of subject and assertion in verb and its immediate complements (or other unmarked focus)	4. Marked distribution of focus, e.g. subject focus, instrument focus, focus on sentence adverbials	
5. Human topics	5. Variety of topics, including natural phenomena	

6. Dynamic, kinetic events	6. Static, descriptive situations	
7. Foregrounding. Event indispensable to narrative	7. Backgrounding. State or situation necessary for understanding motives, attitudes, etc.	
8. Realis	8. Irrealis	

(Modified from Hopper 1979: 216)

Three of the above-defined foregrounding features (listed separately in column 3 of Table 3.2) are crucial to the felicitous lexico-syntactic marking of chronological order. These are event centrality to narrative—the seventh feature of Hopper's list (listed under 1 of column 3)—and two other features: the second feature of Hopper's list (listed under 2 of column 3 and henceforth referred to as the aspectual constraint), and the fourth feature of Hopper's list (listed under 3 of column 3 and henceforth referred to as the given-new constraint). Sample 13b—repeated from 5 above—is felicitous because it conforms to two foregrounding constraints which are systematically violated by our learners: the aspectual constraint and the given-new constraint. Sample 14b—repeated from 6 above—violates the aspectual constraint and 15b—repeated from 7 above—violates the given-new constraint.

13.

a. I got home at five.

b. Then I took the children to the movies.

14.

a. I thought he was wrong.

b. # Then I told him so.

15.

a. The Johnsons had a baby.

b. # Then they called him Tom./They called him Tom.

In what follows, I will say more about the aspectual constraint and the given-new cosntraint and explain how they are violated in 14b and 15b.

The aspectual constraint

To qualify for foregrounding, the event must follow a *completed* preceding event. Vendler (1967) assesses the inherent aspect of the verb and identifies four aspectual categories—states, activities, accomplishments and achievements—depending on whether or not the verb possesses the semantic features of dynamism, telicity (endpoint) and punctility (occurrence at a single point) (cf Table 3.3 below). States are nondynamic, atelic and nonpunctual (as is 'stand' in 'She stood there'), activities are dynamic, atelic and nonpunctual (as is 'walk' in 'She walked '), accomplishments are dynamic, telic and nonpunctual (as is 'build' in 'She built a house') and achievements are dynamic, telic and punctual (as is 'shut' in 'She shut the door').

TABLE 3.3

SEMANTIC FEATURES OF ASPECTUAL CATEGORIES

LEXICAL ASPECTUAL CATEGORIES				
Features	**States**	**Activities**	**Accomplishments**	**Achievements**
punctual	–	–	–	+
telic	–	–	+	+
dynamic	–	+	+	+

(Source: Bardovi-Harlig and Reynolds 1995: 109)

Our assessment is not of the inherent lexical property of the verb alone, which leads to ambiguous assessment of telicity in some cases (cf Dowty 1979). For example, the verb 'walk' can be interpreted as an activity (hence without endpoint) in 'The boy walked' but as an accomplishment (hence with endpoint) in 'The boy walked to school'. Also 'He walked for an hour' and 'He walked in an hour' are 'cases where the verb phrase can be read ambiguously' (Dowty 1979, p 61). For this reason assessment of telicity in this study is made for the denoted situation in the context of its occurrence.

There is another way in which the aspectual assessment here differs from earlier treatments of it. To account for felicitous 'then'/ 'after that' use, it has become necessary to recognise that the completion of events can bring about a resulting associated state. For example, 'got' of 16a is telic, but there is associated with this event the consequential state of being in a state of shock. If the following denoted situation is such that it gives recognition to that continued state, it cannot accommodate 'then'/ 'after that': as in 16b in the context of 16a, where the sobbing uncontrollably clearly happens in the state of shock. When the following denoted situation does not acknowledge this continued state, it does allow for the use of 'then'/ 'after that', as in 16c in the context of 16a.

16.

a. He got the shock of his life when they told him his son had committed suicide
b. (#After that) he started to sob uncontrollably.
c. After that (experience) he basically retired from normal living.

If we now account for the acceptability of 17b, repeated below from 13b, we recognise that besides being in chronological order with respect to 17a, it follows a situation, in (a), completed prior to its commencement, with no acknowledgement of any state associated with (a). Hence the aspectual constraint is met and explicit lexico-syntactic marking of chronological order is felicitous. The same is not true for the chronological ordering in 18b.

17.

a. I got home at five.

b. Then I took the children to the movies.

18.

a. I thought he was wrong.

b. # Then I told him so.

Clause 18a is atelic (that is, it has no end-point); believing is perceived as a state, rather than an event; it does not lend itself to perception as completed. Hence, the aspectual constraint is violated and lexico-syntactic marking of chronological order impermissible.

19.

a. When I came here, I was bored.

b. ? After that I went to school.

The same is true of 19a. Boredom is perceived as a state and is therefore without endpoint. Hence the infelicity of the overt lexico-syntactic marking in 19b.

The given-new constraint

For an event to qualify for foregrounding, there must be 'unmarked distribution of focus in the clause, with presupposition of the subject and assertion in the verb and its immediate complements (or other unmarked focus).' Or, put more simply, the proposition of the clause must be new information at the time of the utterance of the clause. (On the concept of given-new cf Chafe 1976; Clark and Haviland 1977; Halliday 1967; Halliday and Hasan 1976; Horn 1978; Kuno 1972, 1974, 1978, 1979; Prince 1979, 1981.)

There are, however, three types of given information—presupposed, shared knowledge and anticipated—that prevent explicit lexico-syntactic expression of chronological order. (These are three different levels of mutual knowledge between speaker and interlocutor about the event at the time of its denotation.)

Presupposed Event

20.

a. The Johnsons had a baby.
b. (#Then) they called him Tom./Tom they called him.
c. # They gave him a name.

The event of 20b, which was given above under 15, follows the event of 20a in real time, and it occurs after the completion of the event of (a). Hence, the aspectual constraint is fulfilled. But the proposition of 20b is given, rather than new, information at the time of its utterance: it is presupposed information that a baby is given a name after it is born. Hence 20c after 20a is infelicitous.

Shared Knowledge Event

21.

a. I took the Mathematics exam.
b. And (# then) I passed it.

Sentence 21b seems to violate both the aspectual and the given-new constraints. Passing or failing is likely to be perceived as occurring concurrently with the taking of the exam, rather than after it. The proposition of 21b is for this reason not new information at the time of its utterance. That is, it is shared knowledge between speaker and interlocutor, at the time of the utterance of 21b, that I either passed or failed the mathematics exam. Sentence 21b is an instance of this shared knowledge. Hence the given-new constraint is violated.

Anticipated Event

22.

a. I left for class at 9:30.
b. and arrived in the nick of time./ I arrived in the nick of time.

c. and (#then) I arrived in the nick of time.

Sentence 22b, repeated from 12 above, is in chronological order with respect to 22a, but both the above-described constraints are again violated. Whereas the verb of 22a is lexically an achievement, it results in the consequential activity of my being on my way to class, and this is not a situation with endpoint. Hence the aspectual condition is not met. By the same logic, 22b is not entirely new information at the time of its utterance: at the time of the utterance of 22b, it is presupposed that one of a set of actions that can occur after 22a will follow it. When we are told that someone has set off for a particular destination, it is presupposed that s/he will either get there or not get there. The difference from 20b is that at the time of its utterance the proposition of 20b itself is presupposed; it is presupposed that babies are given names. At the time of the utterance of 22b, however, it is presupposed that what follows must be one of two options: I either got there or I did not get there. The presupposition of these two potential outcomes creates anticipation of a selection of one of the two of them. Therefore 22b is highly anticipated, and hence the given-new constraint is violated.

I indicated above that 23b, repeated from 17, meets the aspectual constraint. It also satisfies the given-new constraint: The proposition of 23b is new information at the time of its utterance. That is, there is no presupposed, or shared, knowledge about the denoted event; nor is the event anticipated at the time of the utterance of 23b. All that is mutually known between speaker and interlocutor is that it can felicitously follow the event of 23a.

23.

a. I got home at five.

b. Then I took the children to the movies.

There are three given events, referred to above, that do not allow 'then '/ 'after that' to explicitly express chronological sequencing, but they are given in different ways and this can be syntactically represented: in 24b, repeated from 20, the presupposed event permits preposing.

24.

a. The Johnsons had a baby.

b i. They called him Tom/ ii. Tom they called him.

Sentence 25b, repeated from 21, which is merely shared knowledge, rather than presupposed, does not; it can only be in canonical order.

25.

a. I took the Mathematics exam.

b. i. And I passed it./ ii. # And it I passed.

Although 26c below is felicitous, the passing or failing of the exam is not just shared knowledge here; it is presupposed. That is, at the time of its utterance the hearer is actually attending to failure or success in relation to the taking of the Mathematics exam.

26.

a. I took the Chemistry exam and failed it.

b. But then I took the Mathematics exam.

c. And this I passed.

In 27b, repeated from 22, the temporal follow up of one of two potential events—getting there or not getting there—is presupposed, making the event of 27b itself highly anticipated. This allows VP conjunction, cf 27b(ii).

27.

a. I left for class at 9:30(.)

b. i. I arrived in the nick of time./ ii. and arrived in the nick of time.

We have suggested in the above that to felicitously mark chronological order, the 'then'-/'after that'-marked clause must conform to three grounding constraints. It must conform to the principle grounding constraint, which requires the denoted event to be an informationally key narrative happening. It is also aspectually constrained, that is, it must follow a completed preceding event. In addition, it must uphold the given-new constraint: that is, it must be informationally new, rather than shared knowledge, presupposed or anticipated.

As we will see in the next section, in their marking of chronological order by means of 'then'/'after that', our ESL learners often violate two of the above- described three grounding constraints: the aspectual constraint and the given-new constraint.

3. DATA ANALYSIS

The data for this study comprises 150 short essays written by Vietnamese and Chinese ESL learners. There are a total of 416 instances of 'then'/'after that' used in these essays. A little over two-thirds of this number appear to be felicitously used; the remaining violate one or the other of the above-mentioned two grounding constraints. Although the larger number of temporal adverbials appear to be correctly used, the examination of the significant number of infelicitous cases suggests that all the instances of 'then'/'after that' use follow a distinct governing principle from that which monitors standard usage. As stated above, in native-speaker usage 'then'-/'after that'-marked situations must be informationally central to the narrative, but also informationally new and aspectually telic. In our ESL learner's system 'then'-/'after that'-marked situations are also required to be informationally central to story-line, but while they may also be new and telic, they are not constrained to be either. This is because informational salience is the only necessary condition on their felicitous use. This means that 'then'-/'after that'-marked situations often are both new and telic, because in narrative prose the language user is likely to refer to salient situations which happen to be both informationally new and telic (this accounts for the large percentage of felicitous uses of 'then'/'after that'), but they are also either atelic or nonnew in significant numbers.

The Vietnamese learners of this study were young adults who had spent between ten months and three years in the U.S. at the time these essays were written. All of them were enrolled in a non-intensive preacademic program at a U.S. community college, where they received formal instruction in written and spoken English at four separate levels of instruction. There were four writing courses, each one of a fourteen-week duration. To support free-writing on topics chosen to facilitate the use of appropriate linguistic means of representing TOP, all the students received overt instruction in the basics of the English tense-aspectual system via a traditional pedagogical grammar. In this, the concept of linear time represented through deictic tense is described, and the expression of the internal constituency of denoted situations is shown to be facilitated by such basic aspectual categories as continuity versus completion. They also received some explicit instruction in the use of sentence connectors, including temporal adverbials, but this was limited to illustrating and encouraging their felicitous use, while presupposing knowledge of the constraints that monitor such use[1].

This information about the English tense-aspect system and sentential connectors was introduced in the beginner's writing course and repeatedly revised and updated in the following three courses.

The Chinese learners were freshmen at a Hong Kong university. They had learned English as a foreign language, that is, for a few hours a week, from age three or four to about age twelve, at which time they started using English in most of their classes. It is important to notc that by the age of eighteen, in their freshman year in college, they had had many years of exposure to the English language, but that it was entirely in the context of the classroom and with opportunity largely only to listen to lectures and read textbooks and lecture notes. Their mastery of English, therefore, remained very passive. There was inadequate opportunity to practise writing in their curriculum, and little attention given to grammar consciousness raising. In spite of this, the Vietnamese and Chinese learners of this study are, as one would expect, at separate levels of learning. Yet their use of 'then'/'after that' is entirely alike in that one underlying system of rules governs it for both groups of learners. This is significant in suggesting the challenge that this temporal adverbial poses for learners whose L1 is tense-free.

In what follows, the first complete student narrative is used to show that while each 'then'-marked situation is thematically central to the narrative, four out of the seven situations also appear to violate the aspectual and/or the given-new constraints. Subsequently, further violations of the aspectual and given-new constraints are illustrated using additional student essays. For space constraints, the relevant 'then'-marked clauses are presented in only their immediate discourse context, but with their informational centrality still quite apparent.

Sample 1

My first date

First time, I went out with my girl friend. She invited me to go to her sister birthday party. I went to the birthday party, I saw a lot of people. I felt very nervous with them. There were a lot of strange people because I didn't see them before. She was going to introduce me to her family. At that time I felt a little bit afraid by myself. I didn't know Why? [1]**Then** she found me and her a good place to seat. There were a lot of tables. Every table had 10 chairs. In my table, I and her sat together with 8 more people. They were her sister friend. But every people in my group was very nice and polite. I was sitting next to her, [2]**then** I was talking with her very excited at that time. Some time I tried to talk with another people in my group because I wanted to try friendly with them. [3]**Then** I felt really better now. I didn't feel to afraid by myself anymore. I asked her about the people who sat near her parents. [4]**Then**

> she showed to me everything I wanted to know. [5]**After** (that) the party finished. I came to say good night with family, [6]**then** I kissed her and I said good night. I felt very happy at that night. When I came home I just wanted to go to sleep. [7]**Then** I had a wonderful night sleep. That party was very nice to be. It made me feel very happiness. It was a good time to talk with her. I never forget it. Everytime when I went to another party, it made me to remember that night.

This essay was written by a Vietnamese student in a beginner's course in writing in about the twelfth week of instruction. If we list the 'then'-marked clauses of this narrative, we see that they sum up its key situations.

1.1. She found us a good place to sit.

1.2. I talked to her.

1.3. I felt better (less nervous, less frightened).

1.4. She showed/told me everything I wanted to know.

1.5. The party ended.

1.6. I kissed her goodnight.

1.7. I had a wonderful night's sleep.

However, all but three of these situations do not uphold the aspectual and/or the given-new constraints. Clauses 1.3, 1.5 and 1.6 are felicitously 'then'-marked. In addition to being central to the storyline, they follow completed preceding situations and are informationally new in their respective contexts of appearance. In 1.3, feeling better follows the preceding completed situation of talking/making an attempt to talk to other people. Additionally, 1.3 is neither presupposed, shared knowledge nor anticipated information in the context of its preceding discourse.

(For) some time I tried to talk (talked) to other people.

1.3. Then I felt better.

In 1.5 the party ends after the preceding completed situation, in which the narrator is told what he wants to know by his girlfriend. Clause 1.5 is also neither presupposed, shared knowledge nor anticipated in the context of its preceding discourse.

> She showed (told) me everything I wanted to know.
> 1.5. After that the party finished.

In 1.6, kissing the girlfriend goodnight follows the preceding completed situation of saying goodbye to her family, and 1.6 is also neither presupposed, shared knowledge nor anticipated in the context of its preceding discourse.

> I said goodnight to the family.
> 1.6. Then I kissed her...

In the remaining four 'then'-marked clauses, however, it is not clear that the aspectual and/or the given-new constraints are being upheld. The first 'then'-marked clause in the narrative appears to follow a comment about the narrator's state of mind, which state of mind, being atelic, cannot fulfil the aspectual constraint:

> At that time I felt a little bit afraid by myself. I didn't know why?
> 1.1 Then she found for me and her a good place to sit.

The situation preceding the second key situation is an activity; that is, a situation without an endpoint.

> I was sitting next to her,
> 1 2. Then I was talking with her...

It is possible that an endpoint is intended. This would mean the situation is being interpreted by the speaker as an accomplishment, rather than as an activity, though there is no overt representation of the intended endpoint. If the hearer assumes an implicit endpoint, the sequence seems acceptable. Notice that when an explicit endpoint is introduced, as in 1.2.1 and 1.2.2, the sequence does become felicitous:

> I was sitting next to her for the first hour.
>
> 1.2.1. Then for the next hour I was (actually) talking to her.

> I was sitting next to her.
>
> 1.2.2. After sitting in awkward silence for a while, I picked up a little courage and started talking to her.

Clause 1.4 is anticipated at the time of its utterance and hence violates the given-new constraint:

> I asked her about the people who sat near her parents.
>
> 1.4. Then she showed (told) me everything I wanted to know.
>
> 1.4.1 And she told me everything I wanted to know.

When a question is asked, an answer is anticipated, and therefore 1.4 cannot accommodate sentence-initial 'then'/'after that'; 1.4.1 without 'then'/'after that' is, hence, felicitous. For the same reason, the sequence leading to 1.4.2, below, is felicitous only as child language, or when what happened after the reported asking of the question is not assumed to be forthcoming

> I asked her a question. Then what happened?
>
> 1.4.2. Then she told me everything I wanted to know.

Clause 1.7 again violates the aspectual constraint. The state of wanting of the preceding clause is atelic:

> When I came home I just wanted to go to sleep.
>
> 1.7. Then I had a wonderful night's sleep.

Notice the infelicity of the following similar uses of 'then':

> Last night I wanted to go to a movie.
> #Then/ # After that/So I went./ And I went./ But I couldn't go.

> We were bored with the party.
> # Then/ # After that/So we left.

The awkwardness of using 'then'/'after that' in 1.7 becomes fully apparent when this use of 'then' is compared with its occurrence after situations with endpoint, as in 1.7a:

> I watched the late-night film./I finished my letter./I wanted to sleep.
> 1.7a. After that I had a wonderful night's sleep.

In the following additional examples of aspectual and given-new constraint violations by Chinese and Vietnamese learners, I will separately examine illustrative examples of aspectual constraint violation and given-new constraint violation.

Aspectual violations

> **Sample 2**
> How I Spend my Free Time
> I came to the United States 8 months ago. When I came here, I had a lot of free time but I did not anything. [1]**After that I went to college to study.** Now I only have free time on weekend.

This extract is taken from an essay written by a Vietnamese student enrolled in an intermediate-level writing course (the second course of four).

The event of 2.1 is informationally significant: the narrator, a newcomer to the U.S., joins a college, after an initial period of disorientation in which s/he did nothing at all. But the situation preceding

2.1 cannot be perceived as having an endpoint, nor is one explicitly indicated in the discourse. Notice the infelicity of suggesting the act of going to college occurred after the state of doing nothing, in the following question-answer exchange:

> When did you go to college to study?
>
> ?After I did nothing.

> **Sample 3**
>
> My Favorite Park
>
> Yesterday was a wonderful day. I was there (at the park) from six p.m. to eight p.m. There were many people go there. About seven o'clock p.m., I saw a friend he was walking in the shoulder of the pond. [1]**After that, we had go together**.

This extract is taken from an essay written by a Vietnamese student enrolled in an intermediate-level writing course (the second of four courses).

Clause 3.1 is significant because the narrator, who was making a pleasant but solitary round of the park, is at this point accompanied by a friend. But the act of walking of the preceding clause cannot be perceived as completed. The text is improved by the use of the past tense, as in 3.2, because it is possible, but not necessary, to construe this as the telic event 'he took a walk'.

> About seven o'clock, I saw a friend. He walked in the shoulder of the pond. [2]**After that we walked together**.

But it becomes entirely acceptable only if we, in addition, introduce an explicit end point, as in 3.3.

> About seven o'clock, I saw a friend. He walked in the shoulder of the pond.
>
> [3]**After he was done with that**, we walked together.

Sample 4

Why I Left My Country

When the communism occupied South Vietnam I left my country and live in Saigon city.Itis a big city and noised on the street. [1]**Then I visited some beautiful place in Saigon...**

My country was very poor, about 3.2 millions population. A lot of people did not have job, me too. So I want a new land. [2]**After that my sister guarantee all my family to U.S.A.**

This extract is taken from an essay written by a Vietnamese learner, enrolled in the beginner's course, in about the twelfth week of instruction.

The sightseeing of 4.1 is an obvious priority of visitors to new places, but clearly 'visiting beautiful places' occurred during the period in which this individual lived in Saigon, not after the stay was completed. Hence the aspectual constraint is violated in 4.1.

The event of 4.2 is significant because, here, a family member is responsible for ensuring the narrator's entry to America, thus giving him/her a new lease on life. But 'then' is infelicitous because the aspectual constraint is again violated. The state of wanting of the preceding clause is without endpoint.

Sample 5

Recently I have made quite a great progress in the use of Chinese words. From the beginning our lecturer of the subject modern Chinese writing had provided us with quite a lot of great writings to read. [1]**Then we needed to try to do some exercises which was aiming at finding out some words which were wrongly used.**

This extract is taken from an essay written by a freshman at a Hong Kong university, with Chinese as L1.

In 5.1 doing the exercises is a significant part of learning Chinese vocabulary, but the preceding clausal situation of having been assigned a lot of readings cannot be perceived as having an endpoint. Hence the infelicity of this use of 'then'.

Given-new violations

The following are examples of infelicitous 'then'-marking in which the denoted situation is given information in the context of its occurrence.

Sample 6

After consulting the vet, he told me that he would put some bandage to consolidate her injury.

This extract is taken from the essay of a freshman at a Hong Kong university who uses Chinese as L1.

Diagnosis and treatment are significant in a visit to the vet, but clearly though the information requested is given after the consultation is made, this explication of the necessary treatment is a highly anticipated event in the context of the consultation, and hence the given-new constraint is violated.

Sample 7

After we left home, BB (the dog) finding us not here, then she cried for us because she was afraid that we left her alone.

This is an extract from an essay written by a freshman at a Hong Kong university, with Chinese as L1.

Here the dog's anguish is informationally significant, but the syntactic structure of both the preceding clauses makes a following event inevitable. An event that can felicitously follow must do so in this context; hence the given-new constraint is violated and 'then'-marking is infelicitous.

Sample 8

But striving to survive for our family, my father had never complained on the fate. He even didn't mention his illness before our siblings but **tried to recover his health** by practising some special exercise and taking endless treatments instructed by his doctor. [1]**Then he could really defeat the cancer and survive him.**

This is an extract from an essay written by a Chinese freshman at a Hong Kong university, with Chinese as L1.

The 'then'-marked and preceding clauses are rewritten below to better represent the underlying difference from standard native usage.

He tried to recover his health

1. ?Then he recovered his Health./and in fact recovered it.

The event of recovery is obviously informationally salient, but it is also shared knowledge (in the context of the attempt to recover) that the person will either recover or not recover. Clause 8.1 is an instance of this shared knowledge. Hence the given-new constraint is violated and this use of 'then' is infelicitous.

Sample 9

Every time, I stayed out late at night, [1]**then I have been punish by my uncle.**

This extract is taken from an essay written by a Vietnamese student enrolled in an advanced (third level) writing course.

Here although the act of being punished is noteworthy, the syntactic structure of the preceding clause makes it inevitable that an event that can felicitously follow will follow. Hence the given-new constraint is violated and 'then'-marking is infelicitous.

Sample 10

After I have had graduated high school. I didn't think of going to school no-more. One day my mum came to me and give me some advice about my future. [1]**Then I took her advice and came to college, so here I am**.

This extract is from an essay written by an advanced (level three) Vietnamese student.

Although taking the advice in 10.1 is a significant event in this narrative, it is shared knowledge that the advice given will be either accepted or rejected. Clause 10.1 is an instance of this shared knowledge, and hence the given-new constraint is violated and the 'then'-marking is infelicitous.

Notice that whereas 10.2 below is a felicitous response to its preceding question, 10.3 is awkward because it constitutes a statement of the obvious.

> When did you take your mum's advice?
>
> 10.2. Not immediately after she gave it to me.
>
> 10.3. After she gave it to me.

11.

> After that my family went to find a job. [1]**And then we found a job.**

This extract is taken from an essay written by a Vietnamese student enrolled in the beginner's class, in about the twelfth week of instruction.

Finding the sought-after job is highly significant, but this event is also highly anticipated at the time of the utterance of this clause: It is presupposed that one of a set of events that can felicitously follow the event of the preceding clause will follow it. By the given-new constraint, therefore, 11.1 cannot accommodate the initial temporal adverb.

4. DISCUSSION

It is clear that while this use of the adverbial marking of chronological order is not asystemic in the learners' interlanguage, it differs from its target language counterpart in being governed by less stringent constraints: the lexico-syntactically marked chronologically ordered situation 1) is not constrained to follow a completed preceding event, and 2) while it is of key importance to the narrative, it is not necessarily informationally new: that is, it may be presupposed, shared knowledge or anticipated, at the time of the utterance of the clause that denotes it.

A clear explanation for this idiosyncratic use of temporal 'then' is suggested by the representational systems of TOP marking in the tense-free L1s of these learners: Chinese and Vietnamese. Both languages, along with other tense-free languages such as Malay, use verb-final perfective aspect particles to facilitate the marking of TOP (cf Chao 1968; Hopper 1977; Li and Thompson 1981; Li et al 1982; Li Ping 1989).

In his discussion of the perfective aspect particle in classical Bahasa Malaysia narrative, Hopper indicates that verbs denoting foregrounded events are marked with the perfective particle 'lah'. In the following English translation of a Bahasa narrative taken from Hopper (1977), these verbs are in boldface.

12.

> One day Mr Raffles was talking with his secretary about wishing to send a reply to Prince Rambas, and suddenly **arrived** a Malay man bringing six pieces of durians, thinking Mr Raffles wanted to buy durians, and brought them into the house. He stood at the door and Mr Raffles **got** the smell of the durians and immediately held his nose, **ran** he upstairs, and **amazed** all people to see this thing of running; they didn't know he could not take the smell of durian. And after a moment he called to the sepoy who guarded the door, saying, who brought the durian here? And he pointed to the Malay man, and he ordered him outside quickly, and he gave order to the sepoy, no-one allow to bringing durian through this door. And from that day no-on bold enough to bring durian again. And only then did I realize that Mr Raffles at that time under no circumstances could eat durian. And a moment later **came down** he downstairs, saying: My head aches from the odor of the durian; a most evil food is that. And **smiled** all of us to hear his words because different his habits from other people. A thing which was liked by people was hated by him. And because of that, whenever there were people bringing durian, they were sent away by the sepoy.

This passage also properly indicates the verbs that would be marked with the perfective particle ('le') in Chinese and Vietnamese. Hopper (1979) claims that 1) clauses bearing a perfective particle denote events that are the 'crucial foci of the narrative', and 2) the 'sequentiality property of "lah" involves necessarily a view of the action which it signifies as something completed; the next turn of events in the narrative cannot be initiated, until the preceding event signalled by "lah" has been completed'. However, while the verbs with a perfective particle in the above passage do denote the key situations of the storyline, they do not in fact appear to lend themselves to perception as completed prior to the commencement of the next 'lah'-marked verb. And interestingly, whereas some scholars have supported Hopper's 'completed action' meaning of the perfective aspect marker (cf Chao 1968), others (cf Li and Thompson 1975; Li Ping 1990) argue that what the particle in fact conveys is not 'completed action' but rather 'contrast to previous state'. And it is this meaning of the perfective particle that is in fact evident in the examination of its occurrence in narrative discourse in Chinese, Vietnamese and Bahasa Malaysia. Notice that it is not the case in the above passage that the Malay man arrived ('arrived' is marked with the perfective particle in all three languages) after the secretary had finished talking to Mr Raffles, but rather while the secretary was talking to his boss. And while arrival is telic, the consequential state of being there (which is without endpoint) is acknowledged by the next particle-marked event, of Mr Raffles getting the smell of the durian. Mr Raffles gets the smell because the man is there with the durian. Nor is it possible to suggest that the next particle-marked situation—that Mr Raffles ran up the stairs—occurs after the preceding particle-marked situation of getting the smell of the durian is completed. Though 'got' is telic, the associated state of the smell being there is acknowledged in the particle-marked situation of Mr Raffles running up the stairs. Likewise for the next particle-marked situation, the people were not amazed after Mr Raffles had finished running upstairs. Rather, as is stated in the narrative itself, they were amazed to see him run upstairs.

In fact the 'completed action' interpretation of the perfective particle is not evidenced in any of the verbs with perfective particles in the above passage.

And because the 'completed action' interpretation is not evident and hence, what we referred to earlier under (2) as, the aspectual constraint is not upheld, English translations of clauses containing verbs with the perfective particle in general cannot take temporal 'then'. In 14 'then' is opposed to the on-going quality of the activity denoted in 13; 'when' would accommodate it. 'Then' in 15 and 16 reads as childlike prose; its presence takes away from the consequential relationship that holds between 15 and 14, and 16 and 15, respectively.

13. One day Mr Raffles was talking with his secretary about wishing to send a reply to Prince Rambas.
14. And (?then/afterthat) suddenly there arrived a Malay man bringing durians.
15. And (?then/after that) Mr Raffles caught the smell of the durian.
16. And (?then/after that) he ran upstairs.
17. And (?then/after that) everyone grew amazed to see (this thing of) him runnmg.
18. And (?then/after that) a little later he came downstairs again.
19. And (?then/after that) we all smiled to hear his words.

In addition, most of these clauses are not informationally new, in the way required by the given-new constraint, by which nothing about the situation must be presupposed, shared knowledge or anticipated at the time of the utterance that denotes it: At the time of the utterance of 14, we anticipate that something is about to happen; Clause 14 is an instance of an anticipated situation, and in this context 'then' is infelicitous. Notice the similar anticipated situation of (20b):

20.

a. You'll never believe what happened at the bank: It was crowded with people, and everything was running smoothly,

b. (#After that) suddenly a man pulled out a pistol and...

At the time of the utterance of 15, it is shared knowledge that the situation of 15 is a consequence of the preceding situation, that is, Mr Raffles catches the smell of the durian because the man has brought it. Hence 15 cannot take 'then'. Notice the similar example of 21b:

21.

a. He fell off his horse.

b. i. # Then/after that, he broke his neck/ii. And (he) broke his neck.

Similarly, it is shared knowledge at the time of the utterance of 16 that it is a consequence of 15, that is, Mr Raffles runs upstairs because he smells the durian. Hence, 16 too cannot accommodate 'then'. And at the time of the utterance of 17, it is shared knowledge that it is a reaction to 16. In fact, that everyone is amazed by Mr Raffles running upstairs is explicitly stated in 17. Hence, 17 too cannot accommodate 'then'. Notice the similar example of 22b:

22.

a. He told the funniest jokes I've ever heard.

b. (#Then) we laughed until we cried.

In 18, Mr Raffles came down a little later, but clearly not after everyone was amazed, which is what we would have to conclude if the aspectual constraint held for 18. And finally the observers smiled in 19, as we are explicitly told, in reaction to Mr Raffles' words; Clause 19 therefore comments on a non-key situation (one that is not marked with the perfective particle) and it is not contingent upon the completion of 18.

Clearly key situations in this narrative, like those of the narrative extracts of section 3 above, do not obey either the aspectual or the given-new constraint. As in the ESL narrative extracts by Chinese and Vietnamese learners of section 3, in the above narrative, chronological order is given explicit lexico-syntactic marking when the situation so ordered is central to the storyline, but not necessarily 1) contingent upon the completion of its preceding situation, or 2) entirely new information at the time of its denotation. The suggestion is that in transferring grounding conventions from tense-free languages, learners hypothesise the above-stated somewhat less stringent set of constraints on the lexico-syntactic marking of chronological order.

While it is recognised that the cross-linguistic differences in the conceptualisation of time and/or its formal marking impact L2 acquisition of temporal reference, further research is called for to lend detail to our understanding of the ways in which L2 acquisition is affected. The identification of the above specified differences in the use of the temporal adverb 'then'/ 'after that' by Ll users of a tenseless language aims to contribute at this level of specific details to this understanding. At the level of practical implications, these findings suggest that for Chinese and Vietnamese learners, and very likely speakers of other tenseless languages, the absence in L1 of morphological tense-aspect marking and the use in its place of lexical and discourse anchors does not impact the learner's ability to master English tense and aspect alone. Rather, the whole mechanism facilitating temporal reference is affected, so that teachers cannot assume shared intuitions on the felicitous use of 'so simple a word' as 'then'. Classroom instruction is likely to benefit if target usage is introduced as a subset of the broader functional domain marked out by learners' 'then'. The learner can be made aware that thematic centrality of the denoted situation is not the only condition on felicitous 'then'-marking. In this, negative evidence can be used to illustrate the more stringent constraints, requiring conformity to the above-defined aspectual and given-new grounding conditions. Learners can be given examples of infelicitous 'then'-marking which is the result of either violation of the aspectual constraint, as in 23b, or violation of the given-new constraint, as in 24b.

23.
a. I thought he was wrong.
b. # Then I told him so.

24.
a. The Johnsons had a baby.
b. # Then they gave him a name.

Learners can practise examining examples of both felicitous and infelicitous 'then'-marking to separate out felicitous from infelicitous examples. They can then be encouraged to re-read and edit first drafts of their own writing, to ensure that 'then' and 'after that' show conformity to the target language constraints on their felicitous use.

Notes

1. Encouraging learners to use temporal adverbials, without giving attention to the constraints on their felicitous use may well lead learners to adopt a less rigorously constrained usage of temporal adverbials. But in my considerable experience as an ESL teacher I have not found that all learners, irrespective of their L1, have the type of difficulty with target-like use of 'then'/'after that' that is demonstrated by the Chinese and Vietnamese learners of this study.

References

Andersen R W. 1989. The theoretical status of variation in interlanguage development. In S Gass, C Madden, D Preston and L Selinker (ed), *Variation in Second Language Acquisition* 1, II: *Psycholinguistic Issues*. Clevedon: Multilingual Matters.

Andersen R W. 1991. Developmental sequences: the emergence of aspect marking in second language acquisition. In T Huebner and C A Ferguson (ed), *Second Language Acquisition and Linguistic Theories*. Amsterdam Netherlands: John Benjamins.

Bardovi-Harlig K. 1992. The relationship of form and meaning: a cross-sectional study of tense and aspect in interlanguage of learners of English as a second language. *Applied Psycholinguistics*, 13: 253–278.

Bardovi-Harlig K. 1992a. The use of adverbials and natural order in the development of temporal expression. *International Review of Applied Linguistics*, 30: 299–320.

Bardovi-Harlig K. 1992b. Adverbs, aspect, and tense. In N Bird and J Harris (ed), *Selected Proceedings of the Seventh ILE* (Institute for Language in Education) *Conference: QUILT and QUILL* (*Quality in Language Teaching and Quality in Language Learning*). Hong Kong: Institute of Language in Education, Education Department.

Bardovi-Harlig K. 1992c. The telling of a tale: discourse structure and tense use in learners' narratives. In L Bouton and Y Kachru (ed), *Pragmatics and Language Learning 3*. Urbana-Champaign, Il: DEIL.

Bardovi-Harlig K. 1994. Reverse-order reports and the acquisition of tense: beyond the principle of chronological order. *Language Learning*, 44 (2): 243–282.

Bardovi-Harlig K. 1994a. Anecdote or evidence? Evaluation support for hypotheses concerning the development of tense and aspect. In E E Tarone, S M Gass and A D Cohen (ed), *Research Methodology in Second Language Acquisition*. Hillsdale: Lawrence Erlbaum.

Bardovi-Harlig K and Reynolds D W. 1995. The acquisition of tense in SLA and FLL: a study of learner narratives in English (SL) and French (FL). *Canadian Modern Language Review*, 52: 308–330.

Chafe W. 1976. Givenness, contrastiveness, definiteness, subjects, topics, and point of view. In C Li (ed), *Subjects and Topics*. New York: Academic Press.

Chao Yuen-ren. 1968. *A Grammar of Spoken Chinese*. Berkeley: University of California Press.

Clark H and Haviland S. 1977. Comprehension and the given-new contract. In R Freedle (ed), *Discourse Production and Comprehension*. Hillsdale, N.J.: Lawrence Erlbaum Associates.

Dahl O. 1980. Temporal distance: remoteness distinctions in tense-aspect systems. In B Butterworth, B Comrie and O Dahl (ed), *Explanations of Language Universals*. Mouton Publishers.

Dowty D. 1979. *Word Meaning and Montague Grammar*. Dordrecht: Reidel.

Dry Helen. 1981. Sentence aspect and the movement of narrative time. *Text*, 1 (3): 233–240.

Halliday M A K. 1967. Notes on transitivity and theme in English, Part 2. *Journal of Linguistics*, 3: 199–244.

Halliday M A K and Hasan Ruqaiya. 1976. *Cohesion in English*. London: Longmans.

Hopper P J. 1977. Observations on the typology of focus and aspect in narrative language. *Studies in Language*, 3: 37–64.

Hopper P J. 1979. Aspect and foregrounding in discourse. In T Givon (ed), *Syntax and Semantics: Discourse and Syntax*. New York: Academic Press.

Horn L. 1978. *Presupposition, Theme et Variations*. (ms.)

Kaplan M A. 1987. Developmental patterns of past tense acquisition among foreign language learners of French. In B VanPatten, T R Dvorak, and J F Lee (ed), *Foreign Language Learning: a Research Perspective*. Cambridge, MA: Newbury House.

Klein W. 1986. *Second Language Acquisition* (rev ed., Bohuslaw Jankowski, Trans.). Cambridge University Press. (Original work published 1984).

Klein W, Dietrich R and Noyau C. 1993. The acquisition of temporality. In C Perdue (ed), *Adult Language Acquisition: Cross-linguistic Perspectives*. Vol. 2/*The Results*. Cambridge: University Press.

Kumpf L. 1982. Tense, aspect and modality in interlanguage: a discourse–functional approach. Unpublished paper, UCLA.

Kuno S. 1972. Functional sentence perspective: a case study for Japanese and English. *Linguistic Inquiry*, 3: 269–320.

Kuno S. 1974. Lexical and contextual meaning. *Linguistic Inquiry*, 5: 469–477.

Kuno S. 1978. Generative discourse in America. In W Dressler (ed), *Current Trends in Text Linguistics*. Berlin and New York: de Gruyter.

Kuno S. 1979. *On the Interaction Between Syntactic Rules and Discourse Principles*. (ms.)

Labov W. 1981. Speech actions and reactions in personal narrative. In *Analyzing Discourse: Text and Talk*. Georgetown University Round Table. Washington, DC: Georgetown University Press.

Labov W and Waletzky J. 1967. Narrative analysis: oral versions of personal experience. In J Helm (ed), *Essays on the Verbal Visual Arts*. Proceedings of the 1966 Annual Spring Meeting of the American Ethnological Society. Seattle: University of Washington Press.

Li C and Thompson S. 1981. *Mandarin Chinese: A Functional Reference Grammar*. University of California Press, Berkeley.

Li C, Thompson S and McMillan Thompson R. 1982. The discourse motivation for the perfect aspect: the Mandarin particle LE. In P J Hopper (ed), *Tense, Aspect: Between Semantics and Pragmatics*. Amsterdam: John Benjamins.

Li Ping. 1989. *Aspect and Aktionsart in Child Mandarin*. Unpublished manuscript.

Meisel J M. 1987. Reference to past events and actions in the development of natural language acquisition. In C W Pfaff (ed), *First and Second Language Acquisition Processes*. Cambridge, MA: Newbury House.

Noyau Collete. 1990. The development of means of temporality in the unguided acquisition of L2: cross-linguistic perspectives. In Hans W Dechert (ed), *Current Trends in European Second Language Acquisition Research*. Clevedon: Multilingual Matters.

Prince E F. 1979. On the given/new distinction. In W Hanks, C Hofbauer and P Clyne (ed), *Papers from the Fifteenth Regional Meeting of the Chicago Linguistics Society*. University of Chicago.

Prince E F. 1981. Toward a taxonomy of given/new information. In P Cole (ed), *Radical Pragmatics*. New York: Academic Press.

Reinhart T. 1984. Principles of gestalt perception in the temporal organization of narrative texts. *Linguistics*, 22: 779–809. Mouton Publishers.

Robison R. 1990. The primacy of aspect: aspectual marking in English interlanguage. *Studies in Second Language Acquisition*, 12: 315–330.

Schumann J. 1987. The expression of temporal Basilan speech. *Second language Acquisition*, 9: 21–41.

Vendler Zeno. 1967. Verbs and times. In Z Vendler (ed), *Linguistics in Philosophy*. New York: Cornell University Press.

von Stutterheim C and Klein W. 1987. A concept-oriented approach to second language acquisition studies. In C W Pfaff (ed), *First and Second Language Acquisition Processes*. Cambridge, MA: Newbury House.

4

On the Structure of Enumeration

First published in the *Australian Review of Applied Linguistics* 22 (2) (2001), John Benjamins

INTRODUCTION

A number of researchers (Meyer 1975, 1977a, 1977b; Meyer, Brandt and Bluth 1980; Meyer and Freedle 1984; Carrell 1983; Connor 1984) have claimed that Collection is one of the most rudimentary of expository text configurations. They suggest that unlike expository configurations such as Comparison, Causation and Problem/Solution, it possesses no top-level structure at all. This lack of structural complexity, in their view, accounts for the retention and recall difficulties readers face when dealing with information represented in the form of a collection of items. (This is because less configured information apparently takes up more space in short-term memory than more highly configured information.) While this may be true, one must assume that the lack of configurational complexity of Collection as text will make it a less challenging writing task. The attempts at Collection of the here-examined group of advanced ESL learners, however, suggest otherwise. Examination of the writing of a group of Cantonese-speaking freshmen enrolled in the English department of a Hong Kong university showed that two-thirds of them had difficulty conforming to the configuration that the skilled writer would use. Their nontarget-like output suggests that Collection is in fact not wholly lacking in top-level structure.

To address this finding, in this paper I will re-examine the structure of one type of Collection, by building on a set of claims by Tadros (1994) which suggest, contra Meyer and others, a clear basic rhetorical make-up for Collection as text. I will closely examine a type of Collection referred to by Tadros as Enumeration, to argue that it possesses a well-defined constituent structure and set of inter-constituent relationships. I will then analyse randomly selected samples from a body of twenty student essays to support two principal claims: 1) The majority of the learners here-examined have considerable difficulty conforming to the interconstituent constraints on Enumeration. 2) As a group they show evidence of acquisition of the rhetorical structure of Enumeration at three levels of proficiency. In a final section, I will consider the pedagogical implications of these findings.

Samples of in-class written assignments were collected from twenty freshman English majors at a Hong Kong university. The students had learned English as a school subject from about age three to age twelve, at which point they started using it to study many though by no means all their school subjects. Although by age eighteen, in their freshman year in college, they had had many years of exposure to the English language, it was entirely in the context of the classroom and with opportunity, largely, only to listen to lectures and read textbooks and lecture notes. Their mastery of English, therefore, remained, for the most part, passive. There was inadequate opportunity to practise writing in their curriculum.

The structure of prototypical Enumeration

Tadros (1994) identifies a set of Collection types which she refers to as Prediction, because they are all 'prospective rhetorical devices' (p 71). That is, at one point in the text they predict what is to follow, and by doing so commit the writer to fulfilling this prediction. In 1a below, the writer makes a claim to the existence of several reasons for his/her move to Hong Kong, thereby predicting that these reasons will follow. The prediction commits him/her to instantiate the reasons.

Tadros suggests that all her six categories of Prediction—Enumeration, Advance Labelling, Reporting, Recapitulation, Hypotheticality and Question—conform to the same general top-level structure: each consists of a pair of constituents. The first constituent, the predictive component, marks the prediction, as in 1a, below. This prediction is then realised by the second constituent, the predicted component. Typically there are a number of sentential realisations of the predicted component as in 1b, c, d, and e, below.

1.

Example of Enumeration as a Category of Prediction

a.	I decided to move to Hong Kong for *several* reasons. **numeral Enumeral**	**Predictive component**
b.	It is the most prosperous commercial centre in Asia,	**Predicted component**
c.	it is fast-paced and exciting,	**Predicted component**
d.	it is a happy mix of the East and the West in cultural terms,	**Predicted component**
e.	and finally it takes me back to my roots.	**Predicted component**

Of Enumeration, Tadros says that the *predictive component* 'carries a *signal* that commits the writer to enumerate' (p 71). It contains what she refers to as the Enumeral, one of a set of subtechnical nouns (such as 'advantages', 'reasons' and 'aspects') or discourse reference nouns (such as 'examples', 'definitions' and 'classifications'). The Enumeral is the noun 'reasons' in 1a above. Accompanying the Enumeral is a numeral, which can be exact, as in 'two', 'three' or 'four', or inexact as in 'a few', 'several', or 'a number of'. The numeral is 'several' in 1a above.

It is hence the Enumeral (of the predictive component) along with its accompanying numeral, which commits the writer to enumerate. That is, as stated above, in 1a reference to 'several reasons' for the move to Hong Kong commits the writer to enumerate what these reasons are.

Because of this Tadros claims that the *predicted component* in Enumeration cognitively corresponds to the predictive component, 'that is, a reason signalled must be a reason given' (p 73). She also claims that the predicted component is formally marked by the use of features of 'layout, numbering, punctuation, sequencing marking (first, second, etc), lexical repetition and grammatical parallelism (identical sentence structures)' (p 73).

A closer look at the Enumeration configuration

It follows from Tadros' claims that the interconstituent tie that holds between the two key components of Enumeration can be represented in terms of two defining relationships:

The relationship between Predicted component and Predictive component

Sentences that are predicted components (1b, c, d,and e) are constrained to be instantiations of the Enumeral ('reasons' in 1a) in the number specified by the numeral ('several' in 1a).

The relationship between successive Predicted components

This relationship is made clear by a comparison of the predicted components, one to another. If we examine the successive predicted components of (1), that is, sentences b through e, we notice that a portion of the proposition is the same in all these sentences.

1.

a. I decided to move to Hong Kong **for several reasons**.
b. It is x (where x is something appealing about Hong Kong)
   x = the most prosperous commercial centre in Asia
c. It is x (where x is something appealing about Hong Kong)
   x = fast-paced and exciting
d. It is x (were x is something appealing about Hong Kong)
   x = a happy mix of East and West
e. It is x (where x is something appealing about Hong Kong)
   x = takes me back to my roots.

In b, c, d and e, the open proposition 'It is x (where x is something appealing about Hong Kong)' is sustained from b to e. The realisation of the variable x (the focal component of the sentence) is the only new point of information in each predicted component. This is indicative of the relationship that must hold between successive sentences that are predicted components: *a predicted component sustains the open proposition of the preceding predicted component, adding information only at its focal point.*

The learner must therefore have mastery of these two intersentential relationships in order to properly generate Enumerative prose.

In terms of the basic sentential relationships

If we bring to bear now to our understanding of these relationships two proposed basic sentential relationships, *addition* of a thematically distinct informational point, and its diametrically opposed relationship, *expansion* of the preceding point (cf Beekman and Callow 1974; Fuller 1959), we realise that 1) the predicted sentence is an expansion of the predictive sentence (1b/1c/1d/1e is an expansion of 1a) rather than being a thematically distinct addition to it, and 2) that each predicted component adds information to the preceding predicted component, rather than being an expansion of it.

1.

a.	I decided to move to Hong Kong for several reasons.	
b.	It is the most prosperous commercial centre in Asia,	**expansion of (a)**
c.	it is fast-paced and exciting,	**expansion of (a), addition to b**
d.	it is a happy mix of the East and the West,	**expansion of (a), addition to c**
e.	and finally it takes me back to my roots.	**expansion of (a), addition to d**

In terms of the two basic sentential relationships of addition versus expansion, therefore, we see that each predicted sentence expands on its predictive sentence (by instantiating its Enumeral) and at the same time adds information to its preceding predicted sentence (at its focal point).

THE LEARNING CHALLENGES OF ENUMERATION

Propositional constraints

The need to instantiate the Enumeral monitors the predicted component beyond the general requirement of relevancy that must hold between any pair of successive in-discourse sentences.

2.

Why did you move to Hong Kong?

a. I have been interested in Hong Kong for a long time.
b. (and) I am sure I will become more familiar with Hong Kong in the near future.

Clause 2b, for example, is infelicitous in its context of occurrence. It is informationally relevant to 2a, and also a thematically distinct addition to it, rather than being an expansion of it. But it is not easily construed as an instantiation of the Enumeral; that is, it cannot be easily interpreted as a reason for moving to Hong Kong. Learners can have difficulty monitoring the predicted component to achieve instantiation of the Enumeral, which is a specialised subset of the total set of relevant relationships.

As stated above, predicted components must also add a thematically distinct point to the preceding predicted component, rather than expanding it. The sentence must be interpretable as an addition to the preceding predicted component rather than an expansion of it in an unambiguous way.

3.

Why are you moving to Hong Kong?

a. I have been interested in Hong Kong for a long time(.)

b. (# and/because) Hong Kong is never dull.

...

3.

a. I have been interested in Hong Kong for a long time (.)

c. (? and)I have wanted to gain a deeper understanding of it ...

3.

a. I have been interested in Hong Kong for a long time (,/.)

d. I have been learning Cantonese for some years (,/.)

...

3.

a. I have been interested in Hong Kong for a long time.

e. And I have been learning Cantonese for some years.

3.

a. I have been interested in Hong Kong for a long time.

f. In fact, I have been learning Cantonese for some years.

3.

a. I have been interested in Hong Kong for a long time,

g. (and) I feel compelled to move there because of my dependence on it for continued success in business(./,) ...

Both b and c qualify as expansions of 3a, rather than additions. (This is apparent in their inability to accommodate sentence initial 'and'.) Sentence 3b, in addition, bears a specifiable logical relationship to 3a. It accounts for the writer's interest in Hong Kong, hence accommodating 'because'. The proposition of d after 3a *can* be interpreted as an addition, as in e, but it can also be interpreted as an expansion of 3a, as in f. Its relationship to 3a is therefore ambiguous. Only the proposition of g qualifies unambiguously as an addition in the context of 3a. Learners can have problems understanding addition and expansion as differentiated functions, and hence are often unsuccessful in monitoring prospective predicted sentences to achieve an unambiguous addition to the preceding sentence.

Semantic constraint

Sentences that in their content may qualify as instantiations of the Enumeral, may not be semantically represented in such a way that makes this easily apparent. Compare 4b in the context of 4a, to 4c in the context of 4a below.

4.

Why have you opted to move to Hong Kong?

I have moved to Hong Kong for a number of reasons:

a. I have felt interested in Hong Kong(.)

b. (and) I have felt challenged by it (./,)

4.

a. I have felt interested in Hong Kong(./,)

c. (and) Hong Kong is a difficult place to live in, and I want to feel I can tackle it.

While the informational content of 4b and 4c is the same, 4b sustains the open proposition of 4a:

4.

a. I have felt x (where x is a positive reaction to Hong Kong) x = interest in

b. I have felt x (where x is a positive reaction to Hong Kong) x = challenged by

Sentence 4c does not do this.

Learners can have difficulty expressing the content of the predicted sentence in such a way that the open proposition is sustained. This makes is it more difficult for the reader to process the sentence as a predicted component.

Syntactic constraint

Syntactic parallelism of successive predicted sentences goes hand in hand with a sustained open proposition to ensure readers' recognition of it as a predicted component. Compare 5ab to 5ac. The failure to maintain syntactic parallelism appears to interfere with the interpretation of successive sentences as denoting predicted components.

5.

a. I am interested in Hong Kong,

b. I am challenged by it, ...

5.

a. I am interested in Hong Kong,

c. there is the challenge of Hong Kong...

Learners do not always fully appreciate the need for syntactic parallelism.

Lexico-syntactic constraint

In the prototypical Enumeration, a subset of sentential connectors (e.g. 'and', 'also', 'in addition', for future reference set 1) is used to overtly mark the addition relationship, as in 6 below. Another subset (e.g. 'first', 'second', 'lastly'/'finally', for future reference set 2) is used to overtly itemise successive predicted components, as in 7 below.

The characteristic text structure of Enumeration is also reflected in the constraint on where sentential connectors can occur and where they should occur. There can be no set 1 connectors between the predictive component and the first predicted sentence (e.g. between 6a and 6b) because this first predicted sentence is not an addition to its preceding sentence. However, following predicted sentences can, but need not, take either type of sentential connectors, either the addition-marking set 1 connectors or the itemising set 2 connectors.

6.

a. I decided to move to Hong Kong for several reasons.
b. It is the most prosperous commercial centre in Asia,
c. **and** it is fast-paced and exciting.
d. It is **also** a happy mix of the east and West in cultural terms,
e. and finally it takes me back to my roots.

7.

a. I decided to move to Hong Kong for several reasons.
b. First, it is ...
c. Second, it is ...
d. Third, it is ...
e. and finally, ...

A definite constraint in English Enumeration is the need for an 'and' and/or 'finally' or 'lastly' sentence-initially in accompaniment with the last predicted component (6e/7e).

Learners can have difficulty selecting the appropriate subset of sentence connectors to mark the specialised functions of addition and itemisation.

Foregrounding the predicted sentences

In the Enumeration prototype, the above-described semantic and lexico-syntactic marking serves to foreground predicted sentences (8b, d and f, highlighted below), and separate them from propositions which are mere expansions of these sentences (8c, e, and g). That is, as illustrated in 8b, d, and f below, predicted sentences tend to be either lexically marked for addition relative to the preceding predicted sentence, and/or overtly itemised. They are also in structurally parallel sentences with sustained open proposition. Expansions of these sentences, however, do not come with the semantic and formal marking that signals predicted components.

8.

a. I decided to move to Hong Kong for several reasons.

b. First, it is the most prosperous commercial centre in Asia.

c. There is so much to learn about business.

d. Second, it is fast-paced and exciting.

e. No other place quite matches it in energy.

f. And finally it is a happy mix of the East and the West.

g. One gets the art and culture of Asia and with it the forward-looking vision of the West.

Learners can have difficulty using appropriate semantic and lexico-syntactic means to foreground predicted sentences and set them apart from those that are mere expansions of these predicted sentences.

In summary, learners can have difficulty mastering the propositional constraints that ensure that the predicted sentences are a) proper instantiations of the Enumeral, and b) unambiguous additions to their preceding predicted sentence. Learners can have difficulty with the semantic constraint on predicted sentences, which ensures that the open proposition is clearly sustained across these sentences. They can have difficulty with the need for syntactic parallelism across predicted sentences, and also with the need to use the appropriate sentence connectors. In addition, learners can be challenged by the requirement for strict correlation between the propositional orientation of a sentence (as either an expansion or an addition) and its semantic and lexico-syntactic form. That is, the predicted sentences that add information to the preceding sentence sustain the open proposition and are at the same time syntactically parallel to preceding predicted sentences, appearing often with accompanying set 1 or set 2 connectors. Sentences that merely expand a predicted sentence do not sustain the open proposition, are not syntactically parallel, and do not come with set 1 and set 2 connectors.

It is clear from all this that Enumeration can pose a considerable challenge for the L2 learner. (It is interesting that native speakers who are unskilled writers appear to face similar difficulties, and this is something that follow up studies need to address.)

STUDENT ATTEMPTS

I will now examine five short student essays to illustrate the actual violations of the above-described propositional and representational constraints on successive predicted sentences in some of the attempts at Enumeration by our learners. I will show different degrees of mastery of this set of constraints, and suggest that this evidences acquisition of Enumerative structure at three levels of proficiency. All the essays were written in response to the question 'Why did you choose to be an English major?' as short, 20-minute in-class assignments. Students were not asked to revise their work; the samples were therefore all first drafts.

Non-dichotomous conception of proposition

The following three samples illustrate the learner's failure to recognise the fundamental distinction between propositions that increment information by expanding the preceding sentence, and those that do so by adding a thematically distinct point to the preceding sentence.

Sample 1

There are several reasons for me choosing English major. [1]English is an interesting subject I think since I was in primary school. [2]Studying English is not routine work, because there are so many changes. [3]I want to learn more about English language and literature and have a deeper knowledge in it. [4]Also, I hope I can be an English teacher as my future career. So I choose English as my major subject.

Sample 1 begins with explicit reference to a set of reasons for taking English. The reader, therefore, assumes that instantiation of the Enumeral ('reasons') will follow in a set of predicted sentences. However, propositions 2 and 3 are not additions in their context of appearance, since each proposition is merely an expansion of the preceding proposition, much like the NPs in 1a below:

1.

a. I bought apples; red apples; red delicious apples; red, delicious apples from Spain.

This is more clearly apparent when 2 and 3 are redistributed in the text, with syntactic incorporation and logical connectors used to formally mark their expansion of the preceding proposition, as in 1b:

1b.

[1]I have been interested in English, [3]in gaining a deeper understanding of English language and literature, since I was in primary school, because [2]the subject is full of surprises and is never dull, routinized work. [4]And my goal is to be an English teacher.

Sample 2

> [1]English has been my favourite subject at school, work and leisure. [2]I had used the language for teaching for some years. [3]During my four years stay in Canada, I had more time to read in very resourceful libraries. I found myself falling in love with the great works, authors/journalists. [4]I hope I can be more proficient in the language. [5]Also I wish I can contribute my best to society after graduation.

In sample 2, the reader anticipates an Enumeration in response to the initial question, 'Why did you choose to be an English major?' Predicted components *must*, therefore, follow. But successive sentential propositions in the text are ambiguous as to their mode of information incrementation; it is unclear whether they are intended as additions to preceding sentences and therefore predicted components, or merely expansions of a preceding predicted sentence.

We can disambiguate to mark the unambiguous addition of information of successive predicted components, by introducing set 1 sentential connectors, such as 'also' and 'in addition', as is illustrated in 2a below. All but 4 and 5 are then construable as predicted components.

> 2a.
>
> [1]English has been my favourite subject at school, work and leisure. [2]**Also**, I have used the language for teaching for some years so it makes sense to keep improving my skills. [3]**In addition** during my four years stay in Canada, I had more time to read in very resourceful libraries, and (I) found myself falling in love with the great works, authors/journalists, so for this reason too I want to improve my command of the language. [4]I hope I can be more proficient in the language. [5]Also I wish I can contribute my best to society after graduation.

But the other possibility is that in sentences 2 and 3 the writer is merely expanding on the proposition of sentence 1 as an only predicted component, as in 2b below.

2b.

[1]English has been my favourite subject at school, work and leisure. [2]At work, I've used the language for teaching for some years. [3]In pursing my personal interests, during my four years stay in Canada, I had more time to read in very resourceful libraries and found myself falling in love with the great works, authors/journalists. [4]I hope (that with better English) I can become more proficient in the language, [5]and contribute my best to society after graduation.

In either version, 2a or 2b, 4 and 5 are concluding comments that fall outside the Enumeration organisation.

These two possible interpretations of his/her text suggest that this writer does not appear to have a dichotomous conception of information incrementation as expansion of, or addition to, the preceding proposition.

Sample 3

[1]As English has regarded as an international languages, I would like to know and learn more about it. [2]Besides, being an English major student, I can have lots of chances to practice speaking and writing English. [3]By the way, English also became a part of our daily life. [4]For instance, the instructions of many electrical appliances are written by English. [5]The most important is, being English major student may lead me to a bright future.

In sample 3 the writer is again responding to the same initial question, 'Why did you choose to be an English major?', and therefore the predictive component specifying a number of reasons is evoked, and predicted sentences must therefore follow. Here it is the writer's use of sentential connectors that creates ambiguous information incrementation because, in most cases, these sentence connectors signal relationships to preceding text that are entirely out of consonance with the relation borne by the accompanying proposition. Though sentence 2 is an expansion of the preceding proposition, the sentential connector suggests that it adds to the preceding sentence.

And although 3 is an addition and therefore a predicted component in the informational foreground of the text, the sentence-initial 'by the way' marks it as parenthetical information in the Enumeration. Equally misleading is what seems like a deliberate avoidance of syntactic parallelism across predicted sentences (1, 3 and 5). The writer uses three different constructions, so that there is little chance to signal a sustained open proposition across these sentences.

If these misleading cues are eliminated, and the open proposition 'I want to learn more English because English is/has x (x = some quality of the language)' is sustained in structurally parallel predicted sentences, it is possible to interpret this passage as an Enumeration. The reader is able to separate predicted sentences (1, 3, and 5 in 3a, below) from those which are merely expansions of their preceding predicted sentence (2 and 4 in 3a, below).

> 3a.
>
> [1] **I want to learn more English because it is an international language.** [2]As an English major I have lots of chances to practice speaking and writing English. [3]**I also want to learn it because it has become a part of our daily life**. [4]For instance, the instructions on many electrical appliances are written in English. [5]**But most importantly, I want to learn it because it will give me a brighter future**.

In sample 3 there is, therefore, a consistent clash between proposition-content orientation and the semantic and lexico-syntactic marking. As a result, it is not clear whether this writer conceptually differentiates between the two ways of incrementing information.

Representational means not acquired

The following sample illustrates proper mastery of the proposition constraints and therefore the ability to distinguish between sentences that are additions to, as opposed to being expansion of, the preceding sentence. At the same time, however, the writer is not able to give these distinct modes of information incrementation appropriate semantic and lexico-syntactic representation.

Sample 4

[1]There are a few reasons for me to choose English as a major.

[2]With deep interest in studying languages, especially English, I hope to obtain more knowledge on it. [3]After the course, it can help me on working because I want to be a teacher.

[4]On the other hand, although I have never studied English literature, I think it may be interesting. [5]I hope I will not be disappointed.

Sample 4 differs from 3 because though it shows that the representational means have not been mastered, there is no systematic mismatch between proposition-orientation (as addition or expansion) and its lexico-syntactic marking (as was the case in sample 3). Predicted components are identifiable in the successive sentences 2, 3, and 4, in an unambiguous way. This is primarily because even though the sentence connectors are not appropriate for predicted sentences, they do not mark the relationship of expansion to the preceding proposition, and in doing so go counter to the additive nature of the proposition (as do those of 3).

While predicted components are identifiable, they are nonetheless not appropriately represented semantically and lexico-syntactically: 1) the open proposition is not sustained across predicted sentences. 2) The writer fails to use structural parallelism, a structural aid in sustaining a constant open proposition. 3) In addition, the chosen sentential adverbials of 2, 3 and 4 are not the typical set 1 and set 2 connectors.

If in sentences 2, 3 and 4 we sustain the open proposition 'I want/am interested in/curious about x (x = something that can be achieved through the study of English)' across structurally parallel sentences, and itemise the predicted components, we get the following prototypical Enumeration:

> First, I am deeply interested in studying languages, especially English, and hope to learn more English.
>
> Second, I want to be a teacher and the study of English will help me achieve this goal.
>
> And third, I have never studied English literature, and am curious about it.

Total system in place

The following sample illustrates the learner's ability to properly differentiate between the two types of information incrementation (addition and expansion) as a result of having mastered both proposition constraints and the semantic and lexico-syntactic constraints.

> **Sample 5**
>
> [1]English benefits me a lot in my life. [2]**It is an advantage** in getting a job. [3]If we are proficient in writing, listening and speaking of English, **it is easy** for us to communicate with foreigners. [4]Besides, **we are able to** live in a state of high cultural society all the times. [5]**It is not possible** from being dropped out by the community.

Of all the essays we have examined, sample 5 most closely approximates the prototype Enumeration format. The opening predictive component, claiming the benefits of English in sentence 1, is followed by sentences 2, 3 and 4, which are instantiations of the set of reasons for taking English, each being at the same time a clear addition to its preceding sentence. There is a level of structural parallelism (notice the structures in boldface) accompanying a sustained pattern in the content of these successive predicted sentences: Each one instantiates the heightened opportunity for achieving something desirable as a consequence of knowing English: getting a job, communicating with foreigners, and achieving social acceptance, in sentences 2, 3 and 4, respectively. There is even a set-1 type sentential connector 'besides' accompanying the last predicted component of the Enumeration, in conformity to prototype requirements. The use of still more overt representational features would of course improve the approximation to prototype Enumeration. For example, the following modifications would result in a more transparent rendering of prototypical Enumeration. In 5a, after an opening evocation of a set of three reasons, there is explicit itemisation of these reasons. The open proposition 'Good English is x (x = an advantage of some sort)' is sustained across predicted sentences, and these sentences are syntactically parallel.

> 5a.
>
> [1]I think English benefits me a lot in my life **in 3 principal ways.** [2]**First good English** is an advantage getting a job. [3]**Second if we are proficient** in writing, listening and speaking it is easy for us to communicate with foreigners. [4]**And finally if our English is good**, we gain access to the upper strata of society and therefore [5]cannot become social rejects.

SUMMARISING THE MAJOR FINDINGS

The above findings are suggestive of three levels of proficiency amongst our learners, and therefore a hierarchy of competencies. (This should not be confused with a developmental sequence and its associated stages.):

1. *Level 1: Non-dichotomous conception of proposition*

This learner fails to distinguish between the two distinct ways of incrementing information via the sentential proposition: addition versus expansion. This may be manifest in learners counting each and every proposition as a predicted component (as in Sample 1), or in the ambiguity of the mode of information incrementation of his/her propositions (as in Sample 2), or alternatively in a consistent mismatch between the orientation of the proposition (addition or expansion) and its semantic and formal representation (as in Sample 3).

2. *Level 2: Means of representing the dichotomy not acquired*

This learner differentiates addition and expansion, but is not able to give overt representation to the distinction by use of the appropriate semantic and lexico-syntactic means (as in Sample 4).

3. *Level 3: Total system in place*

This learner has acquired the dichotomous conception of information incrementation and also acquired the corresponding representational equipment (Sample 5).

PEDAGOGICAL IMPLICATIONS

It is significant to note, when considering the pedagogical implications of these findings, that the group of learners of this study had been learning English for approximately sixteen years, at the time the above-analysed essays were written. In spite of this length of exposure to the language, a considerable number of them (at least two-thirds of the total group) failed to master a text-structure which, the organisational intricacies here-demonstrated notwithstanding, is arguably amongst the most rudimentary of text designs. It, therefore, seems reasonable to attempt overt instruction for level 1 and level 2 learners, who are unlikely to acquire what has failed them over so many years without some form of intervention. Of course, without actually testing the outcome of this overt instruction, no definitive statements can be made about its effectiveness.

1. For level 1 learners, therefore, classroom instruction could address the two modes of information incrementation explicitly, by pointing them out as of distinctive function in Enumeration, using exemplification and explanation, and giving students the opportunity to practise using them.
2. And both level 1 and level 2 learners might receive overt instruction on the representational system that distinguishes between these two modes of information incrementation,

a. on the semantic means of enhancing reader recognition of predicted sentences: representation of sustained open proposition from one predicted sentence to the next,
b. on the use of syntactic parallelism to support this,
c. on the use of the addition-marking set 1 and itemising set 2 sentential connectors, and
d. on the manipulation of the total set of above-stated representational means to foreground predicted components and set them apart from sentential propositions that merely add supportive detail to a preceding predicted sentence.

CONCLUSION

I have shown that Enumeration (as one type of Collection) sets well-defined conditions on the proposition content of successive in-discourse sentences and on their semantic and lexico-syntactic representation. I have suggested that mastery of this set of constraints is challenging for the larger percentage of this group of fairly advanced ESL learners, and that learning is achieved at three levels of proficiency, which demonstrate that content-constraints are sometimes acquired independently of their representational counterparts. I have also suggested that learners who, despite their long exposure to the English language, are still at level 1 and level 2 proficiency may benefit from overt instruction on the propositional and representational constraints on successive sentences in Enumerative prose.

This study therefore clearly shows that earlier assumptions about the absence of top-level organisation for the type of exposition commonly referred to as Collection are questionable to say the least, and that the organisational requirements of at least one type of Collection—Enumeration—are in fact sufficiently complex to challenge even advanced learners of ESL.

References

Beekman J and Callow J. 1974. *Translating the Word of God.* Michigan: Zondervan.

Carrell Patricia L. 1983. Some issues in studying the role of schemata, or background knowledge, in second language comprehension. *Reading in a Foreign Language*, 1 (2): 81–92.

Connor Ulla. 1984. Recall of text: differences between first and second language readers. *TESOL Quarterly*, 18 (2): 239–256.

Fuller D P. 1959. *The Inductive Method of Bible Study* (3rd Edn). Pasadena, Fuller Theological Seminary (mimeo).

Meyer Bonnie J F. 1975. *The Organization of Prose and its Effects on Memory.* Amsterdam: North Holland Publishing Co.

Meyer Bonnie J F. 1977a. The structure of prose: effects on learning and memory and implications for educational practice. In R C Anderson, R J Spiro and W E Montague (ed), *Schooling and the Acquisition of Knowledge.* Hillsdale, New Jersey: Lawrence Erlbaum Associates.

Meyer, Bonnie J F. 1977b. What is remembered from prose: a function of passage structure. In Roy O Freedle (ed), *Discourse Production and Comprehension.* Norwood, New Jersey: Ablex Publishing Corporation.

Meyer Bonnie J F, Brandt David M and Bluth George J. 1980. Use of top-level structure in text: key for reading comprehension and ninth-grade students. *Reading Research Quarterly*, 16 (1): 72–103.

Meyer Bonnie J F and Freedle Roy O. 1984. Effects of discourse type on recall. *American Educational Research Journal*, 21 (1): 121–143.

Tadros A. 1994. Predictive categories in expository text. In M Coulthard (ed), *Advances in Written Text Analysis.* London: Routledge.

5

The Encapsulating Sentence and Text-Building

First published in *World Englishes* 24 (1) (2005), John Wiley

INTRODUCTION

In recent examinations of basic text structure, a number of scholars (cf Winter 1994, Hoey 1994, Coulthard 1994, Sinclair 1994, Tadros 1994, amongst others) have identified a principal dichotomy in the modes of incrementing information in written discourse. Sinclair (1994) represents this central distinction most effectively when he distinguishes between two types of text-internal sentences. One sentential type 'contains a single act of reference which encapsulates the whole of the previous text' (p 17) as in 1b/2b (the encapsulating sentence, for future reference).

1.	2.
a. I was on sentry duty.	a. I was on sentry duty.
b. I saw the enemy approaching.	b. (While I was on sentry duty) I saw the enemy approaching.

(from Hoey, 1994)

3.

a. I have only one reason for doing this.

b. I need the money.

The second type of sentence does not 'contain an act of reference' of this kind. It is 'prospected' by its preceding sentence (cf 3b) (the prospected sentence, for future reference).

This central distinction has most often been explored somewhat indirectly, in assessments whose primary objective is to study the sentential sub-types of both the encapsulating and prospected sentences (cf Tadros (1994) on different types of prospected sentences, and Winter (1994), Hoey (1979, 1994), Coulthard (1994), and Grimes (1975) on Problem-solution and other types of encapsulated sentences). There is good reason to look more directly at the basic bifurcation itself, however. This is because there is unequal mastery of text incrementation by the prospected and encapsulating sentences by less experienced writers, which suggests the need for closer assessment of what makes each unique, and an evaluation, concomitantly, of the dissimilar learning issues that their differences give rise to. In this paper, I will address this need by pointing to what amounts to not just a difference but, in fact, a diametric opposition between these modes of incrementing text. I will suggest that this contrast is a major contributor to the difficulty learners have with the proper use of the later-acquired encapsulating sentence. That is, because the means to incrementing text via these sentences are not merely different, but in fact operational opposites, by first mastering the prospected sentence, the learner, unwittingly, becomes less able to use the encapsulating sentence.

After an initial comparison of the most obvious surface-level differences between these two sentence-types, I will closely examine incrementation by the encapsulating sentence. I will describe its core features, and use this assessment to identify two language competencies that are needed for its proper use. I will, then, examine successive text incrementations in two essays, randomly selected from a set of ESL expositions, to show that learners have difficulty applying these competencies in using the encapsulating sentence. I will suggest that this is because of interference from the better-known use of the prospected sentence.

Beyond the very particular insight this study lends to understanding these basic modes of text incrementation and to the learning challenges of the encapsulating sentence, it also makes a broader-based and methodological contribution in the field of text analysis. It gives support to the claim, first articulated by Coulthard (1994), that the examination of 'problematic text' gives us better understanding of the makeup of well-formed text, by highlighting dimensions of preferred structure that are otherwise not readily apparent.

The data for this study consists of 35 short expository student essays. The students were 18–22-year-old freshmen in the Humanities program of a Hong Kong university at the time these essays were written. They had learned English as a school subject in primary school, but by secondary school, from about age twelve, they began to use it as a medium of instruction. At the time they wrote the essays analysed in this study, they had received about sixteen years of exposure to English.

The students were given fifty minutes in class to write these essays, and all the essays were first drafts.

DISTINGUISHING THE ENCAPSULATED SENTENCE FROM THE PROSPECTED SENTENCE

To increment text in a way that generates coherent prose, some element of the preceding text must be retained in the text that follows. We are acknowledging two basic ways of doing this here: by the use of the prospected sentence and the encapsulating sentence.

The prospected sentence realises a prediction made in the preceding sentence.

4.

a. What do you know about Peter?

Implicit: I know certain things about Peter.

b. 1. Peter teaches at St Ann's High School.	1′#. (Because I know certain things about Peter) Peter teaches at St Ann's High School.
2. He has three children.	2′#. (Since Peter teaches at St Ann's School) he has three children.
3. He is planning to go to France this summer...	3′#. (Because he has three children) he is planning to go to France this summer.

Each sentence of 4b is prospected by an opening, implicit claim that the writer knows certain things about Peter. As prospected sentences they cannot retain this initial claim (cf 1′). (Nor can 2 and 3 retain their respective immediately preceding sentence, cf 2′ and 3′.) This means the prospected sentence increments the text without retaining it.

The encapsulating sentence, on the other hand, retains the ideational component of its preceding text, so that, as Sinclair puts it, each encapsulating sentence is at the point of its appearance, in itself, the whole text. So 5b retains 5a, 5c retains 5a and b, and 5d retains 5a, b, and c; this is made explicit in 6a, b, c, and d.

5.	6.
a. I was on sentry duty.	a. I was on sentry duty.
b. I saw the enemy approaching.	b. (While I was on sentry duty) I saw the enemy approaching.
c. I opened fire.	c. (Seeing the enemy approaching while I was on sentry duty) I opened fire.
d. I beat off the enemy attack.	d. (By opening fire, when I saw the enemy approaching while I was on sentry duty,) I beat off the enemy attack.

(from Hoey, 1994)

6′.

a. I was on sentry duty.

b. While I was on sentry duty, I saw the enemy approaching.

c. Seeing the enemy approaching, I opened fire.

d. And by opening fire, I beat off the enemy attack.

A comparison of 6 and 6′ suggests, in addition, that the encapsulation retains not just the information content of the preceding text, but also the hierarchical distribution of successive preceding incrementations, which gives the preceding text its defining configuration. This is evident in the fact that overt representation of the encapsulation (as in, for example, 6b, 6c or 6d) is not equally acceptable for every retained preceding incrementation. In any given encapsulation it is more acceptable to give overt representation to the more foregrounded ideational of the immediately preceding incrementation, rather than the less foregrounded incrementations that precede it (e.g. 6′c rather than 6c, and 6′d rather than 6d). Overt retention of the ideational of the immediately preceding incrementation is allowed and in fact often preferred in academic prose, but the more removed the previous incrementations are from the current incrementation, the less appropriate it is to give them overt expression.

It also follows from the fact that each incrementation encapsulates its preceding text, that each incrementation can be perceived as building the text by answering a certain type of question about its preceding text (cf 7). This projection into dialogue also differentiates between the encapsulating and prospected sentences. The prospected sentence answers a request for clarification question (cf 7′). The encapsulating sentence, on the other hand, answers a question on the logical consequence of, or temporal follow up to, the text (cf 7).

In representing each incrementation as an answer to a question about the preceding text, the projection into dialogue (cf 7), therefore, shows precisely *how* each incrementation encapsulates its preceding text.

7.

a. I was on sentry duty.	1. What happened when you were on sentry duty?
b. (When I was on sentry duty) I saw the enemy approaching.	2. What did you do when you saw the enemy approaching?
c. (When I saw the enemy approaching) I opened fire.	3. What did you manage to do by opening fire?
d. (By opening fire) I beat off the enemy attack.	

7′. I have only one reason for doing this. What is it?

I need the money.

Example 7 also points to the fact that each incrementation has a unique functional role, and consequently proper place, in the linear development of the text (cf Sinclair 1994). The representation of b as an answer to the question of 1 makes it apparent that b describes the problem perceived, in the setting depicted in (a). Similarly, the representation of c as an answer to question 2 makes it apparent that c describes the action taken to address the problem of b. In the same way, representing d as an answer to question 3, makes it apparent that the incrementation of d refers to the consequence of the action taken in c.

It is evident, hence, that at an underlying level the encapsulating sentence contains an initial component that retains the preceding text (that is, the information content, of preceding incrementations, in the configuration that governs its packaging across successive incrementations) in a well-defined relationship to the current incrementation, dependent on where the sentence occurs in the text. Therefore, the recursive use of the encapsulating sentence generates text in a manner represented in A, below:

A

1. a
2. a – b

3. (a – b) – c
4. ((a – b) – c) – d ...

In 2, (a) is the encapsulation of b, which is tantamount to saying b is the answer to a question about a. In 3, b, with (a) as encapsulation, is the encapsulation of c. Or in other words, c is an answer to a question about b, which is an answer to a question about (a). In 4, c with b as encapsulation (which itself has [a] as encapsulation) is the encapsulation of d. Or in other words, d is an answer to a question about c, which is an answer to a question about b, which is itself an answer to a question about (a).

REQUISITE LANGUAGE COMPETENCIES

The above-described defining features can be used to suggest some of the language competencies the learner needs to master to effectively increment text by use of the encapsulating sentence. Two principal requisite competencies are addressed here.

First, after acknowledging that the representation of a particular ideational calls for the use of this type of text development, the learner has to be able to appropriately fragment the non-linear ideational. S/he has to fragment the ideational into a succession of units that, by individually qualifying as encapsulating sentences, can contribute to the development of text of type A (given above). That is, the breakdown of the informational whole must be such that each individual informational unit is able to evoke its preceding text as encapsulation. If we alter the informational breakdown of 5 above, for example, as in 8, below, we find that 8d does not as readily evoke 8a as 5d does its preceding text. That is, 'I beat off the enemy attack' evokes 'I opened fire' far more readily than it does 'I was on sentry duty'. Or put in other terms, 8d cannot be as readily construed as a possible logical consequence of 8a as 5d is of 5c. In fact 8d seems to relate to 8a much more easily as a prospected sentence, taking on an interpretation which is more explicitly expressed in 9, below.

8.	5.
a. I was on sentry duty.	a. I was on sentry duty.
d. I beat off the enemy attack.	b. I saw the enemy approaching.
	c. I opened fire.
	d. I beat off the enemy attack.

9.

a. I was the one who was on sentry duty.

d. I was the one who beat off the enemy attack.

Not only must the ideational or message-whole be fragmented into successive units that are informationally appropriate for evoking the preceding text as encapsulation, but, in addition, each such information unit must be given a textualisation that permits ready evocation of the preceding text. Essentially, this means two things: 1) that each individual unit of information must be appropriately lexicalised, and 2) that in each appropriately lexicalised individual unit, the information must be appropriately packaged.

10.

a. Once in a while a department breaks up into smaller subgroups or cliques.

b. This interferes with its effective functioning, which is not good.

c. As a result, the business of the unit suffers.

b1. Its effective functioning suffers, and this is not good.

b2. Effective functioning is crucial and any interference with this is harmful.

b3. Interfering with the smooth functioning of the department is not good.

b4. Things go wrong and this is not good.

Let us consider first the effective information packaging requirement for a properly lexicalised unit. The distribution of the information in the incrementation can enhance or inhibit the evocation of the encapsulation. This is made apparent by a comparison of the different distributions of the roughly constant proposition in 10b, b1, b2 and b3 above. Of these potential options, 10b makes overt reference to the encapsulation in the clause-initial demonstrative 'this', and b1, in place of 10b, effectively evokes the encapsulation though it does not overtly refer to it (b1′ shows that overt representation of the evoked encapsulation is readily accommodated).

10.

a. Once in a while a department breaks up into smaller subgroups or cliques.

b1′. (Because/When it breaks up into smaller groups or cliques) its effective functioning suffers and this is not good.

Clauses b2 or b3, in place of 10b, on the other hand, do not effectively evoke the encapsulation.

10.

a. Once in a while a department breaks up into smaller subgroups or cliques.

b2′. (Because/When it breaks up into smaller subgroups or cliques) effective functioning is crucial and any interference with this is harmful.

10.

a. Once in a while a department breaks up into smaller subgroups or cliques.

b3′. (Because/When it breaks up into smaller subgroups or cliques) interfering with the smooth functioning of the department is not good.

Because neither b2 nor b3 readily evoke the preceding incrementation as encapsulation, overt representation of this encapsulation is not accommodated by either of them; cf b2′ and b3′. Since the information content is not significantly different in b1, b2 and b3, it becomes clear both that there is a distribution of information in the incrementation that better accommodates the preceding text as its encapsulation, and that every conceivable form of information distribution is not fully effective in doing this.

Clause b4 is a somewhat different case from b2 and b3. It too does not readily evoke sentence 10a as its encapsulation. While it can be framed for interpretation as either an encapsulating (b4′) or prospected sentence (b4″), with no overt sentence-initial marker of its relationship as an encapsulating sentence (e.g. 'hence' or 'in consequence'), it is likely to be perceived as a prospected sentence. But this is not because of the distribution of information in b4.

10.

a. Once in a while a department breaks up into smaller subgroups or cliques.

b4′. (Because/When it breaks up into smaller subgroups or cliques) things go wrong./Hence, things go wrong.

b4″. (That is) things go wrong.

Propositions b1, b2 and b3 are alike in the way they lexicalise their common ideational (since all three refer to the importance of effective or smooth functioning and the harmful effects of interfering with this). In b4 the same ideational is put in entirely different terms. Rather than making reference to the importance of effective functioning and the harmful effects of interfering with it, b4 makes a more general reference to problems arising, in the expression 'things go wrong'. The inability of b4 to evoke the preceding incrementation as encapsulation, therefore, cannot be attributed to a problem with information distribution in the sentence. Rather, b4 suggests that the additional key feature of the incrementation that impacts its ability to evoke the encapsulation is the particular lexicalisation that is given to its ideational.

We have said, then, that the learner, having acknowledged the need for use of the encapsulating sentence in the development of a particular message, or ideational whole, must fracture this ideational into units that are informationally appropriate for evoking the preceding text. We have said, in addition, that each individual unit of information must be given a textualisation which enhances its capacity to effect this evocation, which means that there must be an effective lexicalisation, and an effective information distribution, of each such unit of information.

Data assessment

In what follows, I will examine two representative samples of prose, randomly selected from the total collection, to illustrate learners' difficulties applying the two above-referred to competencies for evoking prior text as encapsulation. I will give evidence, that is, of ineffective 1) fragmentation of the ideational-whole, and 2) textualisation of individual incrementations. I will also account for these message-framing problems by arguing that they result from interference of better-known means of incrementation related to the prospected sentence.

Sample 1 is used to give evidence of the fragmentation problem. To assess the breakdown of its ideational whole, paragraph 1 is compared to an alternative and preferred textualisation of it, labelled 'preferred textualisation', below.

Sample 1

Dealing with the stress of college life

[1]In everyone's life, stress seems to be unavoidable. [2]When one grows up, one will face different kinds of stress in different stages. [3]In the college life, students have to face the stress comes from themselves, from their classmates as well as from their families. [4]Stress will bring to the students a sense of feeling that is unfree or even uncomfortable. [5]Sometimes if stress is not properly deal with, it may cause trouble to the students. [6]Therefore, it is important to deal with the stress of college life properly.

[1]Firstly, the stress students face in college life may come from themselves. [2]Every student like to be praised with their works. [3]However, different students have different abilities in learning [4]and even the same student will not do things good all the time. [5]So students should better know that they sometimes do bad in their homeworks or in the tests and examinations do not represent that they cannot get good results any more. [6]Students can try their best in their college works but should not put too much pressure on themselves, such as setting goals that are out of their abilities. [7]If students find that they are facing great stress, they may share it with others or give themselves a rest to relax.

[1]Secondly the stress of college life may come from students classmates. [2]In a place of people comparison seem to be unavoidable. [3]Students who have tried their best in their works and have not put too much pressure on themselves, will still face stress as they find that other are doing better. [4]In case of this kind, students should notice that if they have really tried their best, comparison of the marks in unnecessary. [5]Besides, if they still face stress, they may make use of the stress as a push force for them to work harder.

Preferred textualisation of paragraph 1

[1]Stress seems unavoidable. [2]One faces it in every phase of life, [3]and each phase comes with its own kind of stress. [4]In college life, students face three types of stress: self-imposed stress, the stress that comes from peer pressure and the stress that comes from parental pressure. [5]The stress of college life, whatever its source, makes people feel trapped and therefore perpetually ill at ease. [6]Unaddressed, it may cause serious health and/or psychological problems. [7]For this reason, it is important to deal with it in effective ways.

It is evident at a point early in the development of paragraph 1 that there is clear intention to use text-incrementation by means of the encapsulating sentence. If incrementation were by means of the prospected sentence, each successive sentence in this paragraph (1–6) would individually instantiate the point made in the title 'Dealing with the stress of college life'. Clearly this is not the case (compare Λ and B below):

A (original paragraph 1)	B
Dealing with the stress of college life	Dealing with the stress of college life
1. In everyone's life, stress seems unavoidable.	1. Students must avoid setting unachievable goals.
2. When one grows up, one will face different kinds of stress...	2. They must learn good time management skills.
3. In the college life, students have to face stress comes from...	3. They must seek the help of counsellors when needed.

Whereas the sentences of B instantiate the opening title, the sentences of A (the original paragraph) do not do this.

But there is a problem with the breakdown of the ideational whole of this paragraph into appropriate successive information units, which results in a failure to generate encapsulating sentences early in the paragraph, and also hinders effective recursive use of encapsulation in the rest of the paragraph.

The title of the essay—'Dealing with the stress of college life'—suggests that the text will address the need to deal with the stress of college life and/or the means of doing this. The opening sentence, however, claims that stress appears to be unavoidable. One expects a reaction to this, hence, not only because readers typically expect a justification in the context of any assertion, but more particularly because this opening assertion contradicts the suggestion of the title, that stress must and/or can be dealt with. In the learner sample, however, the ideational of sentence 1 is not encapsulated in sentence 2 and hence cannot be commented on (cf the projection into dialogue in 11).

11.

Sample 1	**Questions**
1. In everyone's life, stress seems to be unavoidable.	Why?/What follows from this?

2.? When one grows up, one will
face different kinds of stress
in different stages.

Since the ideational of sentence 1 is not encapsulated in sentence 2, it, of course, also follows that it is not encapsulated in any of the sentences that follow sentence 2. The learner has, in fact, selected to textualise it in such a way that sentence 1 and 2 are only connected as prospected sentences of an implicit opening claim, to the effect that there are a number of significant facts about stress (cf 12).

12.

Implicit claim: There are a number of significant facts about stress.

1. In everyone's life stress seems unavoidable.
2. When one grows up one will face different kinds of stress in different stages.

Since neither paragraph 1, nor the essay as a whole, is a mere itemisation of significant facts about stress, it is evident that what is intended is incrementation by encapsulation to make a case for the point of the title, 'Dealing with the stress of college life'. To put in place encapsulation of sentence 1, the preferred textualisation introduces sentence 2: 'One faces it (stress) at every phase of life'. This addition does not alter the information content of the paragraph itself, since the added sentence is in fact implicit in the existing sentence that follows it: 'Each phase of life comes with it own brand of stress'. But its introduction does effect encapsulation of the ideational of sentence 1 in it, and it further brings about the encapsulation of its own ideational in sentence 3 (the original sentence 2). (Refer to the overt representation of the encapsulations that these sentences accommodate in 13, and the projection into dialogue in 14, in which the questions answered by the successive incrementations are indicative of the way in which these sentences relate to the preceding text and, therefore, how they retain it as encapsulation.)

13.

1. Stress seems unavoidable.
2. (Because it is unavoidable) one faces it in every phase of life.
3. And (while stress is a constant feature of every phase of life) each phase comes with its own brand of stress.

14.

	Questions
1. Stress seems unavoidable.	What follows from this?
2. (Because it is unavoidable) one faces it in every phase of life.	Does it follow from this that each phase of life comes with the same type of stress?
3. (While every phase of life is stressful) each phase comes with its own brand of stress.	

In consequence, the otherwise unqualified assertion of sentence 1 is, in fact, addressed in the comments that follow it, and the intended recursive incrementation by encapsulation takes effect for the entire paragraph.

Sample 1, paragraph 2

[1]Firstly, the stress students face in college life may come from themselves. [2]Every student like to be praised with their works. [3]However, different students have different abilities in learning [4]and even the same student will not do things good all the time. [5]So students should better know that they sometimes do bad in their homeworks or in the tests and examinations do not represent that they cannot get good results any more. [6]Students can try their best in their college works but should not put too much pressure on themselves, such as setting goals that are out of their abilities. [7]If students find that they are facing great stress, they may share it with others or give themselves a rest to relax.

Preferred paragraph 2

[1]First, the stress students face in college life may be self-imposed. [2]Students face self-imposed stress when they seek praise all the time without acknowledging that different students have different abilities and no student can do well all the time. [3]Therefore to avoid self-imposed stress students should recognise that an isolated bad performance is not reflective of their true potential. [4]They should try their best without over-pressuring themselves by setting unrealistic goals. [5]However, if these ways of avoiding self-imposed stress do not work, and they are facing great stress, they should seek advice or find ways to rest and relax.

A problem with appropriate fragmentation of the ideational whole is also evident in paragraph 2. Sentence 2 of paragraph 2 by itself does not readily encapsulate its preceding sentence. (Refer to the projection into dialogue in 15.) Though this encapsulation can be achieved by the combined ideational of sentences 2 and 3 (with 4 conjoined), the original packaging of these sentences inhibits the evocation of 1 because 1) there is a formal separation of the ideational whole, needed to evoke 1, into two separate sentential units (namely, 2 and 3 with 4 conjoined to it), and 2) while sentence 2 of the original paragraph does not evoke sentence 1, 3 evokes 2, and 4 also evokes 2 (cf the projection into dialogue in 16).

15.

1. Firstly, the stress students face in college life may come from themselves.	Why/When do students face self-imposed stress?

2. Every student like to be praised for their works.
3. However, different students have different abilities in learning,
4. and even the same student will not do things good all the time.

16.

2. Every student like to be praised for their works.	But do all students have the same capacity to earn praise?

3. (Though every student like to be praised for their work) different students have different abilities in learning.	But are students always consistent in their ability to earn praise? (questions 2)
4. (Though every student likes to be praised for their works) even the same student will not do things good all the time.	

The effective evocations—3 of 2 and 4 of 2 (cf 16)—contrast with the want of ready evocation of 1 by 2, and interfere with the perception of 2 and 3 (with conjoined 4) as an information unit. Once repackaging is implemented to mark this information unit unambiguously (cf 2 of 17), the successive incrementations of this paragraph properly encapsulate their preceding text (as is demonstrated in the projection into dialogue, in 17).

17.

1. First, the stress students face in college life may be self-imposed.	When do students face self-imposed stress?
2. Students face self-imposed stress when they seek praise all the time without acknowledging that different students have different abilities and no student can do well all the time.	How should they avoid self-imposed stress?
3. To avoid self-imposed stress students should recognize that an isolated bad performance is not reflective of their true potential.	How else should they avoid self-imposed stress?
4. They should try their best without over-pressuring themselves by setting unrealistic goals.	

As was the case with the change we made in paragraph 1, the reformulated incrementation here does not change the information content of the paragraph in any way.

Paragraph 3

[1]Secondly the stress of college life may come from students classmates. [2]In a place of people comparison seem to be unavoidable. [3]Students who have tried their best in their works and have not put too much pressure on themselves, will still face stress as they find that other are doing better. [4]In case of this kind, students should notice that if they have really tried their best, comparison of the marks in unnecessary. [5]Besides, if they still face stress, they may make use of the stress as a push force for them to work harder.

Preferred paragraph 3

[1]Second, the stress of college life may be caused by peer pressure. [2](Students experience stress from peer pressure when) **comparison with their peers** puts them under pressure to improve their performance, even if they are doing the best they can. [3](To avoid this kind of stress) students should realize that if they are doing the best they can, a comparison of marks is unnecessary. [4]But if they still feel stress, they can use it to help them work harder.

Inappropriate fragmentation of the ideational whole is also evident in paragraph 3. Like sentence 2 of paragraph 2 above, sentence 2 in paragraph 3 by itself does not effectively encapsulate its preceding sentence (cf the projection into dialogue in 18).

18.

1. Secondly the stress of college life may come from students classmates.	When do students experience stress caused by peer pressure?
2. In a place of people comparison seem to be unavoidable.	

Rather, sentence 3 evokes 1 (cf the projection into dialogue in 19), and the ideational of 2 is actually implicit in 3 (cf boldface portion of 3 below).

19.

1. Secondly the stress of college life may come from students classmates.	When do students' classmates cause them stress?

3. (Students' classmates cause them stress when) students who have tried their best in their works and have not put pressure on themselves, (will) still face stress as (when) **they find that other are doing better**.

The ideational of sentence 2, hence, does not need to be given independent expression, but can be informationally fronted, to reflect its position in the original text (cf preferred text). With this change, which like the preceding changes again adds no new information to the original text, successive sentences encapsulate their preceding sentence, beginning with sentence 1.

If we now assess the way the ideational whole is fragmented in each of these examples, a common information packaging problem becomes apparent. Sentence 2 of paragraph 1, repeated below in 20, fails to evoke its preceding text as encapsulation because it is informationally overloaded.

20.

Paragraph 1

[1]In everyone's life, stress seems to be unavoidable. [2]When one grows up, one will face different kinds of stress in different stages.

It contains two significant propositions: 1) one faces stress at every stage/phase of life, and 2) every phase of life comes with its own distinct kind of stress. The failure to give independent representation to the first of these propositions, as suggested earlier, makes it impossible to evoke sentence 1, as encapsulation. That is, the ideational whole, at this point in its representation is not fragmented into a unit size that effects evocation of the preceding text.

In paragraph 2 of the original, in which sentence 2 fails to evoke sentence 1 as an encapsulation (repeated below in 21), the unit size of the incrementation is, again, a problem.

> 21.
>
> Paragraph 2
>
> [1]Firstly, the stress students face in college come from themselves. [2]Every student like to be praised with their works. [3]However, different students have different abilities in learning [4]and even the same student will not do things good all the time.

Here, the learner over-fragments the ideational whole, and it is by giving sentential expression to the combined ideational of the individual sentences 2 and 3 (with 4 conjoined), in 2 of the revised version of paragraph 2, that sentence 1 is evoked as encapsulation. As we have seen, exactly the same over-fragmentation is also apparent in paragraph 3 (repeated below in 22). In this case, we gave sentential representation to the combined ideational of sentences 2 and 3 of the original in sentence 2 of the revised version.

> 22.
>
> [1]Secondly the stress of college life may come from students classmates. [2]In a place of people comparison seem to be unavoidable. [3]Students who have tried their best in their works and have not put too much pressure on themselves, will still face stress as they find that other are doing better.

It is understandable that achieving an appropriate unit size can prove a challenge for the learner, because what is involved is breakdown of the essentially non-linear ideational into a linear succession of constituent units. I want to suggest that this challenge is made more understandable by the fact that the required breakdown is in direct opposition to one better known to the learner.

In incrementation by the better-known prospected sentence, the information breakdown pointedly disallows fragmentation into a unit size that will evoke the preceding text as encapsulation. Put in other words, text generation by means of the better-known prospected sentence does not allow for an information breakdown that effects a retention, by any one unit of incrementation, of the text that precedes it. In fact, effective incrementation by means of the prospected sentence is only possible when there is no such retention.

23.

a.	Peter has three different jobs.	
b.	He is a part-time teacher.	When does he teach?
c.	He teaches Mondays, Wednesdays and Fridays.	
d.	He (also) cooks at night at a local restaurant.	Where does he cook?
e.	He is a chef at Pagano's.	
f.	And he ...	

Hence 23b which is prospected by 23a cannot retain 23a (cf 24b below).

24.

a. Peter has three different jobs.

b. Since he has three different jobs, he is a part-time teacher.

Clause 24b does not have the same meaning as the prospected 23b. On the other hand, 23c which retains 23b cannot be prospected by 23b. Similarly a comparison of text 25 and 26, below, shows that the retention of the preceding text in 26b makes it impossible to perceive 26b as prospected by 26a (as 25b is by 25a) and hence the message conveyed in 26 is somewhat different from that of text 25.

25.

a. Peter is pursuing many things.

b. He dabbles in this. He dabbles in that.

26.

a. Peter is pursuing many things.

b. Taking on so much at the same time, he (merely) dabbles in this and dabbles in that.

One might ask in addition why learners fail to implement an informational breakdown which allows for retention of the preceding text in the contexts we have discussed above, when they are able to do this elsewhere.

27.

1. In everyone's life stress seems unavoidable.	What follows from this?
2.? When one grows up one will face different kinds of stress in different stages.	(What follows from this?)
(Students face a certain type of stress at college.)	(What type of stress is this?)
3. In college life students have to face (three types of stress):the stress comes from themselves, from classmates as well as from their families.	How does this stress make students feel?
4. (This) stress will bring to the students a feeling that is unfree or even uncomfortable.	What happens if this stress is not properly dealt with?
5. Sometimes if (this) stress is not properly deal with,	What can we conclude from this?

it may cause trouble to the students.

6. Therefore, it is important to deal with the stress of college life properly.

In paragraph 1 (repeated in 27), for example, sentences 4, 5 and 6 properly evoke their immediately preceding text as Encapsulation. (Sentence 3 relates as a prospected sentence to an implicit claim that students face a certain type of stress at college; refer to the projection into dialogue in 27). I think it is possible to find an explanation for the instances of failure to evoke the preceding text, discussed above, in the greater packaging challenge these particular contexts pose for learners who are more familiar with incrementation by the prospected sentence.

In the discussion of our first example, we said that the repackaging of information in paragraph 1 calls for the introduction of sentence 2, which constitutes information already contained in the text that follows it, specifically in sentence 3 (cf the relevant segment of revised paragraph 1, repeated below in 28).

28.

[1]Stress seems unavoidable. [2]One faces **it (stress) at every phase of life**, [3]and **each phase of life comes with** its own kind of **stress.**

This means that the called-for information retention is effected across sentences 2 and 3 (in the revised text above) by means of overt expression (that is, actual lexicalisation) of the retained preceding text. Learners, however, are particularly uncomfortable with retention by overt lexicalisation in the better-known incrementation by prospected sentence. This is because overt lexicalisation that retains the preceding text most readily interferes with the perception of incrementation by the prospected sentence (since retention that is not lexicalised has to be worked out, while retention that is lexicalised is perceived immediately). Hence, if we rephrase b of 29, as in b of 30, the overt retention of this rephrasing makes it difficult to perceive b as one of the jobs prospected by the opening statement.

29.

a. Peter has three jobs.
b. He works in a local restaurant, where he cooks a little, washes dishes and acts as a waiter once in a while.
c. He is a part-time teacher.
d. He also delivers newspapers in his immediate neighborhood.

30.

a. Peter has three jobs.
b. He has three jobs in the restaurant where he works at night.
c. He is a part-time teacher.
d. He also delivers newspapers in his immediate neighborhood.

The retention problems of sentence 2 in paragraph 2, and sentence 2 in paragraph 3 are addressed by repackaging to generate sentences with multiple incorporations. In this regard it is important to acknowledge, again, that text incrementation by means of the prospected sentence does not permit incorporation of the prospecting sentence by the prospected sentence; hence 29b, c or d above cannot incorporate 29a. As we have said earlier, incrementation by the prospected sentence contrasts, in this respect, with incrementation by means of the encapsulating sentence (cf 32, derived by incorporation from 31).

31.

I was on sentry duty.

I saw the enemy approaching.

I opened fire.

I beat off the enemy attack.

32.

By opening fire, when I saw the enemy approaching while I was on sentry duty, I beat off the enemy attack.

Since the better known incrementation by the prospected sentence does not accommodate its use, it is not surprising that learners fail to package information appropriately, when the packaging calls for multiple incorporations.

We can give attention to the point of commonality in the fragmentation problem of sentence 2 of paragraph 1, and that of sentences 2 of paragraph 2 and 2 of paragraph 3 by acknowledging that incorporation also results in overt retention. The suggestion then appears to be that learners package in ways that fail to evoke the preceding text as encapsulation when the required packaging would violate the key constraint of the better-known incrementation by prospected sentence by not just effecting retention, but, more particularly, by effecting overt retention.

We have discussed, above, learners' difficulties with the first requisite competency for incrementation by the encapsulating sentence: the appropriate fragmentation of the non-linear ideational whole. There is also evidence in these essays of ineffectual mastery of the second above-defined requisite competency for incrementation by the encapsulating sentence: the need for an appropriate textualisation (that is, lexicalisation and packaging) of the incrementations. While ineffective textualisations deriving from information packaging problems (cf example 10 above) are not found in this data, informationally appropriate units do fail to evoke their preceding text because they are not given a suitable lexicalisation. In this case we find, again, that learners select inappropriate textualisations when an effective textualisation would result in an overt retention of the preceding text. For example, the successive sentential incrementations of paragraph 4, Essay 2 (cf 33)—2, 3, and 4—are informationally appropriate for evocation of the preceding text, as is demonstrated by the projection into dialogue, in 34.

33.

[1]Finally friends are a source of stress too. [2]It is important to cooperate with classmates and make friends with them in school life. [3]When a student finds there are difficulties to communciate with others, it is hard for him to have a happy school life due to he feels so lonely. [4]He will feel anxious to work with others.

34.

1. Finally friends (classmates) are a source of stress too.	Why are classmates a source of stress?
2. It is important to cooperate with classmates (them) and make friends with them in school life.	What happens when students have difficulty making friends with their peers?
3. When a student finds there are difficulties to communciate with (making friends with) others, it is hard for him to have a happy school life due to he feels so lonely.	What happens when a student finds it hard to cooperate with his peers?
4. He will feel anxious to work (about working) with others (them).	

But this evocation only works with the introduced changes in lexicalisation (the bracketed alternatives to the original words, in the above projection into dialogue, in 34). The failure to select the referring expressions 'classmates' rather than 'friends' in sentence 1, prevents the reference to 'classmates' in sentence 2 from locating a co-referent in sentence 1. This inhibits the evocation of sentence 1 as the encapsulation for sentence 2. In sentence 3, the same problem is caused when the writer selects 'communicating with' as being presumably synonymous with 'making friends with' from sentence 2. This again works against the evocation of sentence 2 as the encapsulation of 3.

These lexicalisation problems, again, seem to stem from the fact that the student avoids overt retention. This is, once more, likely to be because incrementation by the better-known prospected sentence is most readily prevented by overt retention of the preceding text. The fact that learners hardly ever give overt representation to the encapsulation, in sentences that properly evoke the preceding text—although academic prose shows clear preference for this—gives further support to this supposition.

35.

Sample 1, paragraph 2

[1]Firstly, the stress students face in college life may come from themselves. [2]Every student like to be praised with their works.

[3]However, different students have different abilities in learning [4]and even the same student will not do things good all the time. [5]So students should better know that they sometimes do bad in their homeworks or in the tests and examinations do not represent that they cannot get good results any more. [6]Students can try their best in their college works but should not put too much pressure on themselves, such as setting goals that are out of their abilities. [7]If students find that they are facing great stress, they may share it with others or give themselves a rest to relax.

Preferred paragraph 2

[1]First, the stress students face in college life may be self-imposed. [2]**Students face self-imposed stress** when they seek praise all the time without acknowledging that different students have different abilities and no student can do well all the time. [3]Therefore to avoid **self-imposed stress** students should recognise that an isolated bad performance is not reflective of their true potential. [4]To avoid **self-imposed stress**, they should try their best without over-pressuring

themselves by setting unrealistic goals. [5]However, if **these ways of avoiding self-imposed stress** do not work, and they are facing great stress, they should seek advice or find ways to rest and relax.

The sentences of the preferred textualisations in 35, for example, differ from the original sentences in giving overt expression to the encapsulation, even when they are identical to the original sentences in every other way.

CONCLUSION

I have attempted to show that, because text incrementations by the prospected and encapsulating sentences are diametrically opposed operations, fairly advanced learners, who have properly mastered incrementation by the prospected sentence, have difficulty in the effective use of the encapsulating sentence. I have suggested more specifically that these learners have difficulty 1) fragmenting the ideational whole, and 2) textualising the properly fragmented ideational, when these tasks call for overt retention of the preceding text. I have suggested further that this is because overt retention is categorically ruled out by the earlier-acquired incrementation by the prospected sentence.

References

Coulthard M. 1994. On analysing and evaluating written text. In M Coulthard (ed), *Advances in Written Text.* London: Routledge.

Grimes J E. 1975. *The Thread of Discourse.* The Hague: Mouton Publishers.

Hoey M. 1979. *Signalling in Discourse.* Birmingham: University of Birmingham.

Hoey M. 1994. Signalling in discourse: a functional analysis of a common discourse pattern in written and spoken English. In M Coulthard (ed), *Advances in Written Text.* London: Routledge.

Sinclair J McH. 1994. Trust the text. In M Coulthard (ed), *Advances in Written Text*. London: Routledge.

Tadros A. Predictive categories in expository text. In M Coulthard (ed), *Advances in Written Text*. London: Routledge.

Winter E. 1994. Clause relations as information structure: two basic text structures in English. In M Coulthard (ed), *Advances in Written Text*. London: Routledge.

6

Variable Temporal Passage in Storytelling

First published in *Text* 23 (1) (2003), De Gruyter

INTRODUCTION

Scholars interested in the subject of storytelling as a distinct genre of narrative prose have identified what rhetorical conventions must be followed to ensure that the narrator generates a story, rather than a mere report of events that occurred in past time (Labov 1981; Labov and Waletzky 1967; Martin 1984, 1992; Martin and Rothery 1980, 1981, 1984, 1986; Plum 1988; Rothery 1989, 1990, 1995).[1] This article will examine a hitherto unrecognised set of conventions that govern the representation of the passage of time in storytelling.[2]

It is well recognised that passage through past time is suggested in narrative of all types by representing successive past events in chronological order, using independent clauses with verbs of appropriate tense, aspect and mood.

1.

a. I left.

b. I collected my clothes from various parts of the house.
Then I packed them into a travel bag.
After that I left.

Hence the succession of chronologically ordered events in independent clauses, with verbs in the indicative mood and preterite tense of 1b is able to represent passage through past time, while 1a, which is not a succession of such clauses, cannot do this. But while 1b by representing passage through past time qualifies as narrative prose, it does not read as a story. I want to show that those narrators who are telling a story, rather than just reporting events that occurred in past time, use *established means* to bring about *predictable variations* in the passage of time. This is what makes 1c, which follows, distinct from 1b.

1.

c. I collected my clothes from various parts of the house.

They were already tidily stacked in piles of like items, so there was really little to do to get them ready.

I pulled out a large, old travel bag from the back of my bedroom closet, and, dusting it off, took the piles of clothes one at a time and stacked them tightly into the bag.

It was all done rather too quickly.

For a long moment I stared at the bag, unwilling to take the next step.

Then, zipping up the entirety of my small bundle of belongings, I tossed it over my shoulder and left.

Both the pace and the quality of the passage of time varies as the narrative progresses.[3] Unlike 1b, 1c uses three different types of clauses to carry the narrative forward in time: the *then*-marked clause, the clause in canonical order and the VP-conjoined clause. As we will see in the ensuing discussion, each of these clauses marks a distinct pace, and quality, of temporal passage. Example 1c also distributes the narrative into an alternating succession of foregrounded event clauses and backgrounded nonevent clauses (boldface in 1c), suggesting a waxing and waning in the narrative progression, which is not evident in 1b.[4] A particular pattern of such changes in the passage of past time contributes in a crucial way to giving a narrative the recognisable quality of a story.

In what follows, I delineate the nature of this implemented variation in the passage of past time, using two types of evidence to support my claims:

1. I examine the storytelling of skilled writers.[5] I focus exclusively on the novels of Thomas Hardy and the short stories of Somerset Maugham, and provide illustrative descriptions of variable temporal progression in randomly selected thematic segments from Hardy's *Tess of the D'Urbervilles* and Maugham's short story *The Dream.*[6]
2. I also examine a set of ESL learners' written recalls of Maugham's short story *The Dream.* I show that the absence of variable temporal progression in these narratives prevents them from reading as stories.

THE SYSTEM: IMPLEMENTING CHANGE IN THE PERCEPTION OF TEMPORAL PASSAGE

Because representation of the passage through past time is such an integral part of the narrative mode of expression, linguists have addressed this subject in some detail. Common to all the approaches that tackle the issue of temporal progression is the above-mentioned principal claim that temporal progression is effected by representing successive past events in their chronological order (Dahl 1980; Dry 1981; Labov 1981; Labov and Waletzky 1967; Hopper and Thompson 1980, 1979; Hopper 1977, 1979; Reinhart 1984, amongst others). But these studies do not appear to acknowledge that different representations of iconic order can be expressed (cf Tickoo 2002).

Labov (1981) directly addresses the iconic order requirement in what he calls the temporal juncture condition and the 'and then what happened?' test. The temporal juncture condition imposes a relationship between a pair of clauses such that a change in their order also changes the order of the real-world events they denote. Changing the order of clauses 2a and 2b, for example, would result in a change in the order of the real-world events they denote. In the context of 2a, 2b also conforms to the 'and then what happened?' test (refer to example 3). But in 4, while temporal juncture holds between 4b and 4a, 4b fails the 'and then what happened?' test. Yet clearly the sequenced events of 4a and 4b do represent temporal progression. In Labov's formulation of iconic order, therefore, only the temporal progression of 2a–b is acknowledged, while the somewhat different temporal progression represented in 4a–b goes unacknowledged.

2.

a. I got home at five.

b. I took the children to the movies.

3.

I got home at five.

Then what happened?

Then I took the children to the movies.

4.

a. I left for school at 9 o'clock.

b. (#Then) I arrived in the nick of time.

Dry (1981) focuses on the inherent aspectual differences that exist between verbs which push narrative time forward and those that do not. She points out that verbs that are events rather than nonevents facilitate temporal progression. For her, therefore, the sequenced events of both 2a–b and 4a–b represent temporal progression. In her approach, however, the difference between the two types of temporal progression of 2 and 4 is not acknowledged.

Dahl (1980) too recognises the temporal progression of 4a–b. But his 'maximally short narrative discourse', 'Julius Caesar's famous statement' (refer to example 5), is 'altered in an interesting way, specifically in the pragmatic force it carries, when individual clauses are modified to meet Labov's 'and then what happened?' test (in 6).

5.

Veni, vidi, vici.

'I came, I saw, I conquered.'

6.

I came.

Then I saw.

Then I conquered.

The original text (example 5) carries the suggestion of inevitable follow-up at the completion of both the first utterance, 'I came', and the second utterance, 'I saw'. With clause-initial *then* preceding the second and third utterances, this effect of inevitable follow up is lost' (Tickoo 2002). The resulting temporal movement in 6 is not the same as in 5. Like Dry, Dahl also fails to acknowledge the difference between these two types of temporal progression.

In Hopper's (1977, 1979) conception of it, temporal progression is determined by the informational status of denoted situations in their context of occurrence in the discourse ('discourse aspect' in his terminology). The relative informational status of successive denoted situations determines whether and to what extent temporal progression will be effected. The sequence of 7a–b, for example, does not represent temporal progression, in spite of the fact that both 7a and 7b denote events rather than nonevents.

7.

a. He took the exam.

b. He passed it.

c. # Then he passed it.

This is because the event of 7b is not entirely new information, at the time of its utterance. At the time of the utterance of 7b, the hearer already knows that the person referred to either passed the exam or failed it. Though Labov's 'and then what happened?' test would also show that 7a–b is not capable of signalling temporal progression (refer to 7c in the context of 7a), unlike Hopper, Labov does not provide a complete explanation for this fact.

Existing treatments of temporal progression taken collectively do appear to imply that different types of iconic event order are given representation in narrative prose. But to my knowledge focused attention has not been given to that set of predictable changes in the modes of representing iconic order—and hence in the passage of time—which makes a narrative read as a story.

I will describe two different, though related, linguistic means by which differences in the representation of iconic order are implemented to modulate the passage of time; the first of these means of temporal modulation is implemented at the level of the sentence and the second at a level of text organisation. I will show that, at both levels of implementation, a well-defined set of variables is manipulated to effect predictable differences in the passage of time. In discussing the requisite systems for both sentence-level and text-level manipulation of temporal progression, I will suggest that recognised constructs that have other acknowledged functions in narrative (e.g. the marking of the evaluation) are also put to use to modulate the pace and quality of temporal progression.

At the sentence level of manipulation, I will suggest that change in temporal progression is effected by the consonant selection of two features of the denoted situation: (1) its aspect, and (2) the sentential structure of the clause in which it occurs.

At the level of text organisation, I will suggest that the well-recognised narrative organisational principle of grounding (Hopper 1977, 1979), by which narrative is distributed into successive thematically salient and less salient segments, is also manipulated in its distributional design to effect changes in the temporal progression.

It is necessary to acknowledge that the validity of this argument—that the selection of a specific structure (at either the level of the sentence or the text) effects a particular type of temporal progression—clearly rests on the acceptance of an ideal reader's perceptions.

It is also necessary to point out that, in the ensuing discussion, types of temporal progression are described in terms of the pace and quality of the movement, and a failure to use a particular sentence structure, or discourse design, at a particular phase of narrative development, is said to result in an inability to generate the 'right' quality and pace of progression for that phase of narrative development. However, this and like statements, made elsewhere in the article, are not prescriptive; they serve only to describe the constraints that define the system of variable temporal progression as it is used, by at least those skilled storytellers whose works are examined in this study.

It must also be noted that the study constitutes a first attempt at a broad assessment of the subject of variable temporal progression in storytelling. It, therefore, examines core features of the mechanisms of temporal modulation, at both the sentential and textual levels, in a single treatment, while leaving more detailed and separate examination of each of these levels to future studies.

THE SENTENCE-LEVEL MANIPULATION OF READERS' PERCEPTION OF PASSAGE OF NARRATIVE TIME

As already mentioned, variation in the pace and quality of temporal progression is first effected at the level of the sentence. The passage of narrative time is monitored at the level of the sentence, by the selection of a particular internal state of being, that is, aspect, for the situation denoted by that sentence. There are of course a number of ways of representing differentiated aspectual conditions of denoted situations. Different aspectual conditions of denoted situations can be represented by morphological means, as in 8a and 8b.

8.

a. He was leaving in a hurry.

b. He left in a hurry.

But they are also determined by lexical aspect, and therefore by the choice of the verb. Vendler (1967) categorises verbs into four principal aspectual types—states, activities, accomplishments and achievements—depending on whether they possess the semantic features of dynamism, telicity (end-point property) and punctility (occurrence at a single point in time) (cf Table 6.1).

TABLE **6.1**

LEXICAL ASPECTUAL CATEGORIES

LEXICAL ASPECTUAL CATEGORIES				
Features	**States**	**Activities**	**Accomplishments**	**Achievements**
punctual	–	–	–	+
telic	–	–	+	+
dynamic	–	+	+	+

(from Bardovi-Harlig 1995: 109)

States are inherently nondynamic, atelic and nonpunctual (e.g. *stand* in *There it stood*). Activities are dynamic, atelic and nonpunctual (e.g. *walk* in *She walked*). Accomplishments are dynamic, telic and nonpunctual (e.g. *write* in *She wrote a poem*), and achievements are dynamic, telic and punctual (e.g. *leave* in *She left*). (Accomplishments and achievements are often categorised as a single class and together referred to as events.) So there is a potential difference effected in the representation of the aspect of the denoted situation by the choice of one verb over another for its representation, as is suggested by comparing 9b (in the context of 9a) with 9c (in the context of 9a). In 9b, the denoted situation is represented as dynamic, telic and punctual, that is, as an achievement. In 9c, on the other hand, the same happening is represented as nondynamic, atelic and nonpunctual, that is, as a state.

9.

a. What happened to her?

b. A car ran over her.

c. She was in an accident.

Denoted events are the most effective in propelling the narrative forward, while states have the lowest potential for conveying passage of time.

The aspectual state of the denoted situation is also affected by factors other than the choice of the verb. Hopper (1979) acknowledges the contribution of context of occurrence to the aspect of the denoted situation. By this means he is able to recognise dimensions of difference in the aspect of denoted situations that are not captured by a purely lexical-aspectual assessment. Hopper examines not only values of the dynamism, telicity and punctility of the denoted situation, but also its informational, context-dependent features such as its given/new status, and its saliency at the time of denotation. Hopper refers to the total conglomerate of the semantic-cum-informational features that must be examined in a context-based assessment of the aspect of the denoted situation as the transitivity features, and to the resulting context-sensitive conception of aspect as discourse aspect. In Hopper's assessment, denoted situations with more of the transitivity features listed under the category 'perfective' (cf Table 6.2) push the timeline forward, while denoted situations with fewer 'perfective' features (and therefore more 'imperfective' features) are less effective in carrying the timeline forward.

TABLE **6.2**

PERFECTIVE VS. IMPERFECT

Perfective	Imperfective
1. Strict chronological sequencing	1. Simultaneity or chronological overlap of situation C with event A and/or B
2. View of event as a whole, whose completion is a necessary prerequisite to a subsequent event	2. View of a situation or happening whose completion is not a necessary prerequisite to a subsequent happening
3. Identity of subject within each discrete episode.	3. Frequent changes of subject
4. Unmarked distribution of focus in clause, with presupposition of subject and assertion in verb and its immediate complements (or other unmarked focus)	4. Marked distribution of focus, e.g. subject focus, instrument focus, focus on sentence adverbials
5. Human topics	5. Variety of topics, including natural phenomena
6. Dynamic, kinetic events	6. Static, descriptive situations
7. Foregrounding. Event indispensable to narrative	7. Backgrounding. State or situation necessary for understanding motives, attitudes, etc
8. Realis	8. Irrealis

(from Hopper 1979: 216)

When the transitivity features are used in an assessment of the discourse aspect of denoted situations, aspectual differences of the type illustrated by a comparison of 10a and 10b (repeated below from 7) are acknowledged. As was suggested above, the situation of 10a is an event. It is also informationally new. By contrast, 10b, while also an event, is at the same time not informationally entirely new. At the time of its utterance it is given information that the exam was either passed or failed. This shows that some situations, e.g. passing the exam of 10b in the context of taking it, do not propel the narrative forward in time even though lexico-aspectual assessments would consider them suitable for this.

10.

a. He took the exam.

b. (#Then) He passed it.

Similarly, the clauses of 11b, though they do denote events, are not interpreted as carrying the narrative forward along the timeline, because they are not salient to the narrative theme. The clauses of 11b are new information in their context of occurrence, but they do not contribute thematically salient—or in other words storyline—events.[7]

11.

a. The girl went inside and shut the door behind her.
b. The sky darkened and took on the shades of the night. An owl hooted eerily from its tree-top perch.
c. She hesitated for just a brief moment and then, with a resoluteness that was new to her, picked up the phone and dialled that dreaded number.

It is clear from Hopper's more comprehensive representation of aspect that in representing the intended aspect of a denoted situation, the narrator has regulative control over a number of variables, in the form of the transitivity features.[8] It is the assigned values of these variables that collectively determine how the situation will be perceived, and what quality of temporal progression will result in consequence.

If we focus now on only those event verbs that are discourse-aspectually appropriate for propelling the narrative forward (e.g. 'took the exam' of 10a above rather than 'passed it' of 10b) we find that the use of these (1) with somewhat differentiated informational features and/or (2) in structurally differentiated clauses also signals qualitatively differentiated types of forward movement. I will describe three such different movements below, referring to them as Type 1, Type 2 and Type 3 temporal progressions.

Type 1

In Type 1, narrative movement is via an event that is informationally *new* (rather than given), and *salient* (rather than nonsalient). This new and salient event is represented in a clause in canonical (that is, SVO) order. The result of the informational newness and saliency of the event is that the information incrementation it facilitates is perceived as thematically significant. Passage via an event, because of the feature of telicity (end-point property), results in a move to a distinct point in time. The combined result of the newness, saliency and event-like quality of the denoted situation is the suggestion of a thematically and temporally well-defined step forward. The canonically ordered clause marks one level of such a transition.

12.

a. **I collected my clothes from various parts of the house.**

They were already tidily stacked in piles of like items, so there was really little to do to get them ready.

b. **I pulled out a large, old travel bag from the back of my bedroom closet....**

Sentence 12b, for example, presents a new and salient event in a canonically ordered clause, signalling a degree of temporal and thematic transition (in the context of 12a) that is customarily associated with the clause in canonical order.

Because the clause in canonical order marks one level of temporal and thematic transition, temporal movement which involves a higher degree of transition cannot be represented in canonical order. Consider the event sequence of 13a–b below:

13.

a. She had a girl.

b. # She had a boy.

c. Then she had a boy.

In this sequence of events, the transition between 13a and 13b is too great to allow for its representation by means of the clause in canonical order.

Type 2

In Type 2 temporal progression, exemplified in 13c above, and 14b below, an informationally new and thematically salient event occurs in a clause with initial temporal 'then' ('after that' or 'after this' is sometimes used instead of 'then').

14.

a. I collected my clothes from various parts of the house.

They were already tidily stacked in piles of like items, so there was really little to do to get them ready.

I pulled out a large, old travel bag from the back of my bedroom closet, and, dusting it off, took the piles of clothes one at a time and stacked them tightly into the bag.

It was all done rather too quickly.

For a long moment I stared at the bag, unwilling to take the next step.

b. **Then**, zipping up the entirety of my small bundle of belongings, **I tossed it over my shoulder and left**.

c.# Zipping up the entirety of my small bundle of belongings, I tossed it over my shoulder and left.

The *then*-marked structure signals a more significant temporal and thematic transition compared to the clause in canonical order. Canonical order (14c) would not be appropriate in place of the *then*-marked clause of 14b, because it would signal a lower degree of transition than actually holds between 14b and its preceding event.

The uniqueness of the temporal passage signalled by the *then*-marked clause is also apparent in 15, which shows that certain types of event sequences do not meet the conditions for felicitous representation by means of the *then*-marked clause:

15.

a. I left at the last minute.

b. # Then I arrived in the nick of time.

c. And arrived in the nick of time.

The transition between arrival and departure cannot be represented by means of the *then*-marked clause, because the defining conditions for type 2 temporal passage are not met. Arrival is not sufficiently new in the context of departure. Arrival is also not sufficiently (independently) salient in the context of departure.

Type 3

In Type 3 temporal progression, exemplified in 15c, and also in 16b and 16c, the narrative moves via a highly anticipated (rather than new) and thematically (independently) minor (rather than salient) completed event. Because the event is perceived to be anticipated, and hence the inevitable follow up to its preceding event, the transition appears to occur at a faster pace than is suggested by Type 1 or Type 2 progression. The low saliency of each independent anticipated event lends a lightness of touch to the transition. This faster-paced and less independently significant transition is marked by the use of a VP-conjoined clause. It allows for the representation of the successive constituent occurrences of a larger situation, and a depiction hence of the coming about of that larger happening.

16.

I collected my clothes from various parts of the house.

They were already tidily stacked in piles of like items, so there was really little to do to get them ready.

a. I pulled out a large, old travel bag from the back of my bedroom closet, **and**, dusting it off,

b. took the piles of clothes one at a time

c. and stacked them tightly into the bag.

It was all done rather too quickly. For a long moment I stared at the bag, unwilling to take the next step. Then, zipping up the entirety of my small bundle of belongings, I tossed it over my shoulder and left.

At the time of the utterance of 16b, for example, the reader anticipates that something that can felicitously follow 16a will follow it. Likewise, at the time of the utterance of 16c, the reader anticipates that something that can felicitously follow 16b will follow it. Unlike the event of 12b (which appears in a clause in canonical order) and the event of 13c (which appears in a *then*-marked clause), the denoted events of the VP-conjoined clauses are not seen as entirely independent happenings. Rather, because of VP conjoining, *pulled out*, *took* and *stacked* are perceived individually only as constituent actions of a larger action.

As with the sentential types referred to above (canonical order and the *then*-marked clause) VP conjoining can only be used when the event it represents bears the right type of temporal follow up to its preceding event. Consider, for example, the sequence of 17a–b:

17.

a. I had a dream

b. # and had another dream.

c. Then I had another dream.

VP conjunction cannot be used in accompaniment with 17b, because the defining conditions for Type 3 temporal passage are not met: The event of 17b is not anticipated in the context of 17a. It is also independently salient in this context.

While it is true of course that the passage of different intervals of time can be indicated by the use of different temporal adverbials, e.g. *a month later* or *soon after that*, to my knowledge the three above-described quantitatively and qualitatively differentiated types of temporal passage have not been heretofore acknowledged.[9]

We have suggested, therefore, that the narrator has control of the discourse aspect of the denoted situation and hence the ability to monitor the quality of the temporal progression s/he represents. We have suggested further that even when the maximum forward movement via denoted *events* is desired, there is choice between three potential kinds of such progression. The distinct quality of each of these three kinds of temporal progression was evidenced above in their failure to accommodate each and every event sequence. It is also true, however, that many sequenced events are amenable to representation in all three of these ways: Types 1, 2 and 3 temporal progression. This gives the narrator the ability to modulate the temporal progression in a way that best suits his/her narrative purpose.

For example, in excerpt 18a below from Hardy's *Tess of the D'Urbervilles*, the choice of Type 3 narrative progression (formally marked by the use of VP-conjoined clauses) gives the temporal progression a rapid and unlaboured quality of passage and represents the successive occurrences as the constituent elements of a unified larger occurrence. Choice of Type 2 progression in its place would significantly alter the quality of the temporal movement, as is suggested in 18b.

18.

a. 'He leapt up lightly, arranged the reins, and was gone between the tall red-berried hedges.'

(Thomas Hardy, *Tess of the D'Urbervilles*, p 83)

b. He leapt up lightly. Then he arranged the reins. After that he left, disappearing between the tall red-berried hedges.

Choice of Type 2 progression, formally marked by use of sentence initial *then* or *after that*, gives much more thematic significance to the action of each *then*-marked clause. Further, because these actions are no longer regarded as anticipated, but rather are perceived as informationally new at the time of their denotation, the narrative pace loses its light and rapid quality. With each successive occurrence as new and salient, the passage through time moves at a more temporally measured and thematically decisive pace.

That storytellers in fact customarily alternate between different sentential types of temporal progression is evident in excerpt 19 from *Tess of the D'Urbervilles*, in which the narrative starts with the use of Type 3 temporal progression (in boldface), but soon gives way to Type 2 (italicised).

19.

'The harvest men rose from the shock of corn, and stretched their limbs, and extinguished their pipes. ...Tess, having quickly eaten her own meal, beckoned to her eldest sister to come and take away the baby, fastened her dress, put on the bluff gloves again, and stooped anew to draw a bond from the last completed sheaf for the tying of the next.

In the afternoon and the evening the proceedings of the morning were continued...*Then, they all rode home...'*

(Thomas Hardy, *Tess of the D'Urbervilles*, p 98)

The boldface segment of the extract uses VP-conjoined clauses to signal a rapid and unlaboured temporal passage via relatively minor routine activities. The italicised *then*-marked clause, then, signals a significant thematic transition, which in the backdrop of the preceding narrative segment occurs at a slower and more deliberate pace.

EFFECTING TEXT-LEVEL DIFFERENCES IN READERS' PERCEPTION OF PASSAGE OF NARRATIVE TIME

Organisational features of narrative structure are also manipulated to generate predictable differences in the passage of narrative time. The text-level means of temporal modulation described here are evidenced in an examination of (1) randomly selected thematic units from Hardy's *Tess of the D'Urbervilles*, and (2) Maugham's short story *The Dream*. Further support for the key role that temporal modulation plays in the generation of a story is provided by examining how ESL written recalls of Maugham's *The Dream* fail to use variable temporal passage and concomitantly fail to read as stories.

It is widely acknowledged that in narrative a key text-organising principle effects a separation of information into fore- and backgrounded narrative segments. Hopper (1977, 1979) has pointed out that foregrounded narrative segments correlate with denoted situations with more perfective, rather than imperfective, transitivity features. This means that in foregrounded narrative segments denoted situations possess features such as dynamism, telicity, punctility, newness and saliency. Backgrounded narrative segments, on the other hand, correlate with denoted situations with more imperfective, rather than perfective, transitivity features. That is, the denoted situations tend to be stative, atelic, nonpunctual, given and nonsalient.[10]

Because of the difference in transitivity values of denoted situations in the fore- and background, grounding imposes variable temporal passage on the narrative development. It constrains information incrementation to take the shape of a sustained alternation between segments that are more and less effective in propelling the narrative forward along the timeline. The successive pairings, or juxtapositions, of fore- and backgrounded segments can be qualitatively dissimilar. For example, juxtaposing a high transitivity event (20a) to a low transitivity state (20b) results in one type of grounding.

20.

a. We arrived in the late evening.

b. The sky was full of stars—it was a quiet but charming welcome.

Juxtaposing a high transitivity event (one that is new in its context of occurrence, for example, as is 21b) to a lower transitivity event (one that is anticipated rather than new in its context of occurrence, for example, as is 21a) produces another type of grounding.

21.

She picked up her clothes, tied them in a bundle, and

a. tossed them into the river.

b. Then, turning her back on the river, she took the road to...

Though the actual realisations of grounding can vary, therefore, examination of stories written by skilled writers shows that there are certain common design constraints on the distribution of successive fore- and backgrounded segments in a single narrative or a thematically distinct sub-unit of a narrative. That is, there is a well-established way in which the waxing and waning in the temporal passage is manifest.

In his description of the characteristic non-uniformity of narrative development, Longacre (1981) suggests that narrative 'is not spoken or written on a uniform level of excitation or tension' (p 347); rather, 'the flow of discourse seems to quicken and grow more turbulent' (p 347) at one or two points of its development. He uses the term *peak* to refer to such points of excitation/tension. He suggests that the pattern of narrative development first towards and then away from the narrative peak represents the 'profile' of the narrative. This conception of the narrative profile, and the key role of the peak in it, constitutes, in my view, a macro-level account of narrative structure. The non-uniformity of 'excitation or tension' that Longacre refers to is also played out, however, at more micro-levels of narrative development. This means that whereas there are, no doubt, one or two points of maximal 'excitation' in the prototype story, as Longacre suggests, the waxing and waning characteristic of the build up to and movement away from the peak also constitutes a basic unit of narrative progression; so that narrative movement is in fact via a succession of peaks and their complementary troughs. It is with this recognition of its function as a basic building block of narrative progression that the term *peak* is used here.

IDENTIFYING FEATURES OF AN ESTABLISHED MODE OF TEMPORAL VARIABILITY

Peak-to-peak distance

First, for any one thematically distinct unit of a narrative, both peaks and troughs occur at regular intervals. That is, the distribution of peaks (and troughs) is constrained to maintain a roughly constant peak-to-peak distance (and trough-to-trough distance). This is diagrammatically represented in Figure 1.

FIGURE 1

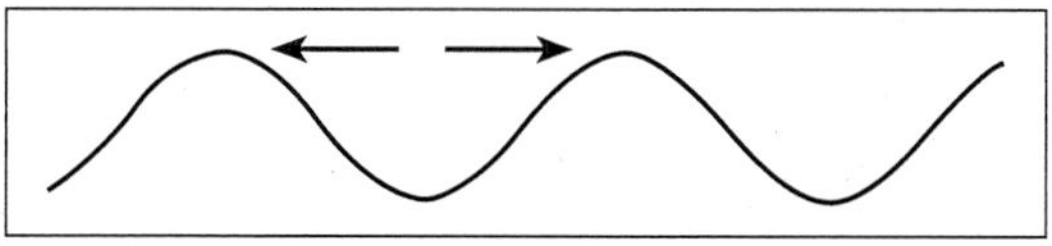

This means the reader has a sense of when the next peak (or trough) will appear from his/her knowledge of when the preceding peak (or trough) was experienced. The following key occurrences are taken from segment V of a thematic unit of *Tess of the D'Urbervilles* that Hardy refers to as 'Maiden'. This particular segment is ten pages in length and contains five key events.

22.

p 33: 'Rising early next day she walked to the hill town...and there **took advantage** of a van...'

p 35: 'She **alighted** from the van at...'

p 37: 'Tess still stood hesitating...when a figure **came forth** from the dark triangular door...'

p 39: 'He **conducted** her about the lawns...'

p 41: 'he **inclined** his face towards her'

(Thomas Hardy, *Tess of the D'Urbervilles*, 'Maiden' V, pp 32–42)

These experiential highs—the peaks—appear in the backdrop of lengthy descriptive passages: the troughs. An illustrative segment, including a stretch of narrative between the second and third peaks from Maiden V, is included in 23 below:

23.

She **alighted from the van at Trantridge Cross, and ascended on foot a hill in the direction of the district known as The Chase**, on the borders of which, as she had been informed, Mrs D'Urberville's seat, The Slopes, would be found. It was not a manorial home in the ordinary sense, with fields, and pastures, and a grumbling farmer, out of whom the owner had to squeeze an income for himself and his family by hook or by crook. It was more, far more; a country house built for enjoyment pure and simple, with not an acre of troublesome land attached to it beyond what was required for residential purposes, and for a little fancy farm kept in hand by the owner, and tended by a bailiff.

The crimson brick lodge came first in sight, up to its eaves in dense evergreens. Tess thought this was the mansion itself till, passing through the side wicket with some trepidation, and onward to a point at which the drive took a turn, the house proper stood in full view. It was of recent erection—indeed almost new—and of the same red colour that formed such a contrast with the evergreens of the lodge. Far behind the corner of the house—which rose like a geranium bloom against the subdued colours around—stretched the soft azure landscape of The Chase: a truly venerable tract of forest land, one of the few remaining woodlands in England of undoubted primeval date, wherein druidical mistletoe was still found on aged oaks, and where enormous yew trees, not planted by the hand of man, grew as they had grown when they were pollarded for bows. All this sylvan antiquity, however, though visible from The Slopes, was outside the immediate boundaries of the estate.

Everything on this snug property was bright, thriving, and well kept; across the glasshouses stretched down the inclines to the copses at their feet. Everything looked like money: like the last coin issued from the mint. The stables, partly screened by Austrian pines and evergreen oaks, and fitted with every late appliance, were as dignified as Chapels-of-ease. On the extensive lawn stood an ornamental tent, its door being towards her.

Simple Tess Durbeyfield stood at gaze, in a half-alarmed attitude, on the edge of the gravel sweep. Her feet had brought her onward to this point before she had quite realized where she was; and now all was contrary to her expectation. 'I thought we were an old family; but this is all new!' she said, in her artlessness. She wished that she had not fallen in so readily with her mother's plans for 'claiming kin', and had endeavored to gain assistance nearer home.

The D'Urbervilles—or Stoke-D'Urbervilles, as they at first called themselves—who owned all this, were a somewhat unusual family to find in such an old-fashioned part of the country. Parson Tringham had spoken truly when he said that our shambling John Durbeyfield was the only really lineal representative of the old D'Urberville family existing in the country, or near it; he might have added, what he knew very well, that the Stoke-D'Urbervilles were no more D'Urbervilles of the true tree than he was himself. Yet it must be admitted that this family formed a very good stock whereon to regraft a name which sadly wanted such renovation.

When old Mr Simon Stoke, latterly deceased, had made his fortune as an honest merchant (some said moneylender) in the North, he decided to settle as a county man in the South of England, out of hail of this business district; and in doing this he felt the necessity of recommencing with a name that would not too readily identify him with the smart tradesman of the past, and that would be less commonplace than the original bald stark words. Conning for an hour in the British Museum the pages of works devoted to extinct, half-extinct, obscured, and ruined families appertaining to the quarter of England in which he proposed to settle, he considered that D'Urberville looked and sounded as well as any of them; and D'Urberville accordingly was annexed to his own name for himself

> and his heirs eternally. Yet he was not an extravagant-minded man in this, and in constructing his family tree on the new basis was duly reasonable in framing his intermarriages and aristocratic links, never inserting a single title above the rank of strict moderation.
>
> Of this work of imagination poor Tess and her parents were naturally in ignorance, much to their discomfiture; indeed, the very possibility of such annexations was unknown to them; who supposed that, though to be well-favoured might be the gift of fortune, a family name came by nature.
>
> **Tess still stood hesitating like a bather about to make his plunge, hardly knowing whether to retreat or to persevere, when a figure came forth from the dark triangular door of the tent.**
>
> (Thomas Hardy, *Tess of the D'Urbervilles*, pp 35–37)

The peak-to-peak distance is maintained across the length of 'Maiden' V, with successive peak occurrences at a distance of about 750 words apart; each trough is hence 700–800 words in length.

Peak height

Another constant of narrative progression is the relative intensity of successive peaks (and troughs) in a single narrative or a thematically distinct sub-unit of a narrative. This is represented diagrammatically as the sustained height of successive peaks (and troughs), as in Figure 2. Like the peak-to-peak (trough–to-trough) distance, the peak (and trough) height remains a constant for a thematically distinct unit of narrative.

What this means is that successive peaks (and troughs) are of roughly comparable transitivity value, that is, they possess comparable perfective features. In the foregoing segment from *Tess of the D'Urbervilles*—'Maiden' V—the peak height is held roughly constant. This is evident in the fact that the same type of denoted situation—an event—occurs in 'took advantage of the van', 'alighted', 'a figure came forth', 'conducted her', and 'leaned his face towards her'. These are all in the backdrop of comparable descriptive passages that represent nonevents; the trough height is therefore also held constant.

FIGURE 2

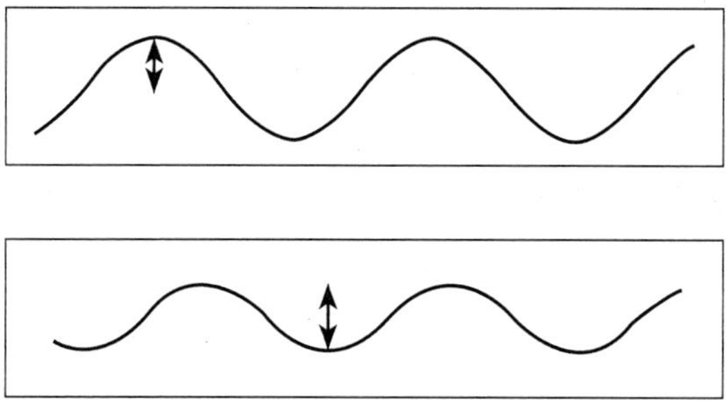

Peak/trough spread

The third constant in the distribution of peaks (and troughs) is what can be referred to as the peak (and trough) spread for successive peaks (and troughs) in a particular narrative or thematic subsection of a narrative. This is diagrammatically represented in Figure 3.

FIGURE 3

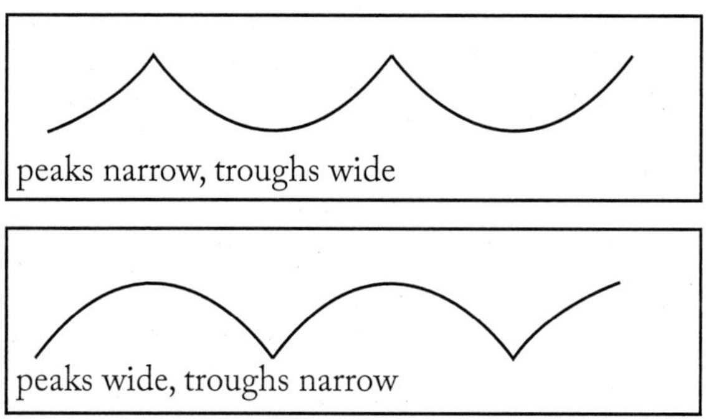

The peak spread is the proportion of narrative assigned to a peak in the stretch of narrative between successive peaks. That is, it is an assessment of what proportion of the stretch of narrative between any two successive peaks contributes to a peak, rather than a trough. The trough spread is the proportion of narrative assigned to a trough in the stretch of narrative between any two successive troughs. That is, it is an assessment of what proportion of the narrative between any two successive troughs contributes to a trough, rather than to a peak. In 'Maiden' V, the peak spread is very small and the trough spread is very wide. This is because a descriptive passage of 700–800 words gives way to an event denoted by a single verb, which is then immediately followed by another descriptive passage of 700–800 words.

Variation in temporal progression is therefore introduced at the level of discourse by a distribution of narrative into a succession of juxtaposed temporal and informational peaks and temporal and informational troughs. This distribution is constrained to sustain peak-to-peak (and trough-to-trough) distance, peak (and trough) height, and peak (and trough) spread for a particular narrative or thematically distinct segment of narrative. It is in this highly regulated way that the discourse design accommodates a variable temporal progression. However, while these three features must remain constant for a particular narrative or a thematic sub-unit of a narrative, the narrator is free to choose what the values of these constants are for a particular narrative, and is also free to change them from one thematic sub-unit of the narrative to the next.

Choice of a particular peak-to-peak distance establishes a particular pace of narrative progression: the shorter the peak-to-peak distance, the more rapid is the movement from one experiential high to another. It is perfectly conceivable, hence, to have a much smaller peak-to-peak distance than the 750 words that Hardy sustains in segment V of 'Maiden'. The effect of such a change on the text would be to hasten the pace of this narrative progression in proportion to the reduction in peak-to-peak distance.

Similarly, the passage of narrative time is affected by selection of a particular peak height. This translates into the selection of a particular quality of experience of narrative progression for a given narrative segment: higher values for peak height would result in temporal progression of heightened intensity, and lower values in temporal progression of decreased intensity. Likewise the choice of a particular value for peak/trough spread lends a unique quality to the narrative progression. This is evident, for example in the thematic unit 'Maiden No More', which immediately follows the 'Maiden' unit. In 'Maiden No More' a number of the dimensions of the narrative progression are altered to effect a difference in the quality of temporal passage. In this segment of about eight pages in length, there are three key events with a space of 750–900 words between the start of any one and the start of the next key event. The peak-to-peak distance has therefore altered a little compared to that of segment V from 'Maiden', but it is not strikingly different. The significant difference is in the peak and trough spread. In 'Maiden' V, the peak spread was minimal and the trough spread therefore wide. In 'Maiden No More', the peak spread is very wide and the trough spread is minimal. The significant events are developed slowly, reach their individual climax and are completed after a stretch of 750–900 words. There are three significant occurrences in this narrative subsection, which portrays Tess's journey home after her departure from the D'Urberville farm. In the first of these occurrences, Tess is stopped on her way home by Alec D'Urberville, who has followed her in the hope of coaxing her to return to him. The encounter slowly builds to a climax and ends with D'Urberville's departure. There is then a very brief hiatus in the experiential high— a stretch of narrative of no more than a 100 words—in which Tess resumes her journey home. The next key event begins immediately after this. Tess is approached by a man who is writing scriptures in red paint on any blank wall he can find. Once more this encounter reaches its climax and is completed again in the span of about 750 words. At this point a trough of very small spread—'she throbbingly resumed her walk'— again quickly gives way to the next key event: the arrival home. Once home, Tess informs her mother of her misfortune. There is once more a slow development of this third event over a length of about 900 words. It is this redistribution of the peak and trough spread, then, that effects a noticeable difference in the quality of temporal passage in this segment of the narrative compared to segment V of 'Maiden', described above.

Learner attempts at story-writing

In the preceding section, I attempted to demonstrate the conformity to certain text-level constraints on temporal modulation in selected samples from Hardy's *Tess of the D'Urbervilles*. In this section, I will use L2 narratives to show that a narrative that does not conform to the above-described modes of temporal modulation concomitantly fails to read as a story. The L2 narratives, while they are recalls of a story, may not necessarily be intended as representations of the recalled events in story format. That is, they may be mere reports of the events of the story. In using L2 narratives, however, I am not claiming that the learners do not generate stories because they cannot. I am merely suggesting that non-use or inadequate use of variable temporal progression, whether intended or otherwise, contributes to the non-story-like quality of their narrative.

L2 study of learners' representation of past time has focused almost exclusively on the use and acquisition of the past tense (cf Anderson 1989, 1991; Bardovi-Harlig 1992; Bardovi-Harlig and Reynolds 1995; Kaplan 1987; Klein 1986; Kumpf 1984; Meisel 1987; Robison 1990; Shumann 1987; von Stutterheim and Klein 1987, amongst others). To my knowledge, Second Language Acquisition (SLA) research has not examined learners' representation of variable temporal progression in storytelling.

In this study, advanced learners of English were asked to read Maugham's short story *The Dream*, and to then write it in their own words. The learners were 18–22-year-old freshmen enrolled in the Humanities program of a Hong Kong university, who used Cantonese as L1. They had studied English as a foreign language, that is, for a few hours a week, from the ages of three to twelve. At age twelve they started to study many, though by no means all, their subjects in the English language.

The students were given fifty minutes to read Maugham's story, and were then asked to write as much of the story as they could from memory in the immediately following hour. There were 35 students in all, and each one of them generated one narrative. These student narratives were examined to assess how well they conformed to the conventions regulating variability of temporal progression.

As suggested above, none of the student narratives actually read as stories; they read, rather, as mere reports of events that occurred in past time. This was because, amongst other things, they neither appropriately nor adequately used the (1) sentence-level and (2) discourse-level means of modulating the temporal progression, described above. In what follows, I will describe the sentential and discourse means of modulating temporal progression that Maugham uses in his story *The Dream*, and compare these to what is done in one randomly selected student attempt at the same story.

24.

Discourse layout of an extract from Maugham's *The Dream*

It chanced that in August 1917 the work I was then engaged in obliged me to go from NY to Petrograd and I was instructed for safety's sake to travel by way of Vladivostok.

I landed there in the morning and passed an idle day as best I could.

The trans-Siberian train was due to start, so far as I remember, at about nine in the evening.

I dined at the station restaurant by myself.

It was crowded and I shared
a table with a man whose
appearance entertained me.

He was Russian, a tall fellow, but amazingly stout, and he had so vast a paunch that he was obliged to sit well away from the table. His hands, small for his size, were buried in rolls of fat. His hair, long, dark and thin was brushed carefully across his crown in order to conceal his baldness, and his huge sallow face, with its enormous double chin, clean-shaven, gave you an impression of indecent nakedness. His nose was small, a funny little button upon that mass of flesh, and his black shining eyes were small too. But he had a large, red, and sensual mouth. He was dressed neatly enough in a black suit. It was not worn but shabby; it looked as if it had been neither pressed nor brushed since he had had it.

The service was bad and it was almost impossible
to attract the attention of a waiter.
We soon got into conversation. The Russian
spoke good and fluent English. His accent was
marked but not tiresome.

He asked me many questions about
myself and my plans

which – my occupation at the time making
caution necessary – I answered with a show of
frankness but with dissimulation.

I told him I was a journalist.
He asked me whether I wrote fiction

and when I confessed that in my leisure
moments I did,

he began to talk of the later Russian

novelists. He spoke intelligently.
It was plain he was a man of education.
By this time we had persuaded the waiter to
bring us some cabbage soup, and

my acquaintance pulled out a small
bottle of vodka

which he invited me to share.

I do not know whether it was the vodka or the natural loquaciousness of his race that made him communicative, but

presently he told me, unasked, a good deal about himself.

He was of noble birth, it appeared, a lawyer by profession, and a radical. Some trouble with the authorities had made it necessary for him to be much abroad, but now he was on his way home. Business had detained him at Vladivostak, but he expected to start for Moscow in a week and if I went there he would be charmed to see me.

(Somerset Maugham, *Collected Short Stories*, pp 227–228)

25.

Discourse layout of student narrative

1. It was a day in August 1917.
2. I was on my way to Petrograd.
3. I had had my dinner at the station
   Restaurant before I got on the tran-Siberian train.
4. I settled down in a chair with a small table.
5. Then, a Russian came in
6. and shared the table with me.
7. He was fat and poorly dressed.
8. We began our conversation.
9. He talked to me about his life.
10. He was a widower.
11. He had a wife before who was married with him for ten years.
12. Her wife was small and thin with bad appearance.
13. She had a bitter tongue.
14. She had strong feeling of jealousy towards him.
15. The Russian began to tell me his relationship with his wife.
16. He started the story by the night he heard the scream of his wife.

17. She had a nightmare that his husband wanted to kill her
18. and threw her over the balusters.[11]
19. She was very frightened.
20. The nightmare changed the impression between the couple.
21. The wife was afraid of having the nightmare.
22. The husband thought that it was easy to throw his wife over the balusters.
23. Then, the Russian's wife had the same nightmare again and again.
24. She was very nervous and
25. asked her husband whether he loved her.
26. The Russian swored that he loved her.
27. He thought that it was the only thing he could do.
28. He was angry about the annoyance of this wife.

Example 24 is a segment from Maugham, and sentences 1–9 of 25 represent the student version of the same narrative segment. In both 24 and 25, I have placed foregrounded or peak occurrences on the right-hand side of the page, and backgrounded occurrences or troughs on the left-hand side.

I want to first look at the sentence means of modulating temporal passage in Maugham's story and compare this to what is done in the student's version of the same story, example 25. Maugham includes a number of event clauses to carry the narrative forward along the timeline. This is exemplified by the clauses placed on the right-hand side of the page in the excerpt from Maugham, in 24. When we compare this to the student version of this excerpt—25, clauses 1–9—the first thing we notice is the significant difference in the number of such clauses; the student uses far fewer: four compared to eight in Maugham's rendition of this segment of the story. When we examine the total number of event clauses in the entire student narrative (refer to the right-hand side of the page in 25), we notice that this low rate of appearance is sustained throughout the narrative. There are only eight event clauses in the student's entire narrative; this is a small fraction (approximately a fifth) of the number of event clauses used by Maugham in his story. The result of the inadequate use of event clauses in the student narrative is significantly less temporal movement than is apparent in Maugham.

When we examine the student's narrative to establish why so few reported happenings qualify as peak events, we find that the aspectual representation of many of the denoted happenings prevents them from being perceived as peak events. For example, early in the narrative in 25—'I had had my dinner at the station restaurant' (clause 3)—the student uses the past perfect. With this aspectual representation, clause 3 of 25 cannot be perceived as contributing to forward movement along the timeline. (The use of the past perfect also happens to be incompatible with the aspectual representation of the same event in the next sentence.) Clause 4 of 25 describes the same event of dining at the restaurant (starting with the act of being seated at a table), but uses the simple past tense: 'I settled down in a chair with a small table'. In this case, the situation is aspectually appropriate for peak event status, and is therefore perceived as contributing to movement along the timeline. The next sequenced event—clause 5 of 25—also contributes to movement along the timeline, and so too do clauses 6 and 8. But the same is not true of the three following denoted happenings. Although when taken individually all three (clauses 9, 15 and 16 repeated in 26) are aspectually appropriate for pushing the timeline forward, they cannot effect temporal passage in their appearance next to each other in the narrative. This is because they do not unambiguously refer to three distinct situations; rather, each can be interpreted as referring to the same situation.

26.

8. We began our conversation...
9. He talked to me about...

15. The Russian began to tell me...
16. He started the story...

In consequence, since they are not informationally new in their context of occurrence, clauses 9, 15 and 16 are not able to effect any temporal movement. In addition, in 16, the potential peak event of 'he heard the scream of his wife' does not appear in an independent clause and hence again fails to contribute to forward movement along the timeline. In short, a number of potential peak events in this student narrative are not given the appropriate representation to carry the narrative forward along the timeline.

The event clauses in the foreground in Maugham are regularly interspersed with juxtaposed backgrounded nonevent clauses (cf the left-hand side of the page in 24). These provide supplementary detail and hence help to flesh out the events of the principal storyline. In the student narrative, however, event clauses are not regularly interspersed with nonevent, backgrounded clauses, and in consequence there is much less fleshing out of the principal storyline. In the first four sequenced events (cf event clauses 4 to 8 of 25), we find only one backgrounded clause: event 7 of 25. Appearing between clauses 6 and 8 of 25, this clause provides a very brief description of the principal protagonist of the story. The next sequence of event clauses (in the narrative segment between clauses 17 and 26 of 25) comes with some backgrounded supplementary information between the sequenced events of 17 and 23. But this too seems inadequate, because clause 23 relative to 17 is a major thematic and temporal transition: 17 is the event of the dream and 23, the repeated occurrence of the same dream. In the original story, much is said by the narrator to lay the ground for this transition. The other sequenced event clauses of this segment are not regularly interspersed with accompanying nonevent backgrounded clauses. In fact, the student appears to show preference for an uninterrupted clustering of event clauses.

In between the two event sequences (clauses 4–8 of 25, and 17–26 of 25), there is a succession of potential peak events which fail to push the timeline forward because, as suggested, they have not been given the right aspectual representation to do this (refer to segments 9–16 of 25). These therefore properly qualify only as part of the narrative background. In this narrative segment, there are also juxtaposed purely descriptive, nonevent clauses, but since they are not accompanying effective peak events, they too cannot contribute to narrative incrementation via a sustained alternation between peaks and troughs.

On the whole, then, there is insufficient use of interspersed backgrounded clauses with those peak event clauses which this learner does use. Some potential backgrounded clauses also accompany events that cannot contribute to the narrative foreground. Therefore these purely descriptive nonevent clauses too cannot be perceived as contributing to the narrative background.

As a result of the insufficient number of both peak events and accompanying backgrounded clauses, while the same broad narrative occurrences are depicted in 25 as in 24, the student narrative represents much less temporal movement of any kind, and shows little of the sustained alternation between peak and trough narrative incrementation that is evident in skilled storytelling.

In addition to failing to effect sufficient temporal movement, the student also fails to use movement of the right pace and quality at the appropriate point of narrative development.[12] Example 27 is a narrative segment from Maugham's *The Dream* which demonstrates the effectiveness of using Type 3 temporal progression in the depiction of one of the climactic events of this story. In this excerpt the protagonist of the story speaks of 'the dream', in which his wife sees him throwing her over the balusters of their house, a fall that would have meant 'certain death'. In the representation of this act, Maugham signals the rapid transition from one of its constituent moves to the next, by using Type 3 temporal progression, marked by the use of VP-conjoined clauses (refer to 27a). Type 3 temporal progression here moves the narrative from one constituent act of the attempted murder—'caught her'—to the anticipated following constituent act—'attempted to throw her over the balusters'—in quick succession, and by so doing gives representation to the coming about of the attempted murder.

27.

She told me that she had had a terrible nightmare; she had dreamt that I was trying to kill her. We lived at the top of a large house and the well round which the stairs climbed was broad. She had dreamt that just as we had arrived at our own floor

a. **I had caught hold of her and attempted to throw her over the balusters.** It was six storeys to floor at the bottom and it meant certain death.

(Somerset Maugham, *The Dream*, p 229)

28.

The comparable portion of one student's narrative:

She had a nightmare that his (her)

a. **husband wanted to kill her and threw her over the balusters.** She was very frightened...

In his/her representation of the attempted murder of the dream in 28, the student conjoins an event ('threw') to a preceding state ('wanted') rather than a preceding event. As a result, the student is not able to depict the quick succession of the constituent moves of a single larger happening, that can be facilitated by use of Type 3 temporal progression.

The learner also shows non-target-like use of Type 2 temporal progression, which, as suggested earlier, is used by skilled writers to signal a more significant temporal and thematic transition than that brought about by either Type 1 or Type 3 progression. Because Type 2 signals the most significant transition of the three possible types of temporal progression, there is only one instance of its use in the whole story in Maugham. It is used to signal the unexpected repeated occurrence of the climactic event of the story: the dream (refer to 29).

29.

The dream had an extraordinary impression upon both of us. It frightened my wife, and she became for a little less bitter and more tolerant. But when I walked up the stairs to our apartment it was impossible for me not to look over the balusters and reflect how easy it would be to do what she had dreamt. The balusters were dangerously low, a quick gesture and the thing was done. It was hard to put the thought out of my mind. **Then some months later my wife awakened me one night.** I was very tired and I was exasperated. She was white and trembling. She had had the dream again.

(Somerset Maugham, *The Dream*, p 230)

The learner's use of Type 2 progression does not show this appreciation of the high degree of transition that it signals. The learner uses a *then*-marked clause very early in his or her telling of the story (refer to clause 5 of 30).

30.

(Repeated from 25)

1. It was a day in August 1917.
2. I was on my way to Petrograd.
3. I had had my dinner at the station restaurant before I got on the tran-Siberian train.
4. I settled down in a chair with a small table.
5. Then, a Russian came in
6. and shared the table with me.
7. He was fat and poorly dressed.
8. We began our conversation.
9. He talked to me about his life.

At the point of the appearance of this *then*-marked clause, there is almost no preceding development of the story. Hence the magnitude (both temporal and thematic) of the suggested transition appears inappropriate. It is interesting that, like Maugham, the student also uses *then* to accompany the reference to the repeated occurrence of the dream (refer to clause 23 of 31).

31.

(Repeated from 25)

17. She had a nightmare that his husband wanted to kill her
18. and threw her over the balusters.
19. She was very frightened.
20. The nightmare changed the impression between the couple.
21. The wife was afraid of having the nightmare.
22. The husband thought that it was easy to throw his wife over the balusters.
23. Then, the Russian's wife had the same nightmare again and again.

But though it appears with the report of the same event, this use of *then* differs significantly from Maugham's. As suggested earlier, in the learner's narrative this *then*-marked clause follows soon after the first reference to the dream—event clause 17 of 31—with just a short and insufficiently developed backgrounded segment between these two peak events. Like the student's earlier use of Type 2 progression, this use of *then*-marking therefore also seems to appear without the thematic and temporal build up that would warrant its use.

When the randomly selected student narrative (25) is compared to the whole set of 35 narratives, it is found to effectively represent the sentence-level treatment of temporal progression of the group. The learners, in general, make insufficient use of peak-event clauses and as a result fail to suggest enough temporal movement of any sort.

Along with this, there is insufficient use of backgrounded nonevent clauses, so that narrative progression via a sustained alternation between peaks and troughs is not properly evident. Learners in general also fail to vary the quality and pace of temporal progression by opting for Type 2 and Type 3 temporal progression when these would be appropriate. Type 3 temporal progression (signalled by VP conjunction) is very rarely used, and the heightened pace of narrative progression (with representation of the internal constituent acts of a larger happening that it effects) is therefore rarely apparent. Type 2 temporal progression is very often inappropriately used in accompaniment with events that are not sufficiently significant to warrant its use. As a result the student narratives are invariably temporally 'flat' and/or marked by counterintuitive temporal fluctuations.

We have said that passage via a sustained alternation of peaks and troughs is what effects variable temporal progression at the discourse level, and we have seen that in skilled storytelling this alternation shows conformity to certain well-defined design constraints. In a single narrative or a thematic subsegment of a single narrative, successive peaks/troughs (1) occur at regular intervals, (2) occur at comparable height, and (3) occur with comparable spread. In this way variability of temporal progression is imposed in a highly predictable manner. The storyteller is free to select the peak-to-peak distance (trough-to-trough distance), peak/trough height and peak/trough spread for a particular narrative or thematic segment, but these selected values must be sustained for the stretch of the narrative or thematic segment of narrative. Maugham shows clear conformity to these discourse level constraints. Close examination shows that his story has a complex two-tier organisational layout. First, there are juxtaposed segments of two types: one is what we might call a peak-bearing, temporal segment, and the second is a purely descriptive, atemporal segment. The peak-bearing segment contains a succession of peaks with accompanying juxtaposed troughs (as is apparent in the segments which are highlighted in

24). This segment is followed by a purely descriptive passage (refer again to 24) which in turn gives way to another peak-bearing segment (highlighted in 24). The distribution of peak-bearing segments to descriptive segments is distributionally roughly even. The dimensions of the peaks and troughs of the peak-bearing segments are also all held roughly constant.

The learner narrative of 25 does not show clear conformity to any discourse-level design constraints. We have said above that a sustained alternation between peak-event clauses and accompanying backgrounded nonevent clauses is not clearly apparent. It is also evident that what is apparent of this alternation between peaks and troughs does not show sustained dimensions of distributional design, that is, peak-to-peak distance, peak height and peak spread. The two brief peak-bearing segments (event clauses 4–8 and 17–27 of 25) are not alike, nor does each individually show an established pattern of distribution of constituent peaks and troughs. Further the intervening narrative segment (event clauses 9–17 of 25) is not entirely descriptive, as are the non-peak-bearing segments of Maugham. Rather, as we suggested earlier, it contains potential peak events (clauses 9, 15 and 16) which are prevented by their aspectual representation from realising peak status.

Example 25 is again representative of the set of 35 student narratives in failing to show proper conformity to the discourse-level means of imposing variable temporal passage. There is little evidence of a sustained alternation between peaks and troughs. Those segments of the narrative that do show evidence of passage via juxtaposed peaks and troughs do not follow any of the design constraints on this distribution. That is, peak-to-peak distance, peak height and peak spread are not kept constant.

CONCLUSION

In this study, an examination of the works of Hardy and Maugham has suggested that storytelling entails a representation of passage through past time, showing a sustained variation in pace and quality in well-defined ways. A predictable pattern of variation in temporal progression is implemented at two levels of linguistic representation: at the level of the sentence, and at the level of discourse organisation. At the level of the sentence, the aspect of the verb and the sentence structure in which the denoted situation occurs are manipulated to effect change in temporal progression. At the level of discourse organisation, a sustained alternation between peak and trough information incrementation imposes a constant variation in the temporal passage. Values for the peak-to-peak distance, peak height and peak spread, which must be held constant for a single thematic segment, are manipulated to effect a particular quality of variation, and they are reassessed in successive thematic units, to bring about potential change in this quality of variation. Learners' narratives do not conform to the constraints on the representation of temporal passage described above and concomitantly fail to read as stories. It is found that there is much less than the expected amount of temporal movement in the learner narratives. There is also a failure to vary the temporal progression that is represented in expected ways, both at the level of the sentence and at the level of discourse organisation.

These findings contribute an understanding of the intricacy and detail of the system of temporal modulation in storytelling that has heretofore remained largely unaddressed. In doing so, they add to our knowledge of the rhetorical structure of this genre of narrative, and support the rather intriguing objective of seeking linguistic insight into the creative enterprise of telling a tale.

It is important to note, however, that these are findings based on the study of a limited database: the works of only two authors belonging to one tradition of storytelling, classic literary English storytelling. Therefore, their applicability to a more general class of storytelling is as yet untested. Further, the study identifies only core principles about variable temporal passage, defining these as they apply to the prototype story of this one tradition of storytelling. It is for these reasons, undoubtedly, a somewhat 'idealised' perception of variable temporal passage in storytelling, the full merit of which can only be properly attested in more comprehensive follow-up studies which examine much larger databases and in far greater detail than is attempted here.

Notes

1. Some of these scholars have, in fact, identified four different genres of narrative prose—recount, anecdote, exemplum and narrative—conforming to not one, but four different kinds of rhetorical organisation (cf Plum 1988; Rothery 1990; Martin 1984, 1992). Of relevance to a basic separation of storytelling from the mere report of past events, however, is the key difference between 'recount' and the other narrative types referred to above. A recount does not include a rhetorical component that is often regarded as the identifying constituent of the prototype story: the evaluation. The evaluation is 'the expression of the speaker or writer's attitude or stance towards, viewpoint on, or feelings about…' the reported happenings (Hunston and Thompson 2000: 5).
2. I think it is possible to view the mode of temporal representation in storytelling as a specialised evaluative device. But while this is an appealing idea, it is not pursued here. I think a full understanding of the representation of temporal progression in storytelling should precede its comparative assessment with the other defining rhetorical conventions of this genre of narrative prose. It is also true that this article delineates only one dimension of the nature of temporal progression in storytelling. There are no doubt other ways of examining temporal progression, addressing dimensions of its systematicity not covered here.
3. We will see in the ensuing discussion that the pace of temporal progression is affected by the typically lexical-aspectual features of denoted situations, e.g. dynamism, telicity and punctility, while the quality of progression is affected by typically informational features, e.g. saliency and newness.
4. The temporal expression *rather too quickly* in 'It was all done rather too quickly' is a descriptive comment on the combined actions of collecting the clothes and packing them into the travel bag. It does not play a part in bringing about the differentiated representation of temporal

passage in the individualised parts of this happening. The following backgrounded clause, *For a long moment I stared at the bag, unwilling to take the next step,* is also a stative clause, rather than an event clause. It cannot play any part in bringing about the differentiated types of temporal movement which are effected by the use of the three types of syntactically distinguished event clauses.

5. Future research must examine a broader database to demonstrate in a conclusive way that the system of temporal modulation described here constitutes a common core of regulations governing all effective storytelling. What should also become apparent through such study is whether—and if so to what extent—practices of temporal modulation differ across dissimilar genres of storytelling.
6. Any chapter, or subsection thereof, overtly signalled by the use of orthographic means (e.g. numbering or labelling) which separate it from preceding and following comparable segments, is regarded as thematically discrete. I have found that the overtly signalled subsections of the narrative consistently identify thematically discrete units in the body of data examined here. Hardy labels his chapters and identifies the thematic subsections within each chapter numerically.
7. Hopper represents saliency as a feature distinct from other transitivity features (feature 7 of Table 6.2) and therefore considers it to be independently assessable. Other scholars besides Hopper subscribe to the view that readers/listeners arrive at common assessments of thematic saliency. Van Dijk (1980) and Renkema (1993) have referred to macrostructure as the discernible core thematic content of a text, which readers/hearers customarily distinguish from subsidiary, noncentral information.
8. Longacre (1981), in his examination of the impact of different clausal types on the represented level of dynamism of narrative passage, also addresses some (but in my assessment not all) the lexical-aspectual-cum-informational features that are explored by Hopper.
9. It is important to note, however, that the limitations of the present database make it impossible to address a number of comparable markers of temporal passage. Follow-up research should, therefore, make a comparative assessment of the three types described above and several other markers of temporal progression. *Suddenly*, for example, appears to be like *then* in that it marks the event as thematically salient and temporally well-defined, but unlike *then* in that it also marks it as unexpected in its context of occurrence. Also, while *but then* appears to differ from

then in ways comparable to *suddenly*, *and then* appears to be a functional hybrid that takes in part from the features of VP-conjunction and in part from the features of *then*, and the combined use of *then* and *after that* in *then after that* seems to accentuate the temporal differentiation between the successive events.

10. In more recent assessments of grounding, the transitivity features of a denoted situation are not assessed in an absolute way, but in comparison to the features of adjacent denoted situations. Transitivity features contribute to fore- or backgrounding, not only by their inherent nature, but also by the comparative value of their impact. This results in an assessment that has been termed 'relative grounding', rather than just grounding.
11. Number 18 is backgrounded because it occurs in a subordinate clause.
12. As suggested earlier, evaluative comments are not intended to be prescriptive. Rather, they acknowledge, and articulate, rules that are adhered to by the skilled storytellers whose works are examined in this study.

References

Andersen R W. 1989. La aquisicion de la morfologia verbal [The acquisition of verbal morphology]. *Linguistica*, 1: 90–142.

Andersen R W. 1991. Developmental sequences: the emergence of aspect marking in second language acquisition. In T Huebner and C A Ferguson (ed), *Second Language Acquisition and Linguistic Theories*. Amsterdam: John Benjamins.

Bardovi-Harlig K.1992. The relationship of form and meaning: a cross-sectional study of tense and aspect in interlanguage of learners of English as a second language. *Applied Psycholinguistics*, 13: 253–278.

Bardovi-Harlig K and Reynolds D W. 1995. The acquisition of tense in SLA and FLL: a study of learner narratives in English (SL) and French (FL). *Canadian Modern Language Review*, 52: 308–330.

Dahl O. 1980. Temporal distance: remoteness distinctions in tense-aspect systems. In B Butterworth, B Comrie and O Dahl (ed), *Explanations of Language Universals*. Amsterdam: Mouton.

Dry Helen. 1981. Sentence aspect and the movement of narrative time. *Text*, 1 (3): 233–240.

Hardy Thomas. 1964. *Tess of the D'Urbervilles*. New York: Washington Square Press.

Hopper P J. 1977. Observations on the typology of focus and aspect in narrative language. *Studies in Language*, 3: 37–64.

Hopper P J. 1979. Aspect and foregrounding in discourse. In T Givon (ed), *Syntax and Semantics: Discourse and Syntax*. New York: Academic Press.

Hopper P J and Thompson S A. 1980. Transitivity in grammar and discourse. *Language*, 59 (2): 251–299.

Hunston S and Thompson G. 2000. *Evaluation in Text*. Cambridge: Cambridge University Press.

Kaplan M A. 1987. Developmental patterns of past tense acquisition among foreign language learners of French. In B VanPatten, T R Dvorak, and J F Lee (ed), *Foreign Language Learning: A Research Perspective*. Cambridge, MA: Newbury House.

Klein W. 1986 [1984]. *Second Language Acquisition*. Revised edition translated by Bohuslaw Jankowski. Cambridge: Cambridge University Press.

Kumpf L. 1984. Tense, aspect and modality in interlanguage: a discourse–functional approach. Unpublished manuscript, UCLA.

Labov W. 1981. Speech actions and reactions in personal narrative. In D Tannen (ed), *Analyzing Discourse: Text and Talk*. (Georgetown University Round Table), Washington DC: Georgetown University Press.

Labov W and Waletzky J. 1967. Narrative analysis: oral versions of personal experience. In J Helm (ed), *Essays on the Verbal Visual Arts*. (Proceedings of the 1966 Spring Meeting of the American Ethnological Society). Seattle: University of Washington Press.

Longacre R. 1981. A spectrum and profile approach to discourse analysis. *Text* 1, 337–359.

Martin J R. 1984. Types of writing in infants and primary school. In L Unsworth (ed), *Reading, Writing, Spelling* (Proceedings of the Fifth Macarthur Reading/Language Symposium). Sydney: Macarthur Institute of Higher Education.

Martin J R. 1992. *English Text: System and Structure*. Philadelphia: John Benjamins.

Martin J R and Rothery J. 1980. Writing project number 1. In *Working Papers in Linguistics*. Sydney: University of Sydney Department of Linguistics.

Martin J R and Rothery J. 1981. Writing project report number 2. In *Work-*

ing Papers in Linguistics. Sydney: University of Sydney Department of Linguistics.

Martin J. R. and Rothery J. 1984. Choice of genre in a suburban primary school. Paper presented at the Annual Conference of the Applied Linguistics Association of Australia, Alice Springs.

Martin J R and Rothery J. 1986. What a functional approach to the writing task can show teachers about 'good writing'. In B Couture (ed), *Functional Approaches to Writing: Research Perspectives*. New Jersey: Ablex.

Maugham W Somerset. 1975. Collected Short Stories, Vol 2. Reading, PA: William Heinemann.

Meisel J M. 1987. Reference to past events and actions in the development of natural language acquisition. In C W Pfaff (ed), *First and Second Language Acquisition Processes*. Cambridge, MA: Newbury House.

Plum G. 1988. Textual and contextual conditioning in spoken English: a genre-based approach. Unpublished Ph.D. thesis, Department of Linguistics, University of Sydney.

Reinhart T. 1984. Principles of gestalt perception in the temporal organization of narrative texts. *Linguistics*, 22: 779–809.

Renkema J. 1993. *Discourse Studies: An Introductory Textbook*. Amsterdam/Philadelphia: John Benjamins.

Robison R. 1990. The primacy of aspect: aspectual marking in English interlanguage. *Studies in Second Language Acquisition*, 12: 315–330.

Rothery J. 1989. Learning about language. In R Hasan and J R Martin (ed), *Language Development: Learning Culture* (*Meaning and Choice in Language: Studies for Michael Halliday*). New Jersey: Ablex.

Rothery J. 1990. 'Story' writing in primary school: assessing narrative type genre. Unpublished Ph.D. thesis, Department of Linguistics, University of Sydney.

Rothery J. 1995. Reading and writing narrative: what can we teach in English? In M L Tickoo (ed), *Reading and Writing: Theory into Practice*. Singapore: RELC Anthology Series 35.

Schumann J. 1987. The expression of temporal Basilan speech. *Studies in Second Language Acquisition*, 9: 21–41.

Tickoo A. 2002. On the use of 'then'/'after that' in the marking of chronological order: insights from Vietnamese and Chinese learners of ESL. *System*, 30 (1): 107–124.

van Dijk T A. 1980. *Macrostructures: An Interdisciplinary Study of Global Structures in Discourse, Interaction, and Cognition.* Hillsdale, NJ: Erlbaum.

Vendler Zeno. 1967. Verbs and times. In Z Vendler (ed), *Linguistics in Philosophy.* New York: Cornell University Press.

von Stutterheim C and Klein W. 1987. A concept-oriented approach to second language acquisition studies. In C W Pfaff (ed), *First and Second Language Acquisition Processes.* Cambridge, MA: Newbury House.

7

Narrative in Support of an Opening End-state Statement

First published in *The EFL Journal* 5:1 January 2014,

INTRODUCTION

There is limited assessment of ESL narrative in the linguistic study of ESL acquisition and use. ESL narrative has been examined in the context of the assessment of other linguistic items/issues rather than as a topic in itself, e.g. language fluency (Wood 2009), lexical richness (Lu 2012), reference (Chen and Pan 2009; Kang 2009; Tickoo 2002), tense and aspect (Ayoun and Salaberry 2008; Chiravate 2011; Bardovi-Harlig 1992, 1994, 1995, 2000; Tickoo 2001, 2005, amongst others). The rationale seems to be that ESL in higher educational settings serves primarily academic purposes, in which narration is assumed to play no significant role.

This assumption, however, overlooks two kinds of robust reliance on narrative in academic writing assignments. First, there is considerable use of personal narrative as a writing task in earlier stages of instruction-in-composition. Second, narrative is frequently used in support of a certain kind of statement: a statement that represents the end-state of a developmental process ('end-state statement' for future reference, e.g. 'Edwardsville is a ghost town today'). Narrative in support of an end-state statement traces a path along successive chronologically sequenced events in the past to the end-state represented by the opening statement. It serves to account for the end state by mapping out the route to its emergence. This is a use of narrative that is exploited across the curriculum in report and research paper writing; hence its importance to the ESL learner with academic goals.

Because all narrational skills are set aside as largely irrelevant to the understanding of ESL for academic purposes, the learning challenges posed by the conventions that shape this particular generic type also remain unaddressed. This paper will carry out a detailed textual assessment of ESL narrative that supports an end-state statement, to arrive at an understanding of the composing challenges this genre poses for the high-intermediate level learner. I will, first, identify key constraints that govern a prototype text, generated by a skilled writer. This will facilitate assessment of learner prose with respect to a conventionally recognised ideal. The assessment measures will gauge the approximation to this ideal, evaluating in relative rather than absolute terms with a measure of less or more skill, rather than as simply 'right' or 'wrong', in order to carry out a careful assessment of whether and, if so, how the identified constraints are implemented in learner prose. Because of space constraints, and in the interest of readability in a short exposition, I will attempt an illustrative assessment of one representative writing sample. But I will also suggest how the identified findings speak to a collective body of 20 comparable essays. All these narratives were written as one-hour, in-class assignments on the topic of 'My relationship with the English language,' as part of a refresher course in academic English for learners of high-intermediate proficiency at a Swedish university. The students came from three different language backgrounds: Spanish, Swedish and Mandarin, but experienced a common set of challenges. These common learning issues are the focus of this preliminary assessment; the subtler differences in learners' use of this genre will be addressed in follow up research.

In what follows, section 1 will examine Sample A, as a prototype realisation of narrative in support of an opening end-state statement, to point to the preferred discoursal conventions for this kind of textual development. Section 2 will then gauge learner use of these conventions, and represent the challenge they pose to the high-intermediate learner. Finally, section 3 will summarise key findings and consider their potential implications.

1. DEFINING A SUBGENRE OF NARRATIVE

Labov (2006, 2004, 2001) and Labov and Waletzky (1967) identify certain general developmental features of narrative prose. At the core of these is the defining constraint that, in narrative representation, past events are captured in their real-world order. For example, when real-world event (a) (riding my bike in the dark) precedes (b) (running into a lamppost), the clausal sequence will be (a) (I rode my bike in the dark) followed by (b) (I ran into a lamppost).

Narrative clauses (1) uphold 'temporal juncture' (a change of clausal order correlates with a change in the order of the events they represent) and (2) respond to the question 'then what happened'?

Prototype narrative also comes with a unique discoursal development along the following well-defined stages: abstract, orientation, complication, evaluation, resolution and coda (Labov 2006, 2004, 2001; Labov and Waletzky 1967). The standard commencement at a summative statement, the abstract, serves to introduce the reader/hearer to the overall happening. The particulars of this happening are then fleshed out in the sequence of events that follow. For example, in response to the question of 1a below ('Have you ever had a near-death experience?'), the narrative of 1b opens with the abstract ('I once came within feet of a 50 foot drop'). This summative statement is then given a more detailed representation in the narrative events that follow. The prototype narrative close in the coda, a concluding statement which serves to return the narrative full-circle to the point of its beginning, is also realised in 1b in the last sentence ('then we had to climb back up: that was a challenge').

1.

a. Question: Have you ever had a near-death experience?

b. Response: **I once came within feet of a 50 foot drop** (abstract). I was with my boyscout troop when we came across a blocked off path. The path was slippery; slippery enough for us to slide down it. We thought that it would be a short cut but little did we know that it came to an abrupt end. It was all we could do to stop ourselves **then we had to climb back up: that was a challenge** (CODA).

Source: uk.answers.yahoo.com

1.1 Macro-design of narrative in support of an opening end-state statement

While the point of commencement of narrative in support of an opening end-state statement is also a statement, it is not summative of the following sequence. Rather, it is the point of culmination of the event sequence that follows.

Sample A

Drug Addiction

[1]Her body no longer produced its own natural chemicals to manage pain, so not having the heroin caused her to become 'dope sick.' [2]When the drug was not replenished, she went into withdrawal. [3]She never experienced this before ... but after time, as she used more and more drug, and needed more and more drug, **the abrupt removal of heroin was devastating....**

[4]She didn't start out that way. [5]When she was in eighth grade she and her friends were given marijuana to try. [6]Most of the kids didn't like it ... **[7]But it agreed with Darcy, who also began to raid the family liquor cabinet when she couldn't buy grass.**

[8]**One day, when she was just past her 14th birthday, she discovered some painkillers in her mother's medicine cabinet.** [9]Her mom had a back surgery and was prescribed X, but only took a couple of them, leaving a nearly full prescription in the bathroom.

[10]Even 14-year-old people can research on the internet and **soon she learned that by grinding the drug and snorting it, the high was intense.**

[11]The chances for addiction were also intense and it didn't take long before Darcy was seeking that euphoric experience over and over.

[12]It was the only time she felt good. **She solicited her friends to steal drugs from their parents.**

[13]Any kind of painkiller would do, but Y and X were preferred, and because they are prescribed so often, getting a supply wasn't all that difficult. [14]**She also became rather clever, as each time she visited the house of a new 'friend' she would secretly check out the medicine cabinets....**

[15]**Darcy soon realized that X was expensive, but heroin on the street was about a quarter the price, so she looked for suppliers. She didn't have to search long.**

from www.drug-addiction-support.org

Sample A is an excerpt from an exposition on drug addiction. The excerpt itself represents how one young person ended up a heroin addict. It begins with a description of the addict's end-state condition: 'not having heroin caused her to become "dope sick". When the drug was not replenished, she went into withdrawal' (sentences 1 and 2). The end-state statement is followed (in sentence 4) by an explicit claim indicating that this was not always her condition: 'She didn't start out that way.' This qualification indicates the temporal specificity of the end-state. It projects narrative as forthcoming to account for the end-state condition, and prospects a return to the relevant point of initiation, in this instance the point of first exposure to drugs: when Darcy realised that marijuana 'agreed with' her, and she 'began to raid her family liquor cabinet when she couldn't buy grass' (sentence 7). This point of initiation is followed by successive changes of state, which are collectively indicative of a growing dependency: She 'discovered...painkillers' (sentence 8), 'discovered... (that when) grinding...and snorting' them the high was more intense (sentence 10), 'solicited her friends to steal...from their parents' (sentence 12), and 'became...clever...visited friends...would check out (their) medicine cabinets' (sentence 14). At the end point of this event sequence, '(she) soon realized that...heroin' was her drug of choice (sentence 15). With this, the narrative that started at the point of first exposure or initiation (sentence 7) has reconnected with the earlier represented end-state condition of dependence on heroin (in sentences 1 and 2).

We can conclude, therefore, that the prototype narrative-support of an opening end-state statement appears to conform to the following distributional envelope.

FIGURE 1

SUMMARY OF THE NARRATIVE ENVELOPE IN SAMPLE A

I. end-state statement:
   Sentences 1 and 2
II. the temporal specificity of end-state statement:
   Sentence 4
III. change of state sequence, in three phases:
   a. *point of first exposure/initiation*:
      Sentence 7
   b. *successive changes of state:*
      Sentences 8, 10, 12 and 14
   c. *reconnection to opening end-state*:
      Sentence 15

1.2 Developmental design features

Also evident in Sample A are the following developmental design features:

a. Narrative once prospected must be embarked upon and followed through to the point of its completion.

Once the narrative has been embarked upon, it cannot, in the normative case, be discontinued or suspended. By the 'then what happened?' condition, every narrative event prospects that another event that can appropriately follow will follow. This need to follow through on what is prospected applies to all genres of discourse. Every discourse type comes with an inherent development design, so the audience has an expectation of receiving the whole unit once it has been embarked upon.

b. Narrative in support of an end-state statement must realise a hyponymic relationship[1] (Finegan 2004) between the overall topic and the individual developmental components used in the treatment of that topic:

In Sample A the overall topic is addiction to drugs. Both the end-state statement (sentence 1) and each change of state of the sequence that follows (sentence 8, sentence 10, sentence 12, sentence 14) are manifestations, or hyponyms, of a single phenomenon, 'addiction to drugs', the hypernym which is the overall topic of Sample A (cf Fig 2 below).

FIGURE 2

REALISING THE RELATIONSHIP OF HYPONYMY

Addiction to Drugs (**overall topic**)	hypernym
a. **end-state**: 'removal of heroin made her dope sick'	hyponym
b. **first exposure**: 'marijuana agreed with her'	hyponym
c. **change of state**: 'discovered painkillers'	hyponym
d. **change of state**: 'discovered grinding and snorting them'	hyponym
e. **change of state**: 'became adept at obtaining them'	hyponym
f. **reconnection**: 'realised heroin was her drug of choice'	hyponym

Hyponymy is not characteristic of all narratives, but rather a unique feature of narrative in support of an opening end-state statement.[2]

c. Narrative in support of an opening end-state statement calls for the use of narrative clauses with verbs in the preterit which are lexico-aspectually achievement-events.

Sample A is in its entirety in the *past tense*. The verbs of successive narrative clauses denote or represent *achievement-events* (that is, events that are not durative). The use of *achievement-event denoting verbs in the past tense* is particularly necessary when the textual development realises the relationship of hyponymy.

We must note that hyponyms are not inherently developmentally differentiated with respect to each other; that is, one hyponym is not necessarily a preceding or following developmental stage of any other. They are, rather, merely alternative manifestations of a single phenomenon, and are readily seen as such in their contiguous appearance in a–f of Fig 3 below, in which the past tense has been removed. Once the past tense is removed, the want of a developmental hierarchy makes it difficult to perceive movement from one to another (a–f), by incremental progression, to an end-state condition.[3]

FIGURE 3

DRUG ADDICTION: WITHOUT THE PAST TENSE

a. removal of heroin makes her dope sick
b. marijuana agrees with her
c. takes painkillers
d. grinds and snorts them
e. is adept at obtaining them...
f. heroin is her drug of choice...

However, the mere use of the past tense is also not enough, as is suggested in the sequence b′–f′ in Fig 3′ below, which remains ambiguous as to the presence or absence of movement in time. It is only the use of the past tense with verbs that are achievement-events (as in b″–f″ in Fig 3″) that conveys movement in time in an unambiguous way.

FIGURE 3′

DRUG ADDICTION: WITHOUT ACHIEVEMENT-VERBS

a removal of heroin makes her dope sick
b′ marijuana agreed with her
c′ took painkillers...
d′ ground and snorted them
e′ was adept at obtaining
f′ knew heroin was her drug...

FIGURE 3″

DRUG ADDICTION: WITH ACHIEVEMENT-VERBS

a removal of heroin makes her dope sick
b″ she **realised** marijuana agreed...
c″ **discovered** painkillers
d″ **discovered** grinding and snorting them
e″ **became** adept at obtaining them
f″ **realised** heroin was her drug of choice

To ensure that hyponymic manifestations of a single hypernym effectively represent temporal passage along constituent developmental points, therefore, requires use of preterit forms of verbs that are semantically achievement-events, rather than accomplishment-events (durative events), states or activities. In fact, as we will see in our assessment of learner prose, the more stringently this requirement is put in place the more acceptable the resulting narrative development appears to be.

d. Nonnarrative clauses in the narrative sequence must mimic the formal characteristics of the narrative clauses they accompany. This is evident in sentences 6 and 9 of Sample A (repeated below) which show both structural and temporal parallelism to their preceding narrative clauses.

Sample A: an extract

6Most of the kids didn't like it ... 9Her mom had a back surgery and was prescribed X, but only took a couple of them, leaving a nearly full prescription in the bathroom.

If this parallelism is removed and 6 and 9 are represented as (1) explicit assertions that are (2) temporally nonspecific (as in 6′and 9′ below), the result is a noticeable break in the narrative flow, and greater difficulty reconnecting to the narrative storyline.

Modified extract of Sample A

5When she was in the eighth grade she and her friends were given marijuana to try. 6′**I think most kids don't like it, because it tastes terrible or they don't like the feeling they get when the effects kick in.** 7But it agreed with Darcy ...8One day, when she was just past her 14th birthday, she discovered some pain killers in her mother's medicine cabinet. 9′**I think people have surgery and are frequently prescribed X, but only take a couple of them, leaving a nearly full prescription in the bathroom.** 10Even 14-year-old people can research on the internet and soon she learned that by grinding the drug and snorting it, the high was intense.

e. There must be an appropriate level of detail in the capture of the events of the narrative sequence to suggest an effective culmination in the end-state.

The emergence of the end state is effected by the representation of successive preceding achievement-events at an appropriate degree of detail. Less than the represented degree of detail would take away this sense of culmination in the end state. Notice the advantage of (2b) over (2a) below, for this purpose:

2.

a. **He fell down.** He hurt himself badly, but luckily broke no bones.

b. **He missed a step, slipped on the thin layer of invisible ice, and landed on his back with a loud thud.** He hurt himself badly, but luckily broke no bones.

It is also true, however, that more than the represented detail in sample A would also diminish the effective build-up to end-state by being perceived as excessively delayed, and therefore laboured. So Sample A represents an ideal, or at least preferred, degree of detail at which the culmination to end-state should be represented.

1.3 Summary of key developmental features

Sample A suggests that narrative-in-support of an end-state statement comes with a defining macro-design which is constrained by a number of developmental features. It opens with the end-state statement, and then makes a statement on the temporal specificity of this end-state. The temporal specificity of end-state in the context of the end-state statement projects narrative as forthcoming, and the narrative must, therefore, follow. The 'then what happened?' condition then ensures that narrative once embarked upon is sustained to the point of its completion.

The narrative, once in place, is implemented in three phases: a point of inception, a following succession of changes of state, and a point of reconnection to the opening end-state. All the points of this development, inclusive of the opening end-state and the concluding reconnection to it, are hyponyms of a single over-arching hypernym, which is the topic of the text. To effect smooth narrative passage along the successive points of this development requires use of achievement verbs in the preterit. Any nonnarrative, intervening statements must mimic the structural and temporal features of the narrative clauses they accompany, to help sustain narrative passage across these intervening nonnarrative clauses. There is also a need to build up to the end state condition, and this build-up is implemented by the use of an appropriate degree of detail in the representation of successive events in the sequence.

2. A LEARNER'S ATTEMPT AT THE NARRATIVE SUPPORT OF AN OPENING END-STATE STATEMENT

I will now describe sample B, written by an L1 user of Spanish, as representative of high-intermediate learners' attempts at narrative in support of an end-state statement.

Sample B

My relationship with the English language

[1]English language is very important in my life nowadays. [2]But this changed a lot along the time.

[3]My relationship with the English language started eighteen years ago, when I was twelve, taking lectures in primary school. [4]In that time I liked English but I didn't learn too much. [5]Actually I think Spanish teaching-learning process in a second language is very bad, teachers don't have a good pronunciation and don't speak English with children, who only translate a lot of sentences word by word.

[6]After that my relationship with English was worse, when I studied in the High School, all the time learning grammar, was boring.

[7]The main reason in my interest about English language in my adult life is that I love travelling and the first time I've been abroad I understood that you can travel wherever you want if you can speak English.

[8]The second reason is I want to be a teacher in a primary school, and as a teacher you can choose different specialties but some of them are very crowded and it's difficult to find a job. [9]And in English specialty is easier to find it. [10]At the moment bilingual schools are coming up in Spain, more and more people want that their children to learn a second language since they are three years old.

[11]Now I'm studying English in another way, I try to give my best and I take lectures with natives by myself because at the university we

are eighty people per classroom, more or less, and it's very difficult to practice skills like speaking or writing, we are too many people and teachers can't spend enough time with each person.

[12]In addition, I hope my Erasmus experience in Sweden help me to improve my English a lot.

2.1 Macro-design of Sample B

Sample B opens with an end-statement in sentence 1 ('English is very important in my life nowadays'). The temporal specificity of the end-state is attempted in sentence 2 ('But this changed a lot along the time'). The change of state sequence follows, starting with a point of first exposure in sentence 3 ('My relationship with the English language started eighteen years ago, when I was…in primary school'). What ought to be successive changes of state to achieve the needed level of narrative detail is attempted in sentence 6 with just one instantiation ('After that my relationship with English…'). It is followed by the reconnection to the opening end-state statement in sentences 7 ("The main reason in my interest about English language in my adult life…'), 8 (The second reason…') and 11 ('Now I'm studying English…').

2.2 Developmental features

a. Narrative once started must be followed through to the point of its completion, with the ideal degree of detail in the representation of the event sequence.

   The return from the end-state condition (sentence 1) to the time of first exposure to English (sentence 3) traces a semi-circle back in time, which then prospects the missing half of the evoked full circle. Sample B does, in fact, follow through, in suggesting that the return path back to the end-state is in place. But the single instance (sentence 6) of what should be a sequence of changes of state along this return path diminishes the needed build up to it, and creates an inappropriate truncation of the narrative.

b. Narrative in support of an end-state statement must realise the relationship of hyponymy.

As suggested above, the statement on the temporal specificity of the end-state normatively comes in the 'this was not always the case' form. Expressed as 'But this changed a lot along the time' (sentence 2), with 'this' referring back to the whole preceding proposition, it suggests that the end-state (sentence 1: 'English is very important in my life nowadays') changed a great deal over time. This cannot be the writer's intent; the end-state (which in the present tense is also the condition at the time of utterance) cannot change in past time. But there is an intent to represent something related to the end-state as changing over time. It is reasonable to conclude that this is the associated hypernym, '*the importance of English in my life*' or more generally '*my relationship with English/my feelings about English*' which is both constant across time, and amenable to differentiated realisation in time. It can take on either positive realisation ('I value English'/'It is important to me') or negative realisation ('I don't value English'/'It isn't important to me.').

It is clear from this that one significant challenge posed by the narrative-support-of-an-end-state-statement is the need to effectively use the relationship of hyponymy. One way of accounting for this challenge is as a purely conceptual difficulty. That is, the difficulty lies in the necessity to (1) conceive of the represented end-state ('English is very important in my life now') as a hyponym of the associated hypernym ('my relationship with English'/'my feelings about English'), and (2) to then regard the hypernym as the broad atemporal constant which can undergo differentiated realisation, to emerge in the end-state in question. The relationship of hyponym to hypernym is less likely to pose difficulty when it holds between meaningful entities (namely, 'rose'/'tulip'/'daisy' to 'flower'), than when it bears between abstract notions (namely, 'English is very important in my life now' to 'my relationship with English').

It is also possible, however, that the challenge may not be a conceptual one at all. It might, rather, be the purely linguistic challenge of knowing how to give appropriate expression to each component, hyponym and hypernym, of the properly conceived relationship of hyponymy. In this case, also, the challenge is more likely to be associated with the realisation of hyponymy by non-entities rather than entities. While in hyponymy between entities both the hypernym and the hyponyms are expressed by NPs (e.g. both 'rose,' the hyponym, and 'flower,' the hypernym, are NPs), this can be (cf 3a and b, below), but does not have to be the case in hyponymy between nonentities.

3.

a. **Drinking** can be a life-long problem.
b. **Drinking moderately** is not a concern, but **drinking heavily** causes serious health problems.

Hyponyms that are nonentities can also be expressed by means of finite clauses (cf 4b below). The corresponding hypernym remains in the nonfinite form, since it is the overarching atemporal constant.

4.

a. **Drinking** can be a life-long problem.
b. If **one drinks moderately** it is not a concern, but if **one drinks heavily** it causes serious problems.

In sample B, the writer does not distinguish between the finite hyponymic realisation of sentence 1 ('English is very important in my life now') and the nonfinite hypernym which is needed in sentence 2 ('the importance of English in my life'). The proper use of 'my relationship with the English language' in sentence 3 (the assigned topic) convincingly evidences a conceptual association as hypernym with the hyponymic 'English is very important in my life now' in sentence 1. But it does not imply complete mastery of its linguistic form. Hence the challenge posed by the use of hyponymy in this instance may well be linguistic, rather than conceptual. The mastery of form has been said to lag behind the mastery of the conceptual in L2 acquisition (cf Bardovi-Harlig 1992), and variable formal accuracy goes hand in hand with this delayed mastery.

c. Verbs in the event sequence must be achievements in the preterit tense.

Sample B does fulfill the general need to realise hyponymy with each successive happening it represents. But because hyponymy places constituent hyponyms on a level or nonhierarchical plane, proper narrative passage requires the use of a succession of achievement-verbs in the preterit tense. To implement such progression, happenings that follow 'started' (sentence 3), which is an achievement-verb in the preterit, must also be framed as achievements in the preterit. This means that the state 'was worse' and the activity 'studied in high school' of sentence 6 should be reframed as 'became worse' and 'entered high school', respectively.

The narrative passage should also be sustained all the way to the culmination in the end-state, and so the state represented in 7, 'I love travelling,' should be re-framed as an achievement in the preterit, as in 'I have realized that I love travelling.' Again, the state 'I want to be a teacher' represented in 8 must be re-framed as an achievement in the preterit as in 'I have realized that I want to be a teacher.'

d. Intervening nonnarrative clauses should mimic the narrative clauses they accompany in structural and temporal features.

Since narrative of all kinds is constrained to sustain a temporal development, intervening nonnarrative clauses are out of synchrony with the narrative mode of textual development.

As suggested in section 1, they are better accommodated when they mimic preceding narrative clauses both in temporality and structure, showing, in consequence, propositional delimitation by the time frame and structure established by the preceding narrative clause(s).

In the second paragraph of sample B, the general comment on the teaching and learning of a second language in the Spanish context (sentence 5) is not sufficiently well tied to the preceding text, which is time-specific and focused on the writer's English language learning experience in primary school. Its connectedness improves if the temporal specificity is made to match that of the preceding narrative clause, by explicit mention of primary school.

But the use of the simple present, and the explicit assertion mode evident in 'I think...' still make the resumption of narration in sentence 6 difficult across this nonnarrative clause. By removing this overt marker of assertion, and putting 5 in the past, the resumption of narration across this intervening clause in sentence 6 becomes much easier (cf 5′ and 6, repeated below).

5′ Spanish teaching-learning process in a second language was very bad both in primary school and at every other stage of learning; teachers didn't have a good pronunciation and didn't speak English with the children, who only translated a lot of sentences word by word.

6. After that my relationship with English was worse, when I studied in the High School, all the time learning grammar, was boring.

3. CONCLUSION

We can conclude that Sample B, a representative high-intermediate learner's attempt at the narrative support of an opening end-state statement, shows a level of conformity to the macro-design of the prototype narrative of this kind. It does so in realising the core macro-design components: opening end-state statement, temporal specificity of end-state, point of initiation/first exposure, succession of changes of state and reconnection to end-state.

In consequence, the broad purpose that this genre of narrative development serves is realised: the text supports the claim, made as an opening end-state statement and qualified in the temporal specificity of the end-state, that English is very important to the writer at the time of the utterance. This support is given by means of retrospective return to the point of first exposure to English, and then backtracking along the path from this point of initiation to the specified end-state.

In this mapping of the passage in past time, however, it does not represent the change of state sequence to anything near the desired degree of detail. This truncation of the narrative diminishes the build-up to the end-state, which is a key objective of the narrative. The sample also shows some lexicalisation difficulties in the consistent realisation of hyponymy, with proper distinction between hyponym and hypernym in sentences 1 and 3, but not in 1 and 2. While this does not lead to misunderstanding, it would be perceived, by the average reader, as taking away from the impactful communication of the message.

Additionally, verbs in the change of state sequence are frequently non-achievements and are also not in all instances in the preterit. Like the insufficient detail in the representation of the event sequence, this decreases the dynamism, the movement in time quality, which is a defining feature of narrative, and therefore works against the core objective of the text. Finally, intervening nonnarrative clauses do not mimic the narrative clauses they accompany in structure and temporality, and therefore put in place a break in narrative flow at the point at which they appear.

This pattern of both conformity and nonconformity to the macro-design of the prototype narrative is representative of the set of 20 learner attempts at narrative in support of an end-state statement, regardless of the differences in linguistic background of the students who produced them. The macro-design is, in general, properly realised. The change of state sequence, however, is evident at less than the desired degree of detail in 18 out of 20 essays. The realisation of hyponymy is also a consistent point of difficulty in all but two of the essays, with significant support for the interpretation of this difficulty as a linguistic rather than conceptual challenge. Fifteen out of twenty students also use achievement-verbs inconsistently in the change of state sequence and twelve show variable use of the preterit for such verbs. Finally, only two students use intervening nonnarrative clauses with the structural and temporal features of their accompanying narrative clauses.

These micro-developmental features work both individually and collectively to put in place the core objective of delineating the narrative development to the stated end-condition. Their imperfect or only partial realisation, therefore, takes away from the particular kind of impact that is, in the prototype case, the functionality or, in more technical terms, discourse-pragmatic effect associated with the selection of this genre. So while conformity to the macro-design signals the use of the genre, the ineffective use of individual, micro-developmental features diminishes its functional impact. This suggests the need for some form of intervention, in the form of classroom practice and appropriate materials, to aid students to better tackle the effective use of narrative in support of an opening end-state statement.

Notes

1. Hyponymy is the relationship that bears between a set and each individual element of it (namely, the relationship of 'dog'/'cat'/ 'tiger' to 'mammal').
2. Consider, for example, the following narrative.

> [1]Last week my friend Mary had the worst experience of her life: **she was mugged**. She was taking an evening stroll down a jogging path at the back of her subdivision, [2]when **a guy jumped out** of nowhere **and held a gun to her head**. [3]**He threatened to blow her brains out** if she didn't do what he said, and [4]proceeded to rob her, taking her wallet, jewellery and even the little small change she had on her person.

3. Hyponymy is, in fact, better suited for an expository rather than narrative rendition.

References

Ayoun D and Salaberry R. 2008. Acquisition of English tense-aspect morphology by advanced French instructed learners. *Language Learning*, 58: 555–595.

Bardovi-Harlig K. 1992. The telling of a tale: discourse structure and tense use in learners' narratives. In L F Bouton and Y Kachru (ed), *Pragmatics and Language Learning*. Monograph Series. Volume 3: 144–161.

Bardovi-Harlig K. 1994. Anecdotes or evidence? Evaluating support for hypotheses concerning the development of tense and aspect. In E Tarone, S M Gass, and A D Cohen (ed), *Research Methodology in Second Language Acquisition.* Hillsdale, N. J.: Erlbaum.

Bardovi-Harlig K. 1995. A narrative perspective on the development of the tense/aspect system in second language acquisition. *Studies in Second Language Acquisition*, 17: 263–291.

Bardovi-Harlig K. 2000. Tense and aspect in second language acquisition: form, meaning, and use. *Language Learning*, 50 (Suppl. 1).

Chen L and Pan N. 2009. Development of English referring expressions in the narrative of Chinese-English bilinguals. *Language and Cognition*, 12 (4): 429–445.

Chiravate B. 2011. The role of narrative structure in the acquisition of English tense-aspect morphology by Thai learners. *Journal of Pan-Pacific Association of Applied Linguistics*, 15 (2): 27–43.

Kang J Y. 2009. Referencing in a second language: Korean EFL learners' cohesive use of references in written narrative discourse. *Discourse Processes*, 46 (5): 439–466.

Finegan E. 2004. *Language: its Structure and Use*. USA: Wadsworth.

Labov W. 2001. *Uncovering the Event Structure of Narrative*. Georgetown University Round Table.

Labov W. 2004. Ordinary events. In C Fought (ed), *Sociolinguistic Variation: Critical Reflections*. Oxford: Oxford University Press.

Labov W. 2006. Narrative preconstruction. *Narrative Inquiry*, 16: 37–45.

Labov W and Waletzky J. 1967. Narrative analysis. In J Helm (ed), *Essays on the Verbal and Visual Arts*. Seattle: University of Washington Press.

Lu X. 2012. The relationship of lexical richness to the quality of ESL learners' oral narratives. *Modern Language Journal*, 96 (2): 190–208.

Tickoo A. 2001. Re-examining the developmental sequence hypothesis for past-tense marking in ESL: transfer effects and implications. *Prospect: A Journal of Australian TESOL*,16 (1): 17–35.

Tickoo A. 2002. On the framing of one kind of indefinite referring expression: learning challenges and pedagogical implications. *International Journal of Applied Linguistics*, 12 (2): 176–194.

Tickoo A. 2005. Re-examining the selective marking of past tense: insights from Indian learners of ESL. *International Journal of Applied Linguistics*, 15: 364–378.

Wood D. 2009. Effects of focused instruction of formulaic sequences on fluent expression in second language narratives: a case study. *Canadian Journal of Applied Linguistics*, 12 (1): 39–57.

8

Information Design and Language Learning

First published in Ashok Thorat (ed), *Pragmatics* (2006),
Institute of Advanced Studies in English, Pune, India

1. INTRODUCTION

One of the less well-studied areas of L2 learning and use is what is commonly referred to as information design or presentation. Information design is the packaging given to the meaning or content of the message to signal the way it is to be perceived. That is, it is a regulatory system that does not generate meaning, but, rather, manages the way meaning is framed. A specific type of packaging is associated with a particular intended perception of meaning, and the same meaning can potentially be given differentiated packaging to be perceived in dissimilar ways.

In this paper, I want to comment on high-intermediate ESL learners' mastery of a fundamental area of information design in written language use. I will put together key findings from a number of my recent assessments of ESL writing, to suggest that they collectively show that at a point in their development at which learners can effectively make meaning, they appear to show only partial mastery of this core area of information design. I will also use these findings to arrive at the specific domains of difficulty posed by the acquisition of this area of information design, and, in concluding, give some initial thought to possible reasons for the lag in the learning of this area of information packaging.

The ESL learners whose prose was examined in the individual studies used in this assessment are all L1 users of Cantonese. They were undergraduates in the Humanities programme of a Hong Kong university at the time they wrote the analysed prose samples. They had learned English for approximately 15 years, but until the age of twelve only as a school subject, and thereafter with limited opportunity to practise their writing skills. In these studies, written samples are taken from individual groups of students, varying in size from approximately 25 to approximately 125. The prose samples are of two main types: some of the studies examine the learners' expository prose, and others look at their attempts at narrative.

Of the potential ways of packaging information, two are very widely acknowledged, and, therefore, serve well to illustrate information packaging and its potentially dissimilar modes of implementation. In one, meaning is packaged to ensure conformity to the communicative objective captured in the Cooperative Principle and the maxims of cooperation (Grice 1989). That is, the packaging of the meaning effects its perception as informationally sufficient, relevant, credible and clear. In the other equally well-acknowledged manifestation of information design, meaning is framed to realise different levels of indirect speech; this form of packaging allows for the perception of the message as face-saving (Brown and Levinson 1987). Of interest here is a more basic form of information design which serves to implement a more fundamental perceptual constraint. The packaging of meaning by this mode of information design serves to make each incrementation of meaning a distinctive informational type, amongst other types that it could potentially be. The distinctive information type functions as an indicator of how the incrementation adds to preceding incrementations, and, therefore, also how it contributes to configuring the informational contour of the message-whole. The general principle—make meaning informationally distinctive—governs every act of meaning-making.

In what follows, I will first illustrate how meaning is framed to make it informationally distinctive.

2. IMPLEMENTING INFORMATIONAL DISTINCTIVENESS: INFORMATION DESIGN FEATURES

The packaging of meaning to make it informationally distinctive is facilitated by manipulating one, or a subset, of a number of information design features, used specifically for this purpose. Three representative selections of these design features, and their modes of use in framing meaning to make it informationally distinctive, are described below:

The notional construct of the set

One design feature used to effect informational distinctiveness is the notional construct of the set. Elements qualify for membership in a particular set by possessing certain shared defining characteristics. One manifestation of informational distinctiveness can be effected, therefore, by packaging the meaning/content of an incrementation as a *well-distinguished* element of a set of elements to which it belongs; that is, it can be fashioned as an element having a feature the other set members do not possess.

1.

a. Do you see those men over there?

b. The man in the red hat is looking at you.

c. The man is looking at you.

As 'the man in the red hat' (1b), the individual referred to is represented as a well-distinguished element of a known-to-hearer set ('those men over there'). If this referring expression were framed as merely 'the man' (1c), the individual referred to would not become informationally well-distinguished from the other same-set elements.

Transitivity

It is also possible to implement an informational distinctiveness by manipulating the transitivity (Hopper 1977, 1979) of the situation represented by a clausal incrementation. Transitivity is a discourse notion of aspect. It is described by Hopper as resulting from the cumulative impact of the individual values of features of a conglomerate which he refers to as the transitivity features (cf Table 8.1). In Table 8.1, positive realisations of these features are represented in the category 'Perfective', and negative realisations appear in the 'Imperfective' category.

TABLE **8.1**

Perfective	Imperfective
1. Strict chronological sequencing	1. Simultaneity or chronological overlap of situation C with event A and/or B
2. View of event as a whole, whose completion is a necessary prerequisite to a subsequent event	2. View of a situation or happening whose completion is not a necessary prerequisite to a subsequent happening
3. Identity of subject within each discrete episode	3. Frequent changes of subject
4. Unmarked distribution of focus in clause, with presupposition of subject and assertion in verb and its immediate complements (or other unmarked focus)	4. Marked distribution of focus, e.g. subject focus, instrument focus, focus on sentence adverbials
5. Human topics	5. Variety of topics, including natural phenomena
6. Dynamic, kinetic events	6. Static, descriptive situations

7. Foregrounding. Event indispensable to narrative	7. Backgrounding. State or situation necessary for understanding motives, attitudes, etc
8. Realis	8. Irrealis

(from Hopper 1979: 216)

A cumulative transitivity value is realised for a clausal situation, by assessing the positive or negative manifestation of each individual transitivity feature for that situation: telicity (end-point property), dynamism, punctility (occurrence at a single point), givenness/newness, informational saliency, realisness/irrealisness, etc.

2.

a. Peter left the restaurant in great haste,
b. walked out into the street without looking,
c. and was instantly run over by a car,
d. and was, in consequence, the victim of a terrible accident.

In 2c, for example, framing the situation as telic, punctual and dynamic represents it as a narrative event in the sequence formed by the preceding two events, namely (a) and b. Framing the same situation as nondynamic, atelic and nonpunctual in the context of (a) and b, instead, as in 2d (that is, as a state) represents it as a purely descriptive incrementation, which, in consequence, cannot contribute to the preceding sequence of events.

Managing the individual values of the transitivity features, therefore, makes it possible to give the represented situation a particular well-distinguished type of informational character, for example, that it is an event rather than a state. That is, the content of the incrementation is represented as a select situational type out of other situational types it could potentially be.

Types of given information

Another way of implementing informational distinctiveness is to regulate in what way an incrementation is given information in the context of its preceding incrementations (On the notion of given/new, cf Halliday 1974; Haviland and Clark 1974; Chafe 1976; Prince 1981, amongst others.)

To be relevant, every incrementation must be to some degree, and in some way, given information in its context of appearance. This simply means some aspect of it must be already known (to hearer/reader) at the point of its appearance. The quality of the given relationship it bears to its preceding incrementations equips the incrementation with a distinct way of contributing to the development of the message.

3.

a. I went out, shopping.

b. I bought some milk.

c. While I was shopping, I ran into an old friend.

In 3, both b and c are relevant to (a), and therefore also, to some extent, given information in the context of (a). In 3b, what is given is that I bought one or more items of food; the new information is the instantiation of a particular item of food: milk. In 3c, it is given that I was shopping; the new information is that while I was so occupied, something else happened, namely, 'I ran into an old friend'. The dissimilar types of given and new relationships that these two incrementations realise gives them distinct ways of building on what precedes them. Thus 3b is a form of expansion on, rather than addition to, 3a, and it constitutes one well-distinguished way of incrementation, or text-building; 3c is a particular way of adding to 3a, rather than expanding on it. This is quite a separate way of incrementation, or text-building.

But one can also alter the givenness type of b to (a), as in 4.

4.

a. I went out, shopping.

b. While I was shopping, I bought some milk.

Now in 4, b adds to (a), rather than expanding on it. Similarly, it is possible to alter the givenness type of c to (a), as in 5. In 5 below, c expands on (a), rather than adding to it.

5.

a. I went out, shopping.

b. I walked all the way to the end of the mall.

c. I ran into an old friend.

d. I had lunch at the new restaurant,

e. and I also bought a little of this and that, too.

So the content of any incrementation is, in fact, deliberately framed, with an acknowledgement of the context in which it appears, to bear a selected type of given relationship to its preceding incrementations.

In the above, I have described three types of information design features—the notional construct of the set, transitivity and givenness/newness— which are used to frame meaning to make it informationally distinctive in three different ways. In what follows, I will provide illustrative examples of the types of challenge ESL learners face applying the make-meaning-informationally-distinctive principle, in three core areas of written language use: 1) reference, 2) temporal representation and 3) text construction.

3. ESL LEARNER ATTEMPTS AT MAKING MEANING INFORMATIONALLY DISTINCTIVE

Reference

Being able to refer effectively is of course an essential language skill. Tickoo (2002a) demonstrates that whereas Chinese learners have no apparent difficulty framing definite NPs (e.g. the highlighted NP in 6b), they are considerably challenged by the proper framing of a defining category of indefinite referring expressions (e.g. the highlighted NP in 7a). This is because successful referring depends on framing the referring expression in a way that will make the referent informationally distinctive amongst same-set entities, and this is a somewhat different task for these two types of referring expressions.

6.

a. Do you see that group of men over there?

b. The man in the red cap has been staring at you.

7.

a. I shared a table with **a man whose appearance intrigued me**.

In the definite NP of 6b, the referent is present and therefore known/given information to not only the speaker, but also the interlocutor. The characteristic that distinguishes the man in question from other same-set entities (the other present men) is, therefore, also visible to both the speaker and the hearer, and hence also mutually known/given information. In the underscored indefinite NP of 7a, however, the referent is new information to the interlocutor. The characteristic used to make the individual distinctive amongst same-set entities (the set of other men) is also new information to the hearer. But in order to get the hearer to recognise the referent in question as properly distinctive amongst same-set entities, the distinguishing characteristic must be one that is generally perceived as capable of making a man distinctive amongst other men. Having an intriguing appearance does, in fact, succeed in doing this. For this type of indefinite reference, hence, it is necessary to use shared knowledge of what would generally be accepted as making an element unique amongst its same-set elements, rather than using specific knowledge of what speaker and hearer mutually know does, in fact, make a mutually known element distinctive in its mutually known set. This use of abstract knowledge, rather than the concrete, poses a challenge for Chinese learners. They generate indefinite referring expressions such as 8a and 8b.

8.

The train made an unexpected stop at Vladislavov, so I went to the station restaurant to get a bite to eat.

a. I shared a table with **a man**.
b. I shared a table with **a fat man**.
c. I shared a table with **a man of extraordinary size**.

Neither 'a man' (8a) nor 'a fat man' (8b) are regarded as distinctive amongst other men. In contrast, 'a man of extraordinary size' (8c) is in fact considered distinctive.

It is evident in this, hence, that a particular needed implementation of the make-meaning-informationally-distinctive principle is either not applied at all (8a) or is improperly applied (8b) in the framing of indefinite reference.

Temporal representation

The use of the past tense

In the area of temporal representation, Tickoo (2001a) demonstrates that Chinese learners attempt to use the past tense to signal one of two contrasting modes of narrative development, on the pattern of a comparable temporal marker in their L1: the perfective particle 'le'. In Chinese, 'le' is used in accompaniment with only verbs representing thematically salient narrative situations, and Chinese learners use the English past tense in like fashion (cf sample 1). That is, they use the past tense to signal an informational distinction that is not, in fact, marked by this means in the English language.

Sample 1

[1]**When I was 14, once time I cleaned my bedroom.** [2]**During this time, I found out so many useless things.** [3]**Then I put them in a rubbish bin.** [4]Useless thing in my mind, there are some of my primary school's friends letters and Christmas cards because of its dust· [5]So, I have taken a very stupid action and **threw them all away.**

In sample 1, the significant acts of cleaning the bedroom, finding 'useless things' and throwing them away, of sentences 1, 2, 3 and 5 are marked with the past tense. Sentence 4, which serves merely to amplify the key point made in these sentences, is not in the past tense.

The use of 'then'/'after that'

Another area of temporal representation where proper application of the distinctiveness-marking principle poses a challenge for these learners is in the use of the temporal adverb 'then'/'after that' (Tickoo 2002b). 'Then'/'after that' is used in English to signal situations that are thematically salient in the narrative and at the same time 1) telic situations occurring after preceding telic situations, and 2) situations which are new, rather than given, information. Because of this it is reasonable to say that 'then'/ 'after that' marks a distinctive type of temporal passage. This is illustrated in 9 and 10.

9.

a. I wanted to go

b. and I went./ and so I went.

c. # Then I went.

Since it is a state, 9a is not a telic happening. Therefore, 'then' is not felicitously used to mark the type of temporal movement of 9b (cf 9c).

10.

a. I left late,

b. and I arrived in the nick of time.

c.# (and) then I arrived in the nick of time.

In 10, b is not new information in the context of (a), since it is anticipated in the context of my having left that I either arrived or I did not arrive. Therefore, 'then' is not felicitously used to mark this type of temporal movement (cf 10c).

This use of 'then'/ 'after that' is not exactly matched by Chinese learners, though they too use it to mark a distinctive type of incrementation and temporal passage. While they also use it to signal situations that are thematically central to the narrative, these situations are not necessarily new information; nor are they necessarily telic situations appearing after preceding telic situations. So both 10c above, and 11b below are acceptable, though 'then' is not accompanying new situations. Likewise, both 9c, above, and 12b are acceptable, though 'then' follows atelic situations.

11.

a. I asked her a question.

b.# Then she told me all I wanted to know./ And she told me all I wanted to know.

12.

a. I wanted to sleep.

b. # After that I had a wonderful night's sleep.

This use of 'then'/ 'after that' is on the exact pattern of the use of the particle 'le' in Chinese, which marks the same informational distinctness. In consequence, the very distinctive type of temporal passage signalled by the proper use of the adverb 'then'/ 'after that' is not marked in this learner's usage.

Text Construction

Micro-level text design: Enumeration

The make-meaning-informationally-distinctive principle is implemented at both the micro- and macro-levels of text construction. As stated under section 2, at the micro-level the type of givenness of a particular incrementation is selected to effect a well-distinguished type of text development. The givenness-type effects a particular type of text development by determining the relationship the incrementation bears to its preceding incrementation.

As demonstrated in section 2, one mode of text development is effected by selecting a givenness-type which expands on a preceding incrementation. Sentences 13b and 13c below expand on 13a by instantiating it. That is, 13a speaks of the move to Hong Kong being made for a number of reasons, and 13b and c expand on it, each by instantiating a particular reason for the relocation. It is also true that each incrementation, at the same time, adds to (rather than expanding on) any preceding instantiations. (13c adds to b, while instantiating (a). It does not instantiate b). Each such instantiation can also be construed as answering a question seeking clarification about (a), as is illustrated in 13.

13.

a.	I moved to Hong Kong for a number of reasons.	What were they? **clarification question**
b.	I was fascinated by the intriguing mix of cultural worlds,	**instantiates (a)**
c.	(and) I was impressed by its international status as a business center,	**instantiates (a) and adds to (b)**...

This particular type of given relationship serves to generate the type of text development which we routinely call Enumeration.

Chinese learners often have difficulty monitoring the givenness of the incrementation, to instantiate a preceding assertion, while at the same time adding to (rather than expanding on) other instantiations of it. In consequence, the very distinctive character of this form of information incrementation and text development is often not evident in their attempts at its use (cf Tickoo 2001b, for full details).

Sample 2

There are several reasons for me choosing English major. [1]English is an interesting subject I think since I was in primary school. [2]Studying English is not routine work, because there are so many changes. [3]I want to learn more about English language and literature and have a deeper knowledge in it. [4]Also, I hope I can be an English teacher as my future career. So I choose English as my major subject.

In the student attempt at enumeration of sample 2, for example, the opening statement suggests that there will be an enumeration of 'several reasons' for the student's choice of English as a major field of study. But the following points don't actually readily lend themselves to perception as independent instantiations of these reasons. Sentence 3 actually explains what the interest of 1 amounts to, and 2 justifies the interest stated in 1. In consequence, 1, 2 and 3 are not making three separate instantiations of the reasons referred to in the opening statement, but rather just one, as is suggested by the repackaging of this paragraph in sample 2a.

Sample 2a

[1]I have been interested in English, [3]in gaining a deeper understanding of English language and literature, since I was in primary school, because [2]the subject is full of surprises and is never dull, routinized work— [4]my goal is to be an English major.

The expansion into dialogue using clarification questions, in sample 2b below also shows that 2 and 3 actually expand on the first instantiation in the sentence labelled 1, rather than adding to it.

Sample 2b

1. I have been interested in English.	**In what way? (clarification question)**
2. (I have been interested) in gaining a deeper understanding of English language and literature	**Why is that? (clarification question)**
3. because the subject is full of surprises and is never dull, routinized work.	

It is clear from this that this learner is unable to make successive independent instantiations of the 'several reasons', and, therefore, also unable to make each one add to, rather than expand on, preceding instantiations.

Micro-level text design: Encapsulation

Another givenness-type effects incrementation and text development of a quite dissimilar character than that used in Enumeration. When an incrementation bears this type of given relationship in its context of appearance, it adds to, rather than expanding on, a preceding incrementation. In one manifestation of this additive relationship, the adding-to happens specifically by retaining the entire preceding incrementation in its addition (cf Hoey 1994).

14.	**Consequence questions**
a. I was on sentry duty.	So, what happened?
b. (While I was on sentry duty) I saw the enemy approach.	So, what happened?
c. (When I saw the enemy approach while I was on sentry duty) I opened fire.	So, what happened?

(Hoey 1994)

14b adds to (a), and it does so specifically by retaining (a) in its addition. Likewise, 14c adds to (b), and it does so, again, by retaining (b) in its addition. Each such addition also answers a question about the temporal follow-up to, or consequence of, the preceding assertion, as is illustrated in 14, rather than answering a clarification question, as was the case in text incrementation by means of expansion, in Enumeration.

This Encapsulating type of incrementation often poses a problem for Chinese learners who have first mastered Enumeration (cf Tickoo 2005). This is because when one instantiates the preceding incrementation (the means of incrementation used in Enumeration) one cannot, at the same time, retain this preceding incrementation.

15.

a. I went to Hong Kong for a number of reasons.
b. # When/While/Since I went to Hong Kong for a number of reasons, I was fascinated by the intriguing mix of cultural worlds.

Hence, the retention of (a) in 15b prevents felicitous instantiation of it. In fact, Encapsulation and instantiation are diametrically opposed as givenness relations: one requires retention of the preceding text; the other entirely rules it out.

Chinese learners who have first mastered instantiation, in constructing Enumerative prose, are therefore, often, negatively influenced by it in their attempts at the diametrically opposed mode of incrementation and text development of Encapsulation.

Sample 3

Dealing with the stress of college life

[1]In everyone's life, stress seems to be unavoidable. [2]When one grows up, one will face different kinds of stress in different stages. [3]In the college life, students have to face the stress comes from themselves, from their classmates as well as from their families. [4]Stress will bring to the students a sense of feeling that is unfree or

even uncomfortable. [5]Sometimes if stress is not properly deal with, it may cause trouble to the students. [6]Therefore, it is important to deal with the stress of college life properly.

In sample 3, the first paragraph of a student essay on the subject of 'Dealing with the stress of college life', there is a break in the continuity, or coherence, at the very beginning, between sentences 1 and 2. This is because sentence 2 does not clearly develop the point made in 1. This is illustrated in sample 3a, in the ineffective expansion into dialogue, using the consequence-seeking question:

Sample 3a

1. In everyone's life, stress seems to be unavoidable.

   What happens in consequence?

2. When one grows up, one will face different kinds of stress in different stages.

The continuity is, however, implemented from sentence 2 to the end of the paragraph. Sentences 4 and 5 and 6 increment the text by encapsulating their preceding sentence, and 3 is an expansion of 2. This is evident in the following expansion-into-dialogue rendition of the paragraph (sample 3b), in which sentence 3 answers a clarification question and the sentences 4–6 answer consequence-seeking questions.

Sample 3b

2. When one grows up, one will face different kinds of stress in different stages.	What kind of stress will one face in college life? (**clarification question**)
3. In the college life, students have to face the stress comes from themselves, from their classmates as well as from their families.	What harmful effects does the stress faced at college have? (**consequence question**)
4. (This) Stress will bring to the	What happens if this stress

	students a sense of feeling that is unfree or even uncomfortable.	is not dealt with? (**consequence question**)
5.	Sometimes if (this) stress is not properly deal with, it may cause trouble to the students.	So what can we conclude from this? (**consequence question**)
6.	Therefore, it is important to deal with the stress of college life properly.	

To make this a coherent paragraph, however, it is necessary to make sentence 2 connect to 1. To do this, sentence 2 can be redistributed into two clauses. The first clause adds to 1 by encapsulating it, and the second clause expands on this preceding clause. This repackaging is illustrated in sample 3c, below:

Sample 3c

1.	In everyone's life, stress seems to be unavoidable.	What happens in consequence? (**consequence question**)
2.	One faces stress at every phase of life, (and) every phase comes with its own kind of stress.	What kind of stress is faced at these different phases of life? (**clarification question**)

This example shows that students, inevitably, need to use the encapsulating type of *additive relationship* as effectively as they use *expansion*, as a means of incrementing text.

Macro-level text design

The above are examples of misapplications of the make-meaning-informationally-distinctive principle at the micro-level of text design. But learners' prose samples also give evidence of its misapplication in ways that impact the macro-design of the text.

At the macro-level, informational distinctiveness gives rise to different genres and sub-genres of discourse. One of the ways of making narrative read as the specific sub-genre of story, rather than a mere report of events in past time, is to implement a distinctive type of temporal passage. The representation of passage through time is a defining feature of all types of narrative. But narrative as story is distinguished by a characteristically variable passage of time (cf Tickoo 2003). The characteristic variability of the temporal passage is implemented in well-defined and predictable ways by two means: sententially, and by orchestrating a specific kind of text organisation.

Temporal movement in narrative is effected by carrying the narrative forward along a sequence of events. In narrative as story, there are three different sentence types which can be used in the representation of situations as events: the clause in canonical (SVO) order (as in 16a), the VP-conjoined clause (as in 16b), and the 'then'-marked clause (as in 16c):

16.

a. I went to the market.
b. and I went to the market.
c. Then I went to the market.

Events appearing in these three sentence-types signal three distinctive modes of temporal passage, differentiated by the pace and quality of the movement (cf Tickoo 2003, for full details).

17.

I got up,

A. I went to the market,

...

I got up,

B. and went to the market.

I got up.

C. Then I went to the market.

Sentences 17A, B and C differ in pace of movement and in the thematic independence of the point to which the temporal move is made in each case. The use of canonical order in A effects a slower and more measured pace than use of the VP-conjoined clause of B, but a somewhat less slow and measured pace than that effected by the 'then'-marked clause of C. A also moves the narrative to a more thematically independent point than does B, though to a less thematically independent point than does C. Of the three, therefore, the VP-conjunction of B effects the most seemingly rapid move, and to the least thematically independent point. It is seen as a constituent step of a larger whole occurrence, made up of it and its preceding conjoined event. On the other hand, the 'then'-marked clause of C effects the most measured move, and carries the narrative to the most thematically independent point.

Narrators are able to implement a variable passage of time by alternating between these three modes of temporal passage and strategically selecting between them a pace and quality that suits their purpose at a particular point in the narrative. In the excerpts from Hardy's *Tess of the D'Urbervilles* of samples 4 and 5, both narratives open with the rapid move from event to event effected by the use of VP-conjoined clauses, but then give way to the more measured pace of the 'then'-marked clause.

Sample 4

'When the passengers were not looking *she stealthily removed the more prominent blooms from her hat and placed them in the basket,* where she covered them with her handkerchief. **Then she fell to reflecting again...**' (p 42)

Sample 5

'Here she dipped her hand into the basin, and fervently drew an immense cross up the baby with her forefinger...**Then their sister, with much augmented confidence in the efficacy of this sacrament, poured forth from the bottom of her heart the thanksgiving...**' (p 101)

(Thomas Hardy, *Tess of the D'Urbervilles*)

At the level of text organisation, the transitivity features are manipulated on successive narrative situations to implement passage along a sustained alternation between happenings of high and low transitivity value.

18.

a. We **left** in the early morning.

b. We **passed** a series of small towns.

c. Then in the early evening we **stopped** at a small motel.

Sentences 18a and c have a higher transitivity value than b; they are dynamic, punctual and telic and also new information in their context of appearance, whereas b is dynamic, but not punctual and telic, and, additionally, not informationally new in its context of appearance. This also translates into movement along happenings of high- and low thematic centrality, since leaving for some destination and getting there are likely to qualify as central points to the narrative theme, whereas the amplifying statement of passing various towns on the way is not (cf Hopper 1977, 1979).

In this sustained alternation between situations of high thematic centrality (peaks for future reference) and situations of low thematic centrality (troughs for future reference), the narrative passage is also, routinely, manipulated by managing the values of three variables of the successive narrative peaks:

1. First, the transitivity value itself is managed for successive peaks (peak intensity, for future reference) to indicate how significant to the theme the happening actually is.
2. The distance between one peak and the next (inter-peak distance, for future reference) is also manipulated, to effect how frequently peaks appear in the narrative.
3. Finally, the stretch of narrative spent on depicting each peak, between successive peaks (the spread for future reference) is also strategically managed to determine the amount of narrative giv-

en to depiction of peaks, rather than to the description of supplementary detail. Selected values for the peak intensitiy, inter-peak distance and peak spread of successive peaks are routinely kept constant for a narrative or thematic segment of it, and altered for following thematic segments (cf Tickoo 2003, for full details).

Sample 6

p 33 Rising early next day she walked to the hill town ... and there **took advantage of** a van...

p 35 She **alighted** from the van at ...

p 37 Tess still stood hesitating...when a figure **came forth** from the dark triangular door...

p 39 He **conducted** her about the lawns...

p 41 he **inclined** his face towards her

(*Tess of the D'Urbervilles*, 'Maiden', pp 32–42)

In sample 6, the represented clauses are the peaks in a ten-page segment from Hardy's *Tess of the D'Urbervilles*, called 'Maiden'. Each peak is an event, in terms of its transitivity value. These events appear roughly two pages apart, as is apparent in the sample above (on pp 33, 35, 37, 39 and 41). That is, the inter-peak distance is considerable, with lengthy descriptive passages between successive peaks. Additionally, the peak spread is very small, since each peak is represented in a single clause. Strategically altering the inter-peak distance by, for example, bringing the peaks closer to each other, and/or the peak spread by, for example, presenting a fuller treatment of each peak than can be achieved in a single clause, would effect a quite different quality of narrative passage.

It is temporal variability in this well-defined and predictable way that contributes to giving narrative the distinguishing character of a story.

Chinese learners have considerable difficulty imposing a variable temporal passage in their attempts at storytelling. At the sentential level of its implementation, they rarely use VP-conjunction, which effects a fast paced movement, along the constituent occurrences of a larger whole event.

Sample 7

[1]It was a day in August 1917. [2]I was on my way to Petrograd. [3]I had had my dinner at the station Restaurant before I got on the tran-Siberian train.

[4]I settled down in a chair with a small table. [5]Then, a Russian came in [6]and shared the table with me.

[7]He was fat and poorly dressed.

[8]We began our conversation.

[9]He talked to me about his life.

[10]He was a widower. [11]He had a wife before who was married with him for ten years. [12]Her wife was small and thin with bad appearance. [13]She had a bitter tongue. [14]She had strong feeling of jealousy towards him.

[15]The Russian began to tell me his relationship with his wife.

[16]He started the story by the night he heard the scream of his wife.

[17]She had a nightmare

that his husband wanted to kill her

[18]and threw her over the balusters.

[19]She was very frightened. [20]The nightmare changed the impression between the couple. [21]The wife was afraid of having the nightmare.

[22]The husband thought that it was easy to throw his wife over the balusters.

[23]Then, the Russian's wife had the same nightmare again and again.

[24]She was very nervous and

[25]asked her husband whether he loved her.

[26]The Russian swore that he loved her.

[27]He thought that it was the only thing he could do. [28]He was angry about the annoyance of this wife.

This is apparent in sample 7, a student's version of Maugham's short story *The Dream* in which VP-conjunction is used only twice in the whole narrative (cf clauses 5 and 6 and 17 and 18). When students do use VP-conjunction, they show evidence of considerable difficulty in its proper use, as is apparent in the conjoined clauses 17 and 18, repeated below from sample 7. In 18, an event ('threw her over the balusters') is conjoined to a preceding state ('wanted to kill'), instead of an event, and in consequence fails to effect the fast-paced movement from one constituent event to another, evident in the original story (cf sample 8).

Repeated from Sample 7

She had a nightmare that his (her) (17) husband wanted to kill her (18) **and threw her over the balusters**. She was very frightened.

Sample 8

'She had dreamt that just as we arrived at our own floor I had caught hold of her and attempted to throw her over the balusters. It was six storeys to floor at the bottom and it meant certain death.'

(Somerset Maugham, *The Dream*)

Additionally, 'then'-marked clauses are over-used and without acknowledgement of the significant thematic transition their use signals. Maugham uses only one 'then'-marked clause in the whole story, and it is at the very significant transition in the story when the wife dreams the dreaded dream of her husband's attempt to kill her for a second time. The student version of the story replicates the use of this 'then'-marked clause (cf sentence 23), but without any of the preceding build-up to it that would mark it as a major transition in the story. The student also uses a 'then'-marked clause very early in the story, at a point where it does not actually accompany movement to a major point of thematic transition (cf clause 5).

At the level of discourse, learners' narratives show little evidence of the basic alternation between peaks and troughs. For example, the event sequences 4, 5 and 6, and 23, 24 and 25, are uninterrupted by intervening descriptive clauses. In fact, event sequences and purely descriptive passages are kept almost entirely separate, as is evident in the fact that 4–8 is an event sequence almost without intervening descriptive clauses, and 10–14 is then a descriptive passage, without intervening event clauses. There is hence no possibility of selecting and maintaining the values for peak intensity, inter-peak distance and peak spread for either the entire narrative or a segment of it, or of altering these values in strategic ways from one narrative segment to the next.

The learner narratives, in consequence, are temporally flat, rather than variable, and hence fall short of true story-like character. In this case, the distinctive character given to temporal passage by the appropriate use of the above-referred-to sentential and textual means is not effected, and, in consequence, story as a genre of narrative is not properly fashioned.

4. DOMAINS OF LEARNING DIFFICULTY

The above-described examples of information design problems at the levels of reference, temporal representation and text construction are indicative of the nature of the challenge that the make-meaning-informationally-distinctive principle poses for the high-intermediate level second language learner who uses Cantonese as L1. A number of significant domains of learning difficulty are revealed in these examples:

1. It has become apparent that when implementation of informational distinctiveness requires use of the abstract notion of what makes an element unique amongst same-set entities, learners have problems framing meaning to make it informationally dis-

tinctive. By contrast, when distinctiveness can be implemented by use of given-/known-to-hearer information about a known element of a known set, making meaning informationally distinctive is unproblematic.

2. We have also seen that syntax is sometimes learned as a means of signalling informational distinctiveness. We have seen that this may pose a learning challenge when the comparable L1 syntactic item is used to effect an information distinction its English counterpart does not share, or shares only partially. The learner, then, attempts to use this feature of English syntax to mark the information distinction its L1 counterpart makes.
3. We have also noted that the type of given information an incrementation realises results in distinctive ways of incrementing, and, thereby, building text. Selecting the appropriate type of givenness and keeping one type separate from another poses a challenge for learners. Additionally, when one type of given relationship, and hence one incremention type/text development type, is the diametric opposite of one learned earlier, learners can be negatively impacted by the earlier learning.
4. Finally, we have established that there is a level of information design that makes one genre of prose, e.g. narration, distinctive from another genre of prose, e.g. exposition. There is also a more specialised level of information design, which, for example, makes one sub-genre of narrative, namely story, distinct from other sub-genres of narrative. This specialised level of information design poses a considerable level of challenge for L2 learners.

Put in more general terms, this collective assessment of the findings garnered from a number of individual studies on the written language use of this group of learners suggests that implementing the make-meaning-informationally-distinctive principle is particularly challenging when the learner is faced with two subtly different modes of its application. It is a problem, that is, when 1) it is applied one way to known entities, but somewhat differently to new ones,

2) when it is applied somewhat differently in L1 and L2, 3) when it is applied differently for different modes of text incrementation, 4) when it is applied differently for an incrementation-mode learned earlier to one learned later, and 5) when it is applied differently in specialised sub-genres of text. When the learner is faced with such subtly different applications, the better known—that is, the application for the given and non-abstract, the earlier-learnt application, the L1 application, and the broader and less specialised application—appears to interfere with the proper use of the other.

5. A POSSIBLE REASON FOR SUSTAINED LEARNING DIFFICULTY IN THIS AREA OF LANGUAGE USE

It is relevant, in closing, to consider why these particular manifestations of the make-meaning-informationally-distinctive principle are only partially acquired at fairly advanced levels of language learning. In addressing this question, it is helpful to note that most of these misapplications, while they contribute to making for a greater information processing challenge for the reader, do not, as a rule, cause misunderstanding. For example, not making the referent in an indefinite referring expression distinctive does not necessarily lead to misunderstanding, since the context generally helps the reader arrive at the writer's intention (as in 19a).

19.

a. When I went for a walk this morning, I saw **a man**. He didn't have a stitch of clothing on.
b. When I went for a walk this morning, I saw **a naked man**. He didn't have a stitch of clothing on.

Similarly, in the selective use of the past tense to mark one of two distinct modes of narrative progression, the context compensates for the lack of consistent marking, so that, again, incomprehension is unlikely, as is made evident in sample 1, repeated below. There is really no possibility of mistaking the clauses unmarked for past tense as occurring in anything other than past time.

Sample 1

[1]When I was 14, once time I cleaned my bedroom. [2]During this time, I found out so many useless things. [3]Then I put them in a rubbish bin. [4]Useless thing - in my mind, there are some of my primary school's friends letters and Christmas cards because of its dust· [5]So, I have taken a very stupid action and **threw them all away**.

In the non-standard use of 'then'/ 'after that', while the adverb itself communicates one type of temporal relationship and incrementation, the sentence itself conveys the relationship it actually bears to its preceding text, as is evident in 20 and 21, repeated below from 11 and 12. Hence, again, though text processing becomes a greater challenge for the reader, incomprehension is unlikely.

20.

a. I asked her a question.
b. # Then she told me all I wanted to know./ And she told me all I wanted to know.

21.

a. I wanted to sleep.
b. # After that I had a wonderful night's sleep.

In storytelling, when the requisite conventions are not upheld, the content does not change. Additionally, since there is a battery of rhetorical conventions which in different ways fashion narrative into a story, the absence of variable temporal passage while it does, in fact, give the narrative a noticeably unstory-like character, does not, in general, suggest that story was not the intended narrative sub-genre. The reader, rather, feels that an ineffective attempt has been made to tell a story.

The fact that these misapplications of the make-meaning-informationally-distinctive principle lead only to a greater processing challenge for the reader, rather than miscomprehension, may well remove the incentive for their proper acquisition. The problem is also very likely exacerbated by the fact that teachers and other facilitators accommodate the greater processing challenge and in so doing inadvertently compensate for the missing dimensions of information design. The greater tolerance for 'imperfect' language use that is a characteristic of today's language classroom may well serve to perpetuate this area of learning difficulty.

References

Brown P and Levinson S. 1987. *Politeness. Some Universals of Language Usage.* Cambridge University Press.

Chafe W L. 1976. Givenness, contrastiveness, definiteness, subjects, topics and points of view. In C N Li (ed), *Subject and Topic.* New York: Academic Press.

Grice P. 1989. *Studies in the Way of Words.* Harvard University Press.

Halliday M A K. 1974. The place of 'functional sentence perspective' in the system of linguistics description. In F Danes (ed), *Papers on Functional Sentence Perspective.* Academia, Prague.

Haviland S E and Clark H H. 1974. What's new? Acquiring new information as a process in comprehension. *Journal of Verbal Learning and Verbal Behavior*, 13: 512–521.

Hoey M. 1994. Signaling in discourse: a functional analysis of a common discourse pattern in written and spoken English. In M Coulthard (ed), *Advances in Written Text.* London: Routledge.

Hopper P J. 1977. Observations on the typology of focus and aspect in narrative language. *Studies in Language*, 3: 37–64.

Hopper P J. 1979. Aspect and foregrounding in discourse. In T Givon (ed), *Syntax and Semantics: Discourse and Syntax.* New York: Academic Press.

Prince E F. 1981. Towards a taxonomy of given-new information. In P Cole (ed), *Radical Pragmatics.* New York: Academic Press.

Tickoo A. 2005. Text building, language learning and the emergence of local varieties. *World Englishes*, 24 (1): 21–38.

Tickoo A. 2003. On variable temporal passage in story telling: identifying constraints and evidencing constraint violation in ESL prose. *Text*, 23 (1): 129–163.

Tickoo A. 2002a. On the framing of one kind of indefinite referring expression: learning challenges and pedagogical implications. *International Journal of Applied Linguistics*, 12 (2): 176–194.

Tickoo A. 2002b. On the use of 'then'/'after that' in the marking of chronological order: insights from Vietnamese and Chinese learners of ESL. *System*, 30: 107–124.

Tickoo A. 2001a. Re-examining the developmental sequence hypothesis for past-tense marking in ESL: transfer effects and implications. *Prospect: A Journal of Australian TESOL*, 16 (1): 17–35.

Tickoo A. 2001b. On enumerative prose in ESL: The rhetorical structure and learning challenges of one type of collection. *Australian Review of Applied Linguistics*, 22 (2): 1–27.

9

Message Undercoding and Language Learning

First published in *The EFL Journal*, 2:1 (2011), English and Foreign Languages University, India

INTRODUCTION

The linguistic system serves to code the speaker's message. It is reasonable to assume, therefore, that the insufficiently coded message will result in a less than complete understanding of the speaker's intent. I will suggest, however, that EFL learners undercode some key conventions for packaging information because it eases message framing, without generating less comprehensible prose. To do this, the paper will examine a large sample of EFL learner prose, to show undercoding of the requisite information-packaging conventions in

1. NP reference framing,
2. the marking of intersentential relations, and
3. the signalling of genre.

NP reference serves to identify entities the language user wishes to talk about, intersentential relations indicate the way successive propositions increment the text, and genre serves to provide an overall perceptual frame for the communicated message. These areas are selected because they are very important aspects of message coding at core levels of text structure. In addition to examining learners' undercoding of information-packaging conventions in these areas, I will assess teacher feedback on this undercoding. I will suggest that this reveals compelling motivation for the sustained use of message undercoding by students who are otherwise at high-intermediate levels of proficiency. Recent literature with interest in the acquisition of information packaging principles in the FL learning context has suggested that students show far less competency in this area than in syntax (Bardovi-Harlig and Dornyei 1998; Walters 1980; Rover 1996; House 1996; Schmidt 1983; Schmidt and Frota 1986; Cohen 1997; Niezgod and Rover 2001). This study will suggest that one significant reason for this lag in learning is the considerable accommodation of undercoded information-packaging conventions in the FL learning context.

The sample of prose examined in this study comprises 50 personal narratives, 60 story-recalls and 20 pieces of expository prose by high-intermediate EFL learners enrolled in the humanities program of a Hong Kong university. All the writing tasks were short in-class assignments, completed in between fifty minutes to an hour and a half. In the personal narratives, students were asked to write on a recent event of some personal significance. In the story recalls, students were given fifty minutes to read Maugham's short story *The Dream* and then asked to write it from memory. In the expository essays, students were asked to explain why they decided to choose English as a major area of study. All the students used Cantonese as L1 and were English users with some fifteen years of experience at the time they composed the essays examined in this study. They had taken English as a school subject until age twelve, at which time they were required to use it as the medium of instruction for most of their school subjects. Their English use was limited to the context of the classroom, however, with significantly more emphasis given to writing over speech.

Written feedback to these essays was obtained from eight trained EFL instructors each with a minimum of two years of EFL teaching experience. The teachers were asked to treat the students' assignments as first drafts and to comment on them as they normally would in response to similar assignments submitted to them in their own EFL courses.

I. THE PHENOMENON OF UNDERCODING

I am using the term 'undercoding' to refer to a certain type of mapping between the coding means and the functional domain it serves to mark. In undercoding, the mapping between the coding means and the functional domain it serves to mark is flawed either because the coding means are unable to capture the functionality to the right degree of specificity, or because the functional specificity of the coding means is not given proper realisation in the use it is put to.

Undercoding is actually, first, evident as an inherent part of the linguistic system. Consider the dissimilar relationships that are all uniformly represented by the English possessive, in 1.

1.

a. John's book = the book that John owns

b. John's father = the male parent of John

c. John's job = the job John is employed to do

The possessive in each of the NPs of (1a–c) serves to modify its accompanying noun. But whereas in 1a the book referred to is the one that John owns, in 1b the father is the male parent of John, not the one John owns, and, similarly, in 1c the job is the one John is employed to do, not the one he owns. There are, in fact, three different modifications of the accompanying NP, in 1, all marked by the possessive. The differences between these NP modifications are not linguistically coded (Blakemore 1992; Grundy 1995). The problem in this case is with the linguistic coding system itself: it is not as discriminating as it needs to be. That is, the coding means are unable to capture the functionality to the right degree of specificity.

But it is also possible to undercode in this way by selecting an insufficiently discriminating coding means, although the right one does, in fact, exist. One can say, for example, 'she cried', when the actual intent is to describe her act of weeping, rather than merely crying.

In the second, above-referred-to kind of undercoding there is a failure to realise the functional specificity of the selected coding means in the use of it. So, to use 'she wept' to describe the less well-specified act of crying would qualify as this kind of undercoding.

There are, therefore, two principal misuses of the linguistic system that result in undercoding:

1. *Type 1 undercoding*

   The selection of an insufficiently discriminating coding means (e.g. 'cry' to represent weeping). This is a problem of choice between existing options. It qualifies as undercoding in failing to capture the intended functional specificity.

2. *Type 2 undercoding*

   The use of a coding means without proper recognition of its level of functional specificity ('weep' to represent crying); the functional specificity is underestimated, in this case. It qualifies as undercoding in failing to realise the right level of functional specificity.

2. STRATEGIC UNDERCODING

It is also true, however, that using language without exploiting its full potential to mark functional specificity is common, and widely perceived as making for both easier and more economical message framing (Grundy 1995). Skilled language users customarily choose to undercode whenever they are in a position to assume that the interlocutor will understand the message in spite of this undercoding.

People, in fact, routinely represent linguistically only what cannot be understood without explicit representation. In this strategic undercoding, shared knowledge and shared context play a crucial role in supporting proper message processing and its full comprehension. Take, for example, the NP 'John's book', of 1a above. It can actually refer to either the book he has authored or the one he owns (example from Grundy 1995). In this case, the undercoding can be strategic when it serves to ease message framing, in a situation where there is enough shared knowledge between speaker and interlocutor to allow the interlocutor to successfully disambiguate the NP.

3. FL LEARNERS AND STRATEGIC UNDERCODING

I would like to suggest that FL learners routinely over-extend the use of strategic undercoding, by applying it to aspects of the linguistic system to which skilled users would not apply it. This is evident in their framing of indefinite reference, their marking of intersentential relations and their signalling of genre.

3.1 Indefinite reference framing (Type 1 undercoding)

The over-extension of strategic undercoding is first evident in the learners' framing of indefinite reference. Whereas our data suggests that learners frame definite reference in standard ways, the same is not true for the framing of indefinite reference. Indefinite NPs show undercoding in significant numbers.

To refer to something successfully, information packaging must be monitored to ensure that the entity referred to is made salient/well-distinguished amongst same-set entities (cf Tickoo 2002a). That is, it must be made to stand out amongst like entities.

2

a. **The man in the red cap** is staring at you.
b. **The man who came to see you yesterday** is here again.
c. I shared a table with **a man whose appearance entertained me**.
d. Yesterday, I saw **a man**.

In 2a, the man the speaker is drawing the hearer's attention to is distinguished from other present men by the selection of the descriptive modifier 'in the red cap', which is known to both the speaker and the hearer as singling him out. In 2b, the man is distinguished by the selection of the mutually known descriptive phrase of the modifying relative clause 'who came to see you yesterday'. In 2c, the indefinite referring expression 'a man' is, similarly, made unique amongst other men by the descriptor provided in the relative clause 'whose appearance entertained me'. This description is recognisable as capable of distinguishing a man amongst other men. But in 2d, the indefinite referring expression, 'a man', is unacceptable, because it is not made unique amongst other men at all.

There is a subtle difference, however, between the way in which definite referents and indefinite referents are singled out. In definite reference, the NP-modifying descriptor that serves to single out the referent ('in the red cap' in 2a and 'who came to see you yesterday' in 2b) is already known to the hearer. In indefinite reference, the descriptor ('whose appearance entertained me' for 'a man' in 2c) is not already known. But what is known is that such a descriptor *can* make the referent unique (as in 2c).

Learners frequently generate insufficiently salient/well-distinguished indefinite referring expressions like 2d above as is illustrated in the examples taken from learner prose in 2e and also 2f and 2g (below), because generating the needed abstract descriptor (like 'whose appearance entertained me', which modifies 'a man' in 2c) is a much greater challenge than using a descriptor known to the hearer (e.g. 'in the red cap' that modifies 'the man' in 2a).

2.

e. i. There were a lot of people. I needed to share a table with **a man**.

   ii. The restaurant was crowded and small, so he shared the table with **a man**.

f. He shared a table with **a tall Russian, with a small nose, (small) hands, long thin hair, black eyes, double chin and large red sensual mouth, in shabby clothes.**

g. i. He shared a table with **a fat man.**

ii. He shared a table with **another man dressed neatly.**

f′. He shared a table **with a man with extraordinarily chiseled features, raven black hair** and the deepest of blue eyes.

g′ i. He shared a table with **a man of enormous size.**

ii. He shared a table with **a man who was immaculately** dressed.

In 2f, the learner attempts to make NP reference well distinguished by generating a list of NP modifiers to delimit the scope of the referring expression and so particularise the referent. But properly well-distinguished NP reference must be made unique to a conventionally established degree. Although the functional scope of the NP in 2f is delimited by the accompanying modifiers, the resulting referring expression still does not qualify as sufficiently salient amongst same-set entities to a conventionally accepted degree. The reformulated NP of 2f′, on the other hand, does.

In 2g (i) and (ii) the learner also attempts to make the NP reference well distinguished. But this too is not done to a conventionally acceptable degree (since only children would consider that simply being fat or neatly dressed can single out a man amongst his peers). The reformulated NPs of 2g(i)′ and 2g(ii)′, on the other hand, are well-distinguished to an acceptable degree, and therefore felicitous.

The assessment of the learner-language data gives evidence that learners undercode in the framing of indefinite reference in the above-illustrated ways. Examination of teacher feedback on the learners' essays serves to provide an explanation for the sustained practice of undercoding in the framing of indefinite reference at even high-intermediate levels of proficiency. What becomes apparent when we examine teacher feedback on student essays is that teachers do not object to this type of undercoding at all. There is nothing in the teachers' comments to suggest that undercoded indefinite reference poses any sort of comprehension problem.

If we return to an examination of the students' use of indefinite reference framing, and now take account of the textual context in which it is used (namely, a story-recall task), we find that the teachers' failure to object to its undercoding is likely to be because in its textual use the intent to use it as well-distinguished is quite clear. In examining the co-text, it becomes evident that indefinite reference invariably comes with a detailed description of the referred-to NP, immediately following it. This is true as much for skilled writing as for the students' prose. In Maugham's short story *The Dream*, the first reference to the protagonist of the story, 'a man whose appearance entertained me' is followed by a detailed description of him (cf 3 below):

3.

He was a Russian, a tall fellow, but amazingly stout, and he had so vast a paunch that he was obliged to sit well away from the table. His hands, small for his size, were buried in rolls of fat. His hair, long, dark, and thin, was brushed carefully across his crown in order to conceal his baldness, and his huge sallow face, with its enormous double chin, clean-shaven, gave you an impression of indecent nakedness. His nose was small, a funny little button upon that mass of flesh, and his black shining eyes were small too. But he had a large, red, and sensual mouth. He was dressed neatly enough in a black suit. It was not worn but shabby; it looked as if it had been neither pressed nor brushed since he had had it.

(Somerset Maugham, *The Dream*, p 227)

This post-NP representation of its saliency is also evident in every student narrative, as is illustrated in 3′, signalling that though the referent is not made unique in its referring expression, there is a clear intent to refer to a unique entity:

3′

I shared table with a man. He was a Russian. He was fat and poorly dressed with a bad appearance.

3.2 Intersentential relations

I will next comment on the learners' undercoding in the use of intersentential relations.

Differentiated ways of incrementing text can be put in place by managing the character of intersentential relations. Different relations can be lexically marked by the use of sentence adverbials (e.g. 'because' in 4′ below, but are not always made explicit in this way as in 4).

4.

a. She liked him.

b. He was very kind.

4′

a. She liked him

b. **because** he was very kind.

Whether they are lexically marked or not, they are apparent in the way in which the propositional incrementation (e.g. in both 4b and 4′b) relates to the proposition that precedes it (as in 4a and 4′a). Both 4b and 4′b increment the text by instantiating a reason for the assertion of 4a and 4′a. It is self-evident that when the intersentential relationship is lexically marked (as in 4′), there must be correlation between the selected adverbial (e.g. *because*) and the relationship that holds between the successive sentence propositions (e.g. the reason for [a], instantiated in b).

Learners' samples, again, show two types of undercoding of intersentential relations:

1. Type 1 undercoding: The implemented relationship between successive propositions is not sufficiently well-specified for the context in which it is used.

2. Type 2 undercoding: The functional specificity of the selected adverbial is not realised by the relationship that holds between the propositions it binds.

3.2.1 *The use of temporal 'then' (Type 2 undercoding)*

I will first comment on learners' undercoding in the use of temporal types of intersentential relations, focusing on undercoding in their use of temporal 'then'.

We can set up a basic distinction between temporal and atemporal modes of incrementing text, and, first, examine learners' use of temporal 'then' as a principal means of marking temporal text incrementation. Learners' use of 'then' qualifies as a type-2 undercoding, because they fail to recognise its functional specificity and, therefore, use it between propositions that convey a less well-delimited type of temporal passage.

'Then' is properly used only when all three of the following informational conditions constrain the proposition it accompanies in the context of its preceding proposition (cf Tickoo 2002b):

1. The event represented in the 'then'-marked clausal proposition is one that is completed, following a completed event represented by the preceding proposition,
2. the 'then'-marked proposition is informationally salient in the context of its preceding proposition, and
3. the 'then'-marked proposition is informationally new (not already known) to the interlocutor in the context of its preceding proposition.

All three of these conditions are properly met in 5, but not 6 and 7.

5.

a. I got home at 4.00 o'clock.

b. Then I took the children to the park.

6.

a. I left at the last minute.

b. # Then I arrived in the nick of time.

7.

a. I wanted to sleep.

b. #Then I fell asleep.

The event represented in the 'then'-marked proposition of 5b is completed and follows the completed event represented by the preceding proposition (as required by condition 1). The 'then'-marked proposition is also informationally salient (as required by condition 2) and new with respect to its preceding proposition (as required by condition 3). Hence all three above-referred-to conditions are met. The same is not true of 6b and 7b.

In the 'then'-marked proposition of 6b, the event of arrival is completed and follows the preceding completed event—departure—of 6a (as required by condition 1). Arrival is also salient in the context of departure (as required by condition 2). But arrival after departure is not entirely new information (as required by condition 3). Rather, arrival is anticipated in the context of departure. For this reason the use of 'then' in 6b is not felicitous.

In 7b, the 'then'-marked proposition represents a completed event—'fell asleep'—but this does not follow a preceding completed event (as required by condition 1), since 'want' is a state rather than an event. For this reason, the use of 'then' in 7b is infelicitous.

Learners, however, systematically use 'then' in contexts like 6b and 7b where the conditions that constraint its proper use are only partially met (as in the examples taken from the learner prose of 8 and 8′, below). That is, it is used to mark a much less well-specified type of temporal passage than it does in skilled usage.

8.

But striving to survive for our family, my father had never complained on the fate. He didn't even mention his illness before our siblings, [a]but **tried to recover** his health by practising some special exercise and taking endless treatments instructed by doctor. [b]**Then** he could really defeat the cancer and survive.

8′

Recently I have made quite a great progress in the use of Chinese words. [a]From the beginning our lecturer of the subject modern Chinese writing **had provided** us with quite a lot of great writings to read. [b]**Then** we needed to try do some exercises which was aiming at finding out some words which were wrongly used.

In 8b, the 'then'-marked propositional event (defeat) does not follow a preceding completed event. Hence 'then' is infelicitously used.

In 8′b, the use of the past perfect gives the act of 'provide with great writings' no end point in the context of the 'doing of exercises' of the clause that follows. Hence 'then' is not felicitously used.

Assessment of teachers' feedback, however, shows no objection to such instances of undercoding. This is again likely to be because the examination of the use of the temporal 'then' in its textual context allows for proper understanding of the intended intersentential relationship. When we examine the use of 'then' in 6b, 7b, 8b and 8′b with respect to the co-text in which it is used, that is, 6a, 7a, 8a, and 8′a respectively, we recognise that it is inappropriately used. But we also recognise that we understand the intended intersentential relationship in spite of the inappropriately used 'then', merely by taking account of the actual relationship that bears between the propositions of 6a and 6b, 7a and 7b, 8a and 8b, and 8′a and 8′b, respectively. Because teachers are able to do this, no misunderstanding results, and, therefore, students also receive no negative feedback.

3.2.2 *The use of atemporal relations (Type 1 undercoding)*

In examining learners' undercoding in the use of atemporal intersentential relations, we must first acknowledge that two basic atemporal intersentential relations constitute key modes of building prose by atemporal means: incrementing by adding an informationally distinct proposition to the preceding proposition (cf Tickoo 2001), and incrementing by expanding the preceding proposition (cf Tickoo 2005).

9.

a. I went to work in Hong Kong for a number of reasons.
b. It is fast paced and exciting.
c. It is an interesting mix of the East and the West.
d. It is a place to make loads of money.

In 9, 9c adds a discrete proposition to 9b, as the second itemisation of the reasons I went to work in Hong Kong, and 9d adds a discrete proposition to 9c, as a third itemisation of the reasons I went to work in Hong Kong.

10.

a. I was on sentry duty.
b. I saw the enemy approaching (when **I was on sentry duty**).
c. I fired (when **I saw the enemy approaching when I was on sentry duty**).

(from Hoey 1994)

On the other hand, 10b and 10c increment the text by using the relationship of expansion. For this reason, 10b retains 10a in its incrementation, and 10c retains 10b.

Learners do not consistently select either addition or expansion as well-distinguished basic ways of incrementing text. Sometimes, the incrementation is not sufficiently well-specified to qualify as either expansion or addition.

11.

Dealing with the stress of college life

[1]In everyone's life, stress seems to be unavoidable. [2]When one grows up, one will face different kinds of stress in different stages. [3]In the college life, students have to face the stress comes from themselves, from their classmates as well as from their families. [4]Stress will bring to the students a sense of feeling that is unfree or even uncomfortable. [5]Sometimes if stress is not properly deal with, it may cause trouble to the students. [6]Therefore, it is important to deal with the stress of college life properly.

In the student sample of 11, for example, expansion is used to increment clause 3 in clause 4:

> Students feel unfree and uncomfortable (clause 4) because **they are stressed** (clause 3).

It is also used to increment clause 4 in clause 5:

> Sometimes it causes trouble (clause 5) when **students feel unfree because they are stressed** (clause 4).

It is also used to increment clause 5 in clause 6:

> It is important to deal with stress (clause 6) when **it causes trouble when students feel unfree because they are stressed** (clause 5).

But expansion does not account for the relationship between clause 1 and 2; nor does addition account for this relationship. (Addition does, however, account for the relationship between clauses 2 and 3). Using expansion between clause 1 and 2 we get:

> # When one grows up one faces different kinds of stress in different stages (clause 2), because **stress is unavoidable** (clause 1).

This is not fully meaningful.

Using addition between clause 1 and clause 2, we get:

> # **Stress is unavoidable** (clause 1) and when one grows up one faces different kinds of stress in different stages (clause 2).

This, too, is not fully acceptable, since addition must be between instantiations of the same kind. (That is, there must be some aspect of parallelism between the units so combined, and this is not the case in the propositions of clauses 1 and 2.)

Teachers' comments, however, do not address this problem. We find once more that an assessment of this lack of intersentential specificity in its broader textual context makes it possible to understand the student's intended sentential relationships. This contextual assessment for clauses 1 and 2, suggests the following intended intersentential relations:

> Stress is unavoidable. (clause 1)

By **expansion:**

> Therefore (because **it is unavoidable** (clause 1)), one faces it at every phase of life (clause 2a).

By **addition:**

> It is also true that every phase of life comes with its own kind of stress (clause 2b).

So, what a contextual assessment gives us is the following:

> Stress is unavoidable. Therefore one faces it at every phase of life. It is also true that every phase of life comes with its own kind of stress.

It is reasonable to assume that teachers use the readily accessible co-text to work out the intended intersentential relations. In consequence, however, there is no misunderstanding, and, therefore, also no negative feedback.

3.3 **Genre (Type 1 undercoding)**

Finally, I will examine learners' undercoding in the marking of genre. Genre represents a perceptual framework within which to process the message, and there are established formal means by which one genre is made well-distinguished from another. For example, a sequence of events in past time can be a story or a mere report of past events, and it is necessary, therefore, to signal which genre of narrative it represents. One way in which 'story' is signalled is by the representation of a passage from past event to past event that varies in pace, rather than being invariant or temporally flat (cf Tickoo 2003). This is done by the use of differentiated clausal types.

For example, a measured pace is indicated by the use of canonical order ('He walked out. He ran into the street …'), a much more rapid pace by the use of the VP-conjoined clause ('He walked out and ran into the street.') and a much slower pace by the use of the 'then'-marked clause ('He walked out. Then he ran into the street.'). When there is a strategic alternation between different clausal types, and hence change, too, in the pace of temporal passage, what the interlocutor perceives is a developing story. Compare, for example, the two versions, 12A and 12B, of the same sequence of events in past time.

12.

A. One night he heard the sound of a piercing scream.
He woke up.
He sat up.
He was startled and confused.
He turned to her.

He asked her what happened.
She had had a nightmare.
She dreamt that he had tried to kill her.
He picked her up.
He threw her over the balusters.
It was a drop of 30 feet to the floor below.
It meant certain death.

B. One night he awoke to the sound of a piercing scream.
He sat up in bed, startled and confused.
Turning to her, he asked her what happened.
She said she had had a nightmare.
She dreamt that he had tried to kill her, that he picked her up and threw her over the balusters, to the floor beneath, a drop of some 30 feet and certain death.

Notice that 12B uses a variety of syntactic constructions and therefore implements a perceptual variation in the represented passage of time; whereas 12A, in using canonical order across all its constituent clauses, marks an invariant or flat passage of time. Sentence 12B, in consequence of marking variable temporal passage, reads much more convincingly as a story.

When we look at student samples of stories, we find a consistent failure to use the requisite syntactic means to mark variable temporal passage, as is illustrated in the extract from one student's rewrite of Maugham's short story *The Dream*, in 13.

13.

The Russian began to tell me his relationship with his wife.
He started the story by the night he heard the scream of his wife.
She had a nightmare that his (her) husband wanted to kill her and threw her over the balusters.

> She was very frightened.
>
> The nightmare changed the impression between the couple. The wife was afraid of having the nightmare.
>
> The husband thought that it was easy to throw his wife over the balusters.

There is an almost exclusive use of canonical order in the successive clauses of this extract.

Yet because 'story' as genre is redundantly signalled by various recognised conventions (including the very standard and widely recognised ones such as 'once upon a time') the learners' intent to tell a story is not in doubt. In consequence, we again find no teachers' comments that point to the failure to mark variable temporal passage, and, therefore, no relevant negative feedback.

4. CONCLUSION

What I have attempted to show is that the FL learning context provides a very supportive environment for undercoding in certain key areas of information packaging, namely, indefinite reference framing, the marking of intersentential relations and the signalling of genre. I have argued that this is because message framing in the FL context occurs principally

1. in the written medium, which allows robust access to co-text in the interpretation of the writer's intent, and
2. with teacher as interlocutor. Teachers are particularly adept at making the co-text relevant to the interpretation of the less skilled writer's intent.

It is these unique features of the context of communication which account for the unproblematic message processing and absence of negative feedback, and, therefore, the sustained use of undercoding at even high-intermediate levels of language proficiency.

References

Bardovi-Harlig K and Dörnyei Z. 1998. Do language learners recognize pragmatic violations? Pragmatic versus grammatical awareness in instructed L2. *TESOL Quarterly*, 32: 233–262.

Blakemore D. 1992. *Understanding Utterances, an Introduction to Pragmatics.* Oxford, UK: Blackwell.

Cohen A. 1997. Developing pragmatic ability: insights from the accelerated study of Japanese. In H Cook, K Hijirida, and M Tahara (ed), *New Trends and Issues in Teaching Japanese Language and Culture* (Technical Report #15). Honolulu: University of Hawaii, Second Language Teaching and Curriculum Center.

Grundy P. 1995. *Doing Pragmatics.* London/New York: Edward Arnold.

Hoey M. 1994. Signaling in discourse: a functional analysis of a common discourse pattern in written and spoken English. In M Coulthard (ed), *Advances in Written Text.* London: Routledge.

House J. 1996. Developing pragmatic fluency in English as a foreign language: routines and metapragmatic awareness. *Studies in Second Language Acquisition*, 18: 225–252.

Maugham, W Somerset. 1975. *Collected Short Stories.* Reading, PA: William Heinemann.

Niezgod K and Rover C. 2001. Pragmatic and grammatical awareness: a function of learning environment? In K Rose and G Kasper (ed), *Pragmatics in Language Teaching.* New York: Cambridge University Press.

Rover C. 1996. Linguistische Routinen: Systematische, Psycholinguistische und fremdsprachendidaktische Uberlegungen. *Fremdsprachen und Hochschule*, 46: 43–60.

Schmidt R. 1983. Interaction, acculturation and the acquisition of communicative competence: a case study of one adult. In N Wolfson and E Judd (ed), *Sociolinguistics and Language Acquisition.* Rowley, MA: Newbury House.

Schmidt R. 1995. Consciousness and foreign language learning: a tutorial on the role of attention and awareness in learning. In R Schmidt (ed), *Attention and Awareness in Foreign Language Learning* (Technical Report #9). Honolulu: University of Hawaii, Second Language Teaching and Curriculum Center.

Schmidt R and Frota S. 1986. Developing basic conversational ability in a second language: a case study of an adult learner of Portuguese. In R Day (ed), *Talking to Learn: Conversation in Second Language Acquisition*. New York: Newbury House.

Tickoo A. 2001. On enumerative prose in ESL: the rhetorical structure and learning challenges of one type of collection. *Australian Review of Applied Linguistics*, 22 (2): 1–27.

Tickoo A. 2002a. On the framing of one kind of indefinite referring expression: learning challenges and pedagogical implications. *International Journal of Applied Linguistics*, 12 (2): 176–192.

Tickoo A. 2002b. On the use of 'then'/ 'after that' in the marking of chronological order: insights from Vietnamese and Chinese learners of ESL. *System*, 30 (1): 107–24.

Tickoo A. 2005. The encapsulating sentence and language learning. *World Englishes*, 24: 21–38.

Walters J. 1980. Grammar, meaning, and sociological appropriateness in second language acquisition. *Canadian Journal of Psychology*, 34: 337–345.